SEA PASSAGES

The British Navy may well have ceased to count its victories. It is rich beyond the wildest dreams of success and fame. It may well, rather, on a culminating day of its history, cast about for the memory of some reverses to appease the jealous fates which attend the prosperity and triumphs of a nation. It holds, indeed, the heaviest inheritance that has ever been entrusted to the courage and fidelity of armed men.

It is too great for mere pride. It should make the seamen of to-day humble in the secret of their hearts and indomitable in their unspoken resolution. In all the records of history there has never been a time when a victorious fortune has been so faithful to men making war upon the sea. And it must be confessed that on their part they knew how to be faithful to their victorious fortune. They were exalted. They were always watching for her smile; night or day, fair weather or foul, they waited for her slightest sign with the offering of their stout hearts in their hands.

JOSEPH CONRAD.

SEA PASSAGES

A NAVAL ANTHOLOGY
AND INTRODUCTION TO THE
STUDY OF ENGLISH

EDITED BY

GEOFFREY CALLENDER

Director of the National Maritime Museum;
Lecturer to the R.N. War and R.N. Staff Colleges;
Hon. Secretary of the Society for
Nautical Research

CAMBRIDGE
AT THE UNIVERSITY PRESS
1943

CAMBRIDGE UNIVERSITY PRESS
Cambridge, New York, Melbourne, Madrid, Cape Town,
Singapore, São Paulo, Delhi, Mexico City

Cambridge University Press
The Edinburgh Building, Cambridge CB2 8RU, UK

Published in the United States of America by Cambridge University Press, New York

www.cambridge.org
Information on this title: www.cambridge.org/9781107659209

First published 1943
First paperback edition 2013

A catalogue record for this publication is available from the British Library

ISBN 978-1-107-65920-9 Paperback

CONTENTS & CHRONOLOGY

ACKNOWLEDGMENTS

It is a pleasant duty to acknowledge the debt which this book owes to the kindness of those who have consented to contribute 'Passages'. My grateful thanks are due to the Prime Minister, the Right Hon. Winston S. Churchill, C.H., for permission to quote in full his speech at the Guildhall on 23 February 1940, 'The Navy is Here!'; to Admiral of the Fleet Lord Chatfield for permission to reprint from *The Navy and Defence* his account of the Battle of Heligoland; to Sir Arthur Quiller-Couch for a generous portion of *Lieutenant Lapenotière* from *News from the Duchy*; to Captain Francis Newbolt for permission to quote verbatim his father's poem *Hawke* from *Poems New and Old* by Sir Henry Newbolt [John Murray]; to the late Mrs R. E. Vernède for permission to make use of her husband's poem *England to the Sea*; and to the Trustees of the National Maritime Museum and the Society for Nautical Research for permission to reprint two extracts from *The Story of H.M.S. Victory*.

I desire also to record my obligation to Messrs Cassell and Co., Ltd. for permission to make use of *Into Battle* for the Prime Minister's speech on 23 February 1940; and to Messrs Wm. Heinemann, Ltd. for similar permission in respect of the Battle of Heligoland from pp. 124–126 of *The Navy and Defence*.

Permission has also been granted for the passage from R. L. Stevenson's essay *English Admirals* by Mr Lloyd Osbourne; for the passage from Froude's *English Seamen in the Sixteenth Century* by Messrs Longmans Green and Company; for the extracts from Thomas Hardy's *The Trumpet-Major* and *The Dynasts* by Messrs Macmillan and Co. and the trustees of the Hardy Estate; and for the extract from Swinburne's poem *Trafalgar Day* by Messrs Wm. Heinemann, Ltd.

G. C.

June, 1943

INTRODUCTION

I

IN THE ROYAL NAVY and in the Merchant Navy, as in other professions, the capacity to write good English will always prove (other things being equal) the sure and certain pathway to Success. It is, therefore, obviously the duty of every youth who follows a sea-career to do his utmost to become proficient in expressing his thoughts in his mother tongue adequately, fluently and lucidly—on paper.

As in handwriting the most desirable quality is to be legible, so in the writing of English the most desirable quality is to be intelligible: and this is not nearly as easy as might at first appear. Indeed it is hardly an exaggeration to say that most writers assume that they themselves are always intelligible, and that it must be some relative or friend or acquaintance who is at fault, if he, or she, is unable immediately to grasp the meaning of a letter sent to him, or to her, through the post.

In order to illustrate how obscure such an ordinary everyday piece of English may be, let us examine a letter from one naval rating to another, in which the writer is describing a recent incident which took place on board his ship and which was attended by unpleasant consequences to both the parties concerned.

H.M.S. *Calypso*.
Tuesday, 14 October.

Dear DUSTY,

Since this old hooker left Pompey, Nobby and I have parted brass-rags. About three weeks since, Nobby was lined up by the Jaunty before the Bloke and got weighed off with fourteen penn'orth! Poor old Nobby had unhooked Buck's caulker, having dropped his own in the ditch; so the pusser got into a flat spin as slops are running low. Nobby always was a trump card at dripping, especially when he's been striking it down; and this time, being chocker, he threatened to coil up his cable. Why Nobby should reckon that his raggie should blow the gaff, when there are crushers everywhere, leaves me guessing; but there it is. In the last dog he rounded on me and called me a white rat. I got stroppy and told him he was shooting a line: but all he said was, 'Oh! choke your luff! I'm looking for another oppo you snivelling sand-scratcher.' So that looks like paying off.

I must pipe down now. So cheerio, my old China,

Yours PINCHER.¶

There is nothing in this letter which an active service rating could fail to understand. On the other hand it is equally safe to say that the letter would convey less than nothing at all to a Minister of Religion, a Justice of the Peace, or other responsible personage, to whom those desiring help in an hour of need are commonly advised to resort.

Let us then 'translate' or convert this letter into correct English, which would enable a Minister of Religion, a Justice of the Peace, or other adviser of those in trouble, to possess himself of the facts leading up to what Ordinary Seaman Martin describes as the parting of brass-rags.

Dear MILLER,

Since this ship left Portsmouth, Clarke and I have, I regret to say, brought our old-established friendship to a close. About three weeks ago, Clarke was paraded by the Master-at-Arms before the Commander as a defaulter and was condemned to fourteen days in cells. Clarke, it appears, had taken possession of Taylor's overcoat, having lost his own overboard. As stocks of

¶ To certain English surnames, nicknames are always automatically attached by the lower deck. All Bennetts are 'Wiggie', all Millers 'Dusty', all Martins 'Pincher', all Greens 'Jimmy', all Woodses 'Stinger', all Taylors 'Buck' or 'Snip', all Days 'Happy', all Wellses 'Kitty', all Clarkes 'Nobby', all Ewarts, or Hewitts, 'Nobby', all Youngs 'Brigham', all Welshmen 'Taffy', all left-handed men 'Lefty', all men of short stature 'Shorty', and their opposites 'Lofty'. The list might be unduly extended.

clothing are running low, the Senior Accountant Officer took a serious view of the offence. Clarke always was notorious for grumbling especially after drinking too freely; and on this occasion, being at the end of his tether, he threatened to commit suicide. Why he should imagine that his best friend should turn King's evidence, when it is the duty of the ship's police to detect and report larceny, I fail to understand. But between six and eight o'clock last evening Clarke rounded on me and called me a sneak and a tell-tale. I naturally became annoyed and told him that such an insinuation was incredibly far-fetched. 'That's enough from you,' he replied, 'I'm looking for another shipmate, one that is above currying favour with his superiors.' This, therefore, looks like the end.

I must now bring this letter to a close; and with all good wishes to you, old friend, I remain,

Yours ever,

J. D. MARTIN.

The concealment of its meaning in the original letter was occasioned by the use of Slang. In other words, Slang is one of the chief hindrances to the writer of English, who seeks on paper to make himself intelligible.

What is Slang?

Slang, believed by some authorities to be a Gypsy word, may have stood in times past for words and expressions which Gypsies employed among themselves, to the bewilderment of ordinary men. To-day it stands for words and expressions employed by ordinary men and women in familiar conversation among themselves; and often serves among like-minded folk of similar occupation or similar tastes as the badges, labels, watchwords or trademarks of their class and a mystery to all outside it.

Sailors are by no means the only lovers of slang; their preference is shared by hunting people and racing touts; by cockneys, tinkers, housebreakers and cracksmen, schoolboys, undergraduates and stockbrokers. But it is open to question whether any of these rivals can compete on equal terms with the sailor at his breeziest.

There are two main reasons why sea-going folk should make such extensive use of slang.

In the first place, sailor language proper paves the way to it and encourages new developments. Sailor language comprises all words and expressions properly applied to a ship; words and expressions which may not on any account be replaced by shore-going terms. The sailor, once on board, stands, not on floors, but on 'decks'. Around him rise not walls, but 'bulkheads'. To proceed from one level to another he does not use staircases, but 'hatch-ways'. He does not go upstairs, but 'topsides'; and being on the upper, or uppermost, deck, he does not proceed downstairs, but goes 'below'. He does not go to bed, but 'turns in'. He does not get up at the call of duty, but 'shows a leg'. He does not get one half-day off a week, but indulges in a 'make and mend'. These terms and many others are *not* slang; but professional phraseology. None the less, the sailor, forcibly reminded at every turn by the contrast between sailor language and that used ashore, can hardly be blamed if to objects of everyday life he attaches a salty vocabulary of his own. He refers to his own uniform, jumper, collar and bell-bottomed trousers, as 'square rig'; the double-breasted coat and peaked cap of other ratings as 'fore and aft rig'. With some slight irreverence he calls the Chaplain the 'Devil dodger' and the ship's Surgeon the 'Sawbones'. Torpedo-dropping aircraft he dismisses as 'cuckoos'; torpedoes as 'tin fish'; and when he dons his steel helmet, he calls it his 'battle-bowler'. On the mess deck he makes merry with his bill of fare: eggs are 'farmyard nuggets', sausages 'mystery torpedoes', tapioca pudding 'fish-eyes', tins of potted meat or potted fish 'depth charges'; and the pepper-pot is the 'lighthouse'.

It must not be supposed that, when he comes ashore, the sailor is incapable of any language but that which he uses afloat. Such is very far from being the case. Except in foreign parts, he has no difficulty in making himself understood: and as his apprenticeship to the sea involves a close study of a number of text-books on technical matters such as gunnery and seamanship; and, as he is in daily contact with officers, who in their orders and instructions provide excellent models of correct English, he talks to his friends and intimates ashore in a style conforming closely to their own, though more fluent and picturesque. And where shore-dwellers and home-keeping folk halt or falter in their narrative, he gladly and instantly comes to the rescue with a word or phrase coined at sea. When, for example, the wooden ship in the eighteen-fifties found the shell-gun too much for her, she protected her vitals with steel plates and the Press began to wonder what the new craft should be called. With ready wit the men in blue, who had already christened themselves 'Bluejackets', invented the word 'Ironclad'; and the editors of dictionaries took it to their hearts at once. In the same manner 'Jack Ashore' has enlarged and indeed enriched the English language with words and ex-pressions many of which are hardly recognized at times as having a maritime origin—'Above board', 'Look out for squalls!', 'The coast is clear', 'Under false colours', 'Davy Jones's Locker', 'Stand by', 'Carry on', 'Sheet anchor', 'Mainstay', 'Take the wind from his sails', 'By and large', 'Taken aback', 'Catch a crab', 'Plain sailing', 'On his beam ends'. These words and ex-pressions, with hundreds more, came into existence in the same manner as those used by Pincher Martin in the letter quoted above; but in the passage of time they have lost their identity and risen, through adoption by the world at large, from Slang to Idiom. No doubt history will repeat itself; and some slang words, current at the present time, will perhaps undergo the same promotion. But that possibility does not entitle the young writer of to-day to utilize sea-going slang, if he wishes his written English to be correct. We speak of our language as the 'King's English'. It is not for the King's lieges to take liberties with what is uni-versally admitted to be a proud national inheritance.

Another stimulus in the sailor to resort to slang is the desire, or ambition, which the young sailor shares with speakers and writers of every kind, to lend force or emphasis to his words; to drive home his meaning by the use of a simile or image which has not been utilized before. The story is told of a young stoker, who was being questioned about the mental capacity of a shipmate. 'Intellect?' he replied scornfully, 'Yes! it sticks out all over him like feathers from a pig.' Another story explains the nickname given to the eighth officer to join a certain ship already in commission. The officer in question had ink-black hair and a swarthy jowl, but he stood 6 feet 4½ inches in his socks; and the ship's company promptly dubbed him 'Snow-White'. For beside him, you see, the other members of the Ward Room looked like 'Seven Little Dwarfs'. These two examples of appropriate emphasis lack nothing in drollery and wit; and they are characteristic of the British sailor's humour and inventiveness. Who but he would have christened the Long Service and Good Conduct Medal 'fifteen years of undetected crime'; or H.M.S. *Vengeance* 'the Lord's own'; or a cooked joint surrounded by roast potatoes 'a schooner on the rocks'; or a shore establishment a 'Stone Frigate'; or weak tea 'water bewitched'; or the group of warships named after garden flowers 'the Herbaceous Border'?

In the old days of oak and hemp when a ship was homeward bound with a fair wind abaft; when every sail was drawing and a big bow-wave gave the impression that, like the horse to its stable, the vessel knew where she was going, the sailors used to say that the girls at home were hauling on the tow-ropes. Another example of emphasis, though dating from times long past, is still quoted to-day, especially when anything particularly unpleasant has to be done, 'Who would not sell his farm and go to sea?'

These two quotations are of literary quality and might be borrowed from one of the older dramatists, whose plays are still performed. But the inventive brains that fashioned them also gave rein to their fancy when they called a straw mattress 'a donkey's breakfast', a useless rating 'a King's hard bargain', a rehearsal 'a dummy run', the art of visual communications by hand 'flag wagging', an empty bottle 'a dead marine', the ship's cook 'a grub spoiler', switching off the light 'dowsing the glim', and entrance into the blessed state of matrimony 'getting spliced'.

All of which examples and many more besides only go to show that in his efforts to lend point and emphasis to his remarks, the navigator in the perilous seas of English composition is all too apt to wreck his craft on the insidious shoals of Slang.

II

Another serious obstacle in the path of the young writer who has decided to avoid slang and write intelligible English is Vagueness; and this hindrance to progress is very difficult to surmount and can only be removed by most patient and painstaking care. Vagueness is the opposite of Clearness or Lucidity. Like the bad helmsman's 'trail of the serpent', the writer, convicted of vagueness, fails to keep a steady course, fails to make his meaning understood. The causes of vagueness are mainly two; uncertainty as to what should be written; and uncertainty as to the order in which collected information should be arranged.

The early navigators and explorers came back from their voyages very greatly impressed by the experiences they had undergone; and they were only too glad to impart information to those who were anxious to listen. But in answer to such questions as 'When was that?' 'Which day of the week and of the month?' 'Which way was the wind blowing?' 'Were you under courses and reefed topsails?' 'In what direction was the shoal of porpoises?' 'How large was the iceberg?' 'For how many days were you down to half-a-pint of water per man per day?' and scores of similar questions, he had two alternatives before him; either honestly to admit that after two years at sea he could not for the life of him remember; or else to draw upon his imagination and make rough guesses to satisfy his audience. If the audience was gathered round his own fireside, his guesses or approximations would doubtless be politely accepted, whatever responses were made: but if his audience was made up of his employers, who had sent him forth on his venture to obtain definite intelli-

gence, then any vagueness or lack of accuracy on the part of the
navigator would be most unwelcome and unsatisfactory.

English ventures into distant seas began in the reign of Henry VII
(1485–1509); but the navigators were at first all foreigners like
John and Sebastian Cabot. Our next king, Henry VIII, not only
founded Trinity House for the training of home-bred navigators,
but he insisted that all English navigators should keep journals of
their voyages, or Log Books. Log Books have changed in details
since then; and slightly different methods of keeping them have
been adopted by the Royal Navy and the Merchant Navy; but
the principle is always the same. For a Sea Journal, or Log (as it
is called for short), is a book wherein is registered an exact and
regular account of the various occurrences that happen on board
a ship during her voyage; but more particularly those concerning
the ship's way, in order that her situation may be exactly known
at any time required.

When Nelson sailed the seas, there was kept in the steerage, or
some other convenient part of the ship, a large blackboard, called
the Log Board, which was divided vertically into six columns;
the first for the hours of the day, the second and third for the
knots and fathoms which the ship ran in half a minute (or miles
and tenths of a mile in an hour); the fourth for the course or
courses steered by the compass; the fifth for the wind; and the
sixth for various remarks, such as the state of the weather, the
sails set or taken in, and whatever else appeared necessary or
remarkable. The log was hove once every hour; and at noon
every day the particulars, as ascertained by observation or calculation, were neatly entered in a book, divided exactly like the
Log Board and called the Log Book. The resulting fair copy would
appear as on the page opposite.

Finally, with the help of this page, the navigating officer could
not only render a precise account of the varied happenings of an
eventful and busy day, and the order of their occurrence; but
with the calculations made at the close of the previous day's work
and by a knack acquired during long experience and perpetual

practice he could very quickly inform the Captain of the ship (unless of course he was himself the Captain) that the *Britomart*, shaping a course to the south-west had, in spite of bad weather, made forty-one miles in the twenty-four hours; that her position

SHIP *BRITOMART* FROM ENGLAND TO MADEIRA

H.	K.	F.	Courses	Wind	Remarks Saturday, 19 June 1805
1	6	6	W. by S.	S. by W.	Strong breezes with rain, attended with hard squalls, thunder and lightning
2	6	2			
3	6				In first reef of topsails
4	5				
5	5				Tacked
6	5		S.E. by S.	S.W. by S.	Squally. In topgallant sails
7	5				In second reef of topsails
8	4				Down top-gallant yards
9	4		S.S.E.	S.W.	
10	4				Hard squalls. Handed the mainsail and mizzen top-sail
11	3				
★12	3				Close reefed; handed the fore and main topsails, and brought the ship to under a foresail, mizzen, and main staysail
1	—		{Up S. by E. {Off S.E. by E.		
2	—				
3	—		{Up W. by S. {Off N.W. by W.	Variable	Wore ship
4	—				
5	3		W. by N.	S.W. by S.	At daylight more moderate. Set the topsails doubly reefed and the mainsail. Up top-gallant yards
6	3				
7	4				
8	4	6	West	S.S.W.	Fair weather. Out all reefs of the topsails. Set top-gallant sails
9	4	2			
10	4				
11	4				
12	4				

★ Called by landsmen 'midnight'.

at the moment was in 43° 50′ North Latitude, 11° 17′ West Longitude; and that Cape Finisterre, bearing S.E. by E. ¼ E., lay one hundred and two miles away.

There are thus three processes to be observed in the keeping of a Log. There is, firstly, the voyage itself with its accompaniment of entries on a surface which admits of erasure and amendment, when an accidental slip has been made, or a wrong letter entered. Secondly, there is the transcript, or fair copy, in which the details collected are set out in their final form, tidily and concisely; appealing to the eye almost as much as to the brain; abbreviated like shorthand, simple as the A.B.C. And, finally, there is the narrative, the recital, or the report, based on the fair copy of the notes compiled; exploiting to the limit of their usefulness the facts laboriously collected; omitting mere details that are now superfluous, and concentrating on the pith or essence or real substance of the matter in hand.

He who would write clear, intelligible, lucid English could not do better than imitate the procedure of the 'Master' (as he was called in the olden days), that is, the navigator of the ship. Let him first make the voyage with its accompaniment of rough notes; then the carefully set forth summary, or compendium of the facts observed; and finally the completed work, the attempt at connected English prose, the composition, or Essay.

The 'voyage' may take the essayist into the country to study the nesting of birds, the varieties of wild flowers, or the habits of wild animals; to the city or town to watch the thronging streams of traffic, the business of the market-place or the entertainments of the theatre or the cinema; to the local or central library to consult the books of reference on the open shelves or special volumes dealing with a hobby or pursuit; to the long cross-country walking-tour; the passage of a coastwise steamboat; the ascent of a mountain, the descent of a mine; the visit to a museum or an art-gallery; to a concert or to private theatricals; to dreamland after a busy day; or to fairyland on the flying carpet of Imagination. But the impressions made by such 'voyages' fade almost as quickly as they are registered. Like the camera which, in addition to its eye or lens, needs a sensitized film, or plate, behind it on which to register the impressions which it brings to a focus; so the busiest and liveliest mind will require rough notes, from which the summary of things observed can be compiled. In this summary, which should be compiled without undue haste, care must be exercised in the sifting of the material, in the assemblage of related facts, figures or opinions, and in their arrangement in an orderly methodical array, which commends itself to the brain or the imagination as reasonable or attractive, or both. The final presentation in connected narrative will then prove, not merely a practicable task, but often enough a real pleasure.

III

Mention has been made in the preceding section of a visit to a Library and the reference books on its open shelves or the volumes dealing with some special subject, hobby, or pursuit. Often enough it will be found, in fact far more frequently than not, that the information required has to be gathered, like the sweet levy of the honey-bee, from many sources of supply. But occasionally it will happen that the information sought for is obtainable from some single book or set of volumes; from some single newspaper, pamphlet or speech, or a sequence of newspapers, pamphlets or speeches. Then will it be necessary to study the matter in hand with special intensity, seizing upon the essentials only and discarding what is not indispensable. This useful exercise is called writing a Précis [pronounced *pray-see*]; and the rules for Précis-writing may be quickly summarized. In the first place, it is necessary to reduce the original to one-third of its original length. Secondly, in spite of this severe compression, no important fact must on any account be omitted. Thirdly, the summary of the essential facts must be (a) clear, (b) concise, and (c) complete.

Real success in précis-writing can come only with long practice; but the tedium of failure may be shortened and made more tolerable, if the following words of advice are borne in mind:

(1) Read the passage through carefully and with concentration, so as to discover what it is about.

(2) As you go through the passage, mark lightly with a pencil the point at which one section of the subject ends and another begins. Then re-write the passage as a continuous narrative, taking

the gist of each marked section in order, but omitting anything not absolutely necessary to the sense or compressing sentences together for the sake of conciseness. As it is essential to follow out the author's train of thought, you may, by going over the main points in succession in your head, make sure that you have omitted nothing of importance.

(3) Re-read the passage to make sure that you have your essentials clearly presented.

(4) Go carefully over what you have written, in order to see that it is clear and well expressed.

N.B. *Be careful to rub out all pencil marks in the book after the précis is finished.*

Here is a passage descriptive of 'Greek Mariners', taken from a travel book called *Eothen*★ by A. W. Kinglake.

'The crew receive no wages, but have all a share in the venture, and in general, I believe, they are the owners of the whole freight. They choose a captain, to whom they entrust just power enough to keep the vessel on her course in fine weather, but not quite enough for a gale of wind; they also elect a cook and a mate. The cook whom we had on board was particularly careful about the ship's reckoning; and when, under the influence of the keen sea-breezes, we grew fondly expectant of an instant dinner, the great author of *pilafs* would be standing on deck with an ancient quadrant in his hands, calmly affecting to take an observation. But then, to make up for this, the captain would be exercising a controlling influence over the soup, so that all in the end went well. Our mate was a Hydriot, a native of that island rock which grows nothing but mariners and mariners' wives. His character seemed to be exactly that which is generally attributed to the Hydriot race; he was fierce and gloomy and lonely in his ways. One of his principal duties seemed to be that of acting as counter-captain or leader of the opposition, denouncing the first symptoms of tyranny and protecting even the cabin-boy from oppression.

★ A Greek word meaning 'Out of the East'.

Besides this, when things went smoothly he would begin to prognosticate evil, in order that his more light-hearted comrades might not be puffed up with the seeming good fortune of the moment.'

If you count the words in this passage, you will find that they number 251. Therefore our précis must not exceed eighty-three words in all. Here it is:

PRÉCIS

The crew are all co-partners in the venture. They elect a captain with full authority in calm weather, a mate and a cook. But the cook at dinner-time would be found taking an altitude of the sun, though as a counter-balance the captain would be superintending the cooking. The mate was fierce and aloof as befitted a native of Hydria. He continually opposed the captain, fiercely resenting any suspected tyranny and prophesying misfortune when he thought his companions optimistic. [Total = 78 words.]

Artists who desire to draw pictures of human beings are warned in the art-schools that they must study the skeleton first; otherwise their figures will look lifeless, heavy, inert and ridiculous. Précis-writing may be described as cutting down an articulated body of English prose to the irreducible minimum of a skeleton.

So much then for précis-writing.

But to return to the artist and his preliminary training. Once he has acquired sufficient knowledge of anatomy to serve his purpose, he need not always be drawing skeletons. It will be sufficient if he can draw with accuracy the external forms which mask the bony structure and encase the muscles that move the limbs and lend variety to posture. Then he can think about clothing his puppet with whatever garments he cares to take from his wardrobe.

So the writer of English prose, when he has sufficiently mastered the necessary technique of précis-writing and has acquired the knack of dissecting passages, chapters, journals and books and extracting their irreducible minimum, can leave the valley of dry bones behind him and, like the artist, trust himself to draw a rough sketch or preliminary picture in outline, before proceeding to clothe his figure, or figures, with appropriate costume—the dingy dress of the workaday world, the gayer garments of holiday wear, or the gorgeous raiment of a gala or a festival.

Let us examine the following abstract of a short passage from a famous book. It is not a précis, technically so called: a real 'skeleton' of the same passage would appear more cadaverous. Here the flesh already covers the bones and makes the irreducible minimum sufficiently comely. But for all that, as the sequel will show, it is an *outline* only; a preliminary sketch for the more elaborate, more highly coloured picture to follow. It may, however, serve as a pattern or model of how such an outline should appear to the eye before the final pigments are laid on. The tale-teller, it should be understood, is calling to mind a visit to a fisherman's cottage, paid by him, many years earlier, when he was only a small boy.

NARRATIVE IN OUTLINE

Looking all round me, I could see no trace of a house, although we were approaching a big black barge drawn up on shore above the high-water mark. On receiving my companion's assurance that this was indeed his home, I was amused to discover that it was roofed in and had a door and windows in its sides. As it had not been designed as a dwelling, but as a fishing-boat and had spent much of its existence in the sea, its charm to my childish mind increased enormously. Inside, it was extremely clean and tidy; and I noticed at once, in addition to a table and Dutch clock, a chest of drawers with many objects of interest on the top. The walls were hung with coloured pictures of Scripture subjects; and, over the mantelpiece, a framed model of a Sunderland lugger, the joint work of a painter and a carpenter, excited in me both wonder and envy. There were inexplicable hooks in the ceiling, and lockers and boxes along the walls afforded convenient seats. The bedroom allotted to me was in the stern of the vessel; and the rudder-hole was glazed and served as a window. A looking-glass framed in shells, a patchwork quilt on the narrow cot, and a mug of sea-weed did much to brighten the tiny apartment; while a strong smell of fish in every part of the dwelling proclaimed the owner's occupation.

Now let us turn to the actual book from which this drab outline has been made and notice what animation and vitality the author infuses into the sketch and with what gay and colourful loveliness he invests it.

'I looked in all directions, as far as I could stare over the wilderness, and away at the sea, and away at the river, but no house could I make out. There was a black barge, or some other kind of superannuated boat, not far off, high and dry on the ground, with an iron funnel sticking out of it for a chimney and smoking very cosily; but nothing else in the way of habitation that was visible to me.

"That's not it?" said I, "That ship-looking thing?"

"That's it, Mas'r Davy," returned Ham.

If it had been Aladdin's palace, roc's egg and all, I suppose that I could not have been more charmed with the romantic idea of living in it. There was a delightful door cut in the side, and it was roofed in, and there were little windows in it; but the wonderful charm of it was, that it was a real boat which had no doubt been upon the water hundreds of times, and which had never been intended to be lived in, on dry land. That was the captivation of it to me. If it had ever been meant to be lived in, I might have thought it small, or inconvenient, or lonely; but never having been designed for any such use, it became a perfect abode.

It was beautifully clean inside, and as tidy as possible. There was a table, and a Dutch clock, and a chest of drawers, and on the chest of drawers there was a tea-tray with a painting on it of a lady with a parasol, taking a walk with a military-looking child who was trundling a hoop. The tray was kept from tumbling down, by a Bible; and the tray, if it had tumbled down, would have smashed a quantity of cups and saucers and a teapot that were grouped around the book. On the walls there were some common coloured pictures, framed and glazed, of Scripture subjects; such as I have never seen since in the hands of pedlars, without seeing the whole interior of Peggotty's brother's house again, at one view. Abraham in red going to sacrifice Isaac in blue, and Daniel in yellow cast into a den of green lions, were the most prominent of these. Over the little mantelshelf, was a picture of the *Sarah Jane* lugger, built at Sunderland, with a real little wooden stern stuck on to it; a work of art, combining composition with carpentry, which I considered to be one of the most enviable possessions that the world could afford. There were some hooks in the beams of the ceiling, the use of which I did not divine then; and some lockers and boxes and conveniences of that sort, which served for seats and eked out the chairs.

All this, I saw in the first glance after I crossed the threshold—childlike, according to my theory—and then Peggotty opened a little door and showed me my bedroom. It was the completest and most desirable bedroom ever seen—in the stern of the vessel; with a little window, where the rudder used to go through; a little looking-glass, just the right height for me, nailed against the wall, and framed with oyster-shells; a little bed, which there was just room to get into; and a nosegay of seaweed in a blue mug on the table. The walls were whitewashed as white as milk, and the counterpane made my eyes quite ache with its brightness. One thing I particularly noticed in this delightful house, was the smell of fish; which was so searching, that when I took out my pocket-handkerchief to wipe my nose, I found it smelt exactly as if it had wrapped up a lobster. On my imparting this discovery in confidence to Peggotty, she informed me that her brother dealt in lobsters, crabs, and crawfish; and I afterwards found that a heap of these creatures, in a wonderful conglomeration with one another, and never leaving off pinching whatever they laid hold of, were usually to be found in a little wooden outhouse where the pots and kettles were kept.'

IV

The passage quoted above is from *David Copperfield* by Charles Dickens.

How is the young writer, who has determined to keep his writing of English free from the taint of slang and the zig-zag paths of obscurity and vagueness, how is he to achieve the same measure of success as Charles Dickens in the passage quoted above?

All branches of knowledge fall into two main divisions, Sciences and Arts. Sciences teach a man *to know*. Arts teach him *to do*. The science of Chemistry treats of the properties of substances, both elementary and compound, and the laws of their combination and action one upon another. The science of Physics treats of the general properties of matter as affected by energy or force. By contrast, the Art of Music enables a composer so to combine sounds as to please the ear, an instrumentalist to master the technique of his instrument, the conductor to direct the concerted efforts of his orchestra. The art of Architecture enables its exponent to draw plans and elevations of houses and shops, factories and palaces, and to supervise the work of the contractors and builders who enable him to erect them.

According to such definitions, English composition is undoubtedly an 'Art' and must be handled as such: and the main requisites are constant and unwearied practice, and the close study of suitable models and congenial examples. The pianist or violinist cannot hope to qualify, still less to attain proficiency or excellence, without intense and assiduous application to his chosen instrument; and the same thing is true of the architect at his drawing-board or the sculptor at his modelling in clay. The same truth, also, holds good in the writing of English. Anyone can utter vague remarks, or lend his conversation pungency by resort to slang. But to write correct English needs the same unwearied and constant practice as the mastery of the piano or violin, or the planning of a little country-house or a palatial cinema.

In the tedious process of acquiring the art there is no help comparable to that of the living instructor; but the best teacher in the world cannot do more than supervise and correct. The learner must do the writing himself; and before the writing can begin, the theme of the composition must be chosen and the mind stimulated to activity by concentrating on the subject-matter. In the pages that follow, themes are supplied with an accompaniment of short questions to set the student at work on the process of digesting the subject-matter, on which his mind has been browsing. When the theme has been duly selected and its accompanying questions answered, the student should follow the advice given to the keeper of a Log; and when his composition is complete, should submit the result to his teacher, or some other candid critic, and listen carefully to the verdict, both in its general purport and in its particular corrections.

Great progress may be made in this way. No doubt it will seem slow at first. But for all that, it will be imperceptibly gradual; and perceptible also, if earlier essays are preserved for comparison with later. But something more is required.

There was once a young artist, who was already making a name for himself and receiving commissions to paint portraits, at what was then called Plymouth Dock and is to-day called Devonport, when a sailor friend offered to take him on a cruise to the Mediterranean. The kind invitation was eagerly accepted, and in 1749 the young artist, who already had in him a keen desire to improve, found himself in Italy, with the chance of visiting all the famous picture-galleries in a country where the art of painting may almost be said to have been born. That he profited by his unique opportunity will readily be believed. Constantly before his eyes were canvases painted by artists infinitely more talented than he himself then was. His admiration rose to the highest pitch. He stared and studied: studied, and still stared. His notes show that he made hurried copies of a picture by Rubens, by Titian or by Rembrandt, to see 'how the thing was done'. Quite consciously he was imitating, and at the same time analysing:

that is to say, at one and the same time he was craving to be able to do half as well, and taking the picture, which he could not too much admire, unceremoniously to pieces, as it were, to discover, if he could, how its irresistible charm had been effected. 'Why was that flame-coloured drapery introduced? or that half of the face thrown completely into shadow?' In due time he returned to his native land; and, with a full-length portrait of the sailor friend who had taken him abroad—painted, not in the manner then customary in England, but in a style of his own unconsciously derived from all that he had learned from all the famous artists whose works he had studied and admired—took the world of fashion by storm, and lived to become Sir Joshua Reynolds, first President of the Royal Academy.

The art of writing needs the same study of approved examples. Robert Louis Stevenson, the author of *Treasure Island*, in the forming of his own literary style, tells us that he played the 'sedulous ape', until his pen could move by itself. He means that he was following, in his own chosen profession, the same course pursued by Sir Joshua Reynolds in his. Of all creatures in the animal kingdom the ape is the most imitative: the chimpanzee, as everyone knows, has only to watch what men and women do, and he will take off his hat, sit down in a chair and pour himself out a cup of tea. But mere imitation is not enough. Imitation, as Stevenson said, must be 'sedulous'; that is, industrious, persevering, plodding, painstaking, thinking no kind of drudgery too dull.

No writer can acquire proficiency without reading; but the reading that will prove helpful must not be casual or unwilling or perfunctory [that is, done merely as a duty to be rushed through, passed over, and put behind one]. The passage read must be thoroughly understood and its meaning studied until it is completely grasped. Everyone doubtless can find some reading-matter to hold and interest him; the jockey in the racing news, the farmer in fat-stock prices. But the student, who desires one day to write well himself, must not confine his reading to what helps his physical digestion. He must follow the example of Reynolds and Stevenson; seek for models worthy of close study and imitation, and get to grips, like a wrestler determined to win.

In the pages that follow will be found passages that provide the necessary models. They should be read again and again; not with the intention of memorizing them, or learning them by heart, but in order to qualify as a 'sedulous ape'; in order, that is, to answer any question concerning the passage itself, the meaning of any of its words or phrases, of its allusions to persons and things. When that stage has been reached, then will be the time to select one of the subjects set 'For an Essay', following the method specified above in section II and adopting as nearly as memory, admiration, or both, make possible, the style or manner of the author from whom the model has been derived.

There is a story told of Thomas Alva Edison, which points the straight road to eventual success in difficult undertakings; and among such, to many folk, the writing of an essay ranks high. The great American had just evolved one of the remarkable inventions which have put humanity so deeply in his debt. All agreed that the new discovery was the work of *Genius*. But then arose the question: 'What *is* Genius?' 'Wouldn't you say', enquired one of the flatterers around him, 'that it is just *Inspiration*?' 'One per cent, *perhaps*,' replied the inventor unmoved, 'the other ninety-nine per cent is *undoubtedly* perspiration.'

'Work hard!' that is the moral. Avoid slang, avoid vagueness; collect your material and note it down as you jog along life's road; arrange it with neatness and precision and method; study your model or models before writing yourself; read your own composition critically when it is finished: and some day perhaps you will be able to write as well as Admiral Lord Nelson, or that other writer, who served before the mast, the novelist, Joseph Conrad.

N.B. A Glossary of nautical terms occurring in the Passages that follow will be found at the end of the book. But the wise student will do well to provide himself also with a *Dictionary of the English Language*, if only of the pocket variety. Sir James Barrie, Bart., O.M., in one of his whimsical outbursts of confidence, once told his listeners that he always kept a dictionary by his side. 'I may not keep it busily employed,' he said, 'but it gives me a wonderful feeling of security.' If it is remembered that the English language is known to comprise upwards of four million words, the most highly educated man alive cannot be expected to know them all, and Sir James Barrie's example is one that deserves to be widely and consistently followed.

CHARLES KINGSLEY

THE COMING OF THE ARMADA

[INTRODUCTORY NOTE. In Queen Elizabeth's reign the countries which
we now call Holland and Belgium formed part of the Spanish Empire,
and their obedience was claimed by King Philip II at Madrid. The harsh
government of his viceroys and their cruel oppression at last goaded the
people of the 'Low Countries' to revolt; and strong as Philip's armies were,
suppression was not easy because there was no connection by land between
Madrid and Brussels. The most practicable route from Spain to the Low
Countries was by sea: but, by the international law then recognized, the
English Channel was exclusively English property and use could only be
made of it in comfortable fashion if our Island Race agreed. As the
English people sympathized with the sufferings of the Low Countries, they
put every obstacle in the way of the Spaniards—without asking or receiving
permission to do so from their Queen. Before very long it became clear
to Philip II that, if he was to suppress the Revolt of the Netherlands, he
would first have to take possession of the Channel; and that of course meant
the invasion of England, the occupation of London, and the overthrow of
Queen Elizabeth. For this purpose the 'Invincible Armada' set out in
1588.]

CHATTING in groups, or lounging over the low wall which
commanded a view of the Sound and the shipping far below,
were gathered almost every notable man of the Plymouth fleet,
the whole posse comitatus of 'England's forgotten worthies'.
The Armada has been scattered by a storm. Lord Howard has
been out to look for it, as far as the Spanish coast; but the wind
has shifted to the south, and fearing lest the Dons should pass him,
he has returned to Plymouth, uncertain whether the Armada will
come after all or not. Slip on for awhile, like Prince Hal, the
drawer's apron; come in through the rose-clad door which opens
from the tavern, with a tray of long-necked Dutch glasses, and
a silver tankard of wine, and look round you at the gallant
Captains, who are waiting for the Spanish Armada, as lions in
their lair might wait for the passing herd of deer.

See those five talking earnestly, in the centre of a ring, which
longs to overhear, and yet is too respectful to approach close.

Those soft long eyes and pointed chin you recognize already; they are Walter Raleigh's. The fair young man in the flame-coloured doublet, whose arm is round Raleigh's neck, is Lord Sheffield; opposite them stands, by the side of Sir Richard Grenville, a man as stately even as he, Lord Sheffield's uncle, the Lord Charles Howard of Effingham, Lord High Admiral of England; next to him is his son-in-law, Sir Robert Southwell, captain of the *Elizabeth Jonas*: but who is that short, sturdy, plainly dressed man, who stands with legs a little apart, and hands behind his back, looking up, with keen grey eyes, into the face of each speaker? His cap is in his hands, so you can see the bullet head of crisp brown hair and the wrinkled forehead, as well as the high cheek-bones, the short square face, the broad temples, the thick lips, which are yet firm as granite. A coarse plebeian stamp of man: yet the whole figure and attitude are that of boundless determination, self-possession, energy; and when at last he speaks a few blunt words, all eyes are turned respectfully upon him;—for his name is Francis Drake.

A burly, grizzled elder, in greasy sea-stained garments, contrasting oddly with the huge gold chain about his neck, waddles up, as if he had been born, and had lived ever since, in a gale of wind at sea. The upper half of his broad visage seems of brick-red leather, the lower of badger's fur; and, as he claps Drake on the back, and, with a broad Devon twang, shouts, 'Be you a-coming to drink your wine, Francis Drake, or be you not?—saving your presence, my lord,' the Lord High Admiral only laughs, and bids Drake go and drink his wine; for John Hawkins, Admiral of the port, is the patriarch of Plymouth seamen, if Drake be their hero, and says and does pretty much what he likes in any company on earth.

So they push through the crowd, wherein is many another man whom one would gladly have spoken with face to face on earth. Martin Frobisher and John Davis are sitting on that bench, smoking tobacco from long silver pipes; and by them are Fenton and Withrington, who have both tried to follow Drake's path round the world, and failed, though by no fault of their own. The man who pledges them better luck next time, is George Fenner, known to 'the seven Portugals', Leicester's pet, and Captain of the galleon which Elizabeth bought of him. That short prim man in the huge yellow ruff, with sharp chin, minute imperial, and self-satisfied smile, is Richard Hawkins, the complete seaman, Admiral John's hereafter famous and hapless son. The elder who is talking with him is his good uncle William, whose monument still stands, or should stand, in Deptford church; for Admiral John set it up there but one year after this time; and on it record how he was, 'A worshipper of the true religion, an especial benefactor of poor sailors, a most just arbiter in most difficult causes, and of a singular faith, piety and prudence'. That, and the fact that he got creditably through some sharp work at Porto Rico, is all I know of William Hawkins; but if you or I, reader, can have as much or half as much said of us when we have to follow him, we shall have no reason to complain....

The talk of all the groups was interrupted by an explosion from old John Hawkins.

'Fail? Fail? What a murrain do you here, to talk of failing? Who made you a prophet, you scurvy, hang-in-the-wind, croaking, white-livered son of a corby-crow?'

'Heaven help us, Admiral Hawkins, who has put fire to your culverins in this fashion?' said Lord Howard.

'Who? my lord! Croakers! my lord! Here's a fellow calls himself the captain of a ship, and her Majesty's servant, and talks about failing, as if he were a Barbican loose-kirtle trying to keep her apple-squire ashore! Blurt for him, sneak-up! say I.'

'Admiral John Hawkins,' quoth the offender, 'you shall answer this language with your sword.'

'I'll answer it with my foot; and buy me a pair of horn-tips to my shoes, like a wraxling-man. Fight a croaker? Fight a frog, an owl! I fight those that dare fight, sir!'

'Sir, sir, moderate yourself. I am sure this gentleman will show himself as brave as any, when it comes to blows: but who can blame mortal man for trembling before so fearful a chance as this?'

'Let mortal man keep his tremblings to himself, then, my lord, and not be like Solomon's madmen, casting abroad fire and death, and saying, it is only in sport. There is more than one of his kidney, your lordship, who have not been ashamed to play Mother Shipton before their own sailors, and damp the poor fellows' hearts with crying before they're hurt, and this is one of them. I've heard him at it afore, and I'll present him, with a vengeance, though I'm no churchwarden....'

'There is no croaking aboard of us, we will warrant,' said twenty voices, 'and shall be none, as long as we command on board our own ships.'

Hawkins, having blown off his steam, went back to Drake and the bowls.

'Fill my pipe, drawer—that croaking fellow's made me let it out, of course! Spoil-sports! The father of all manner of troubles on earth, be they noxious trade of croakers! "Better to meet a bear robbed of her whelps", Francis Drake, as Solomon saith, than a fule who can't keep his mouth shut. What brought Mr Andrew Barker to his death, but croakers? What stopped Fenton's China voyage in the '82, and lost your nephew John, and my brother Will, glory and hard cash too, but croakers?...'

'And what', said Drake, 'would have kept me, if I'd let 'em, from ever sailing round the world, but these same croakers? I hanged my best friend for croaking, John Hawkins, may God forgive me if I was wrong, and I threatened a week after to hang thirty more; and I'd have done it too, if they hadn't clapped tompions into their muzzles pretty fast.'

'You're right, Frank. My old father always told me—and old King Hal (bless his memory!) would take his counsel among a thousand;—"And, my son," says he to me, "whatever you do, never you stand no croaking: but hang mun, son Jack, hang mun up for an ensign...." Those were his words, and I've found mun true.—Who com'th here now?'

'Captain Fleming, as I'm a sinner.'

'Fleming? Is he tired of life, that he com'th here to look for a halter? I've a warrant out against mun, for robbing of two Flushingers on the high seas, now this very last year. Is the fellow mazed or drunk, then? or has he seen a ghost? Look to mun!'

'I think so, truly,' said Drake. 'His eyes are near out of his head.'

The man was a rough-bearded old sea-dog, who had just burst in from the tavern through the low hatch, upsetting a drawer with all his glasses, and now came panting and blowing straight up to the High Admiral,—

'My lord, my lord! They'm coming! I saw them off the Lizard last night!'

'Who? my good sir, who seem to have left your manners behind you.'

'The Armada, your worship,—the Spaniard: but as for my manners, 'tis no fault of mine, for I never had none to leave behind me.'

'If he has not left his manners behind,' quoth Hawkins, 'look out for your purses, gentlemen all! He's manners enough, and very bad ones they be, when he com'th across a quiet Flushinger.'

'If I stole Flushingers' wines, I never stole Negurs' souls, Jack Hawkins; so there's your answer. My lord, hang me if you will: life's short and death's easy, 'specially to seamen; but if I didn't see the Spanish fleet last sundown, coming along half-moon wise, and full seven mile from wing to wing, within a four mile of me, I'm a sinner.'

'Sirrah,' said Lord Howard, 'is this no fetch, to cheat us out of your pardon for these piracies of yours?'

'You'll find out for yourself before nightfall, my Lord High Admiral. All Jack Fleming says is, that this is a poor sort of an answer to a man who has put his own neck into the halter for the sake of his country.'

'Perhaps it is,' said Lord Howard. 'And after all, gentlemen, what can this man gain by a lie, which must be discovered ere a day is over, except a more certain hanging?'

'Very true, your lordship,' said Hawkins, mollified. 'Come here, Jack Fleming—what wilt drain, man? Hippocras or Alicant, Sack or John Barleycorn, and a pledge to thy repentance and amendment of life.'

'Admiral Hawkins, Admiral Hawkins, this is no time for drinking.'

'Why not, then, my lord? Good news should be welcomed with good wine. Frank, send down to the sexton, and set the bells a-ringing to cheer up all honest hearts. Why, my lord, if it were not for the gravity of my office, I could dance a galliard for joy!'

'Well, you may dance, Port Admiral: but I must go and plan: but God give to all captains such a heart as yours this day!'

'And God give all generals such a head as yours! Come, Frank Drake, we'll play the game out before we move. It will be two good days before we shall be fit to tackle them, so an odd half-hour don't matter.'

'I must command the help of your counsel, Vice-Admiral,' said Lord Charles, turning to Drake.

'And it's this, my good lord,' said Drake, looking up, as he aimed his bowl. 'They'll come soon enough for us to show them sport, and yet slow enough for us to be ready; so let no man hurry himself. And as example is better than precept, here goes.'

Lord Howard shrugged his shoulders, and departed, knowing two things; first, that to move Drake was to move mountains; and next, that when the self-taught hero did bestir himself, he would do more work in an hour than anyone else in a day.

Westward Ho.

HELPS

Posse comitatus [*Latin*, power of the county]. Men called out by the Sheriff to assist him in the execution of his duty.

Elizabeth Jonas. A ship christened by Queen Elizabeth and meaning, 'May the Lord deliver me from the power of the Spaniard as he delivered Jonah from the belly of the whale!'

Lord High Admiral. A highly placed Government Official responsible in Queen Elizabeth's day for the duties now performed by the Board of Admiralty.

Admiral of the port. The magistrate responsible within the limits of his jurisdiction for the trial and punishment of offences at sea, e.g. piracy, collision, etc.

Mother Shipton. A reputed prophetess, generally of doom, destruction and catastrophe.

QUESTIONS

[N.B. If you cannot get anyone to repeat the questions and listen to your answers, write down your replies and correct them by re-reading the passage.]

(1) What is the meaning of the word 'croaker'? Is the word idiom or slang? What equivalent word is used in the war against Hitler?

(2) Who was Prince Hal? To what action of his is mention made in this passage?

(3) Give the place and date of the scene described.

(4) What was the name of Sir Robert Southwell's ship?

(5) What made George Fenner famous?

(6) Who set out on an unlucky voyage to China in 1582?

(7) Of what did Sir John Hawkins accuse Captain Fleming; and of what did Captain Fleming accuse Sir John Hawkins?

(8) Explain 'Flushinger', 'Don', 'Sirrah', 'Old King Hal', 'Murrain', 'Galleon', 'Galliard', 'Hippocras', 'Sack', 'John Barleycorn'.

(9) What other motive induced Drake to continue playing bowls besides a love of the game?

(10) What was the occupation of a 'drawer'?

(11) To what does Kingsley compare the English captains waiting for the Armada's arrival?

(12) Quote, as nearly as you can remember them, Kingsley's descriptions of (a) Sir Francis Drake, (b) John Hawkins, (c) Richard Hawkins.

(13) Who was an 'especial benefactor of poor sailors'?

(14) The passage mentions the names of seventeen famous Elizabethan seamen. How many can you recite from memory?

FOR A PRÉCIS

Write a précis of John Hawkins's remarks from 'Fail? Fail?' to '...though I'm no churchwarden'.

FOR AN ESSAY

(1) Imagine yourself to be the landlord of the 'Rose and Crown' at Plymouth, and describe the company assembled on your bowling-green when the news came of the Armada's arrival.

(2) Write a letter to a friend (Martin Killigrew), as from one of the junior officers in attendance on the Lord High Admiral, describing the principal events leading up to Drake's resolve to finish the game of bowls.

THE LIGHTING OF THE BEACONS

NIGHT sank upon the dusky beach, and on the purple sea;
Such night in England ne'er had been, nor e'er again shall be.
From Eddystone to Berwick bounds, from Lynn to Milford Bay,
That time of slumber was as bright and busy as the day.
For swift to east and swift to west the ghastly warflame spread:
High on St Michael's Mount it shone; it shone on Beachy Head.
Far on the deep the Spaniards saw, along each southern shire,
Cape beyond cape, in endless range, those twinkling points of fire.

    ✻   ✻   ✻   ✻   ✻   ✻

Southward from Surrey's pleasant hills flew those bright couriers
    forth;
High on bleak Hampstead's swarthy moor they started for the
    north;
And on and on, without a pause, untired they bounded still;
All night from tower to tower they sprang, they sprang from hill
    to hill
Till the proud Peak unfurled the flag o'er Darwin's rocky dales;
Till like volcanoes flared to heaven the stormy hills of Wales;
Till twelve fair counties saw the blaze on Malvern's lonely height;
Till streamed like crimson on the wind the Wrekin's crest of light;
Till, broad and fierce, the star came forth on Ely's stately fane;
And tower and hamlet rose in arms, o'er all the boundless plain;
Till Belvoir's lordly terraces the sign to Lincoln sent
And Lincoln sped the message on, o'er the wide vale of Trent;
Till Skiddaw saw the fire that burned on Gaunt's embattled pile,
And the red glare on Skiddaw roused the burghers of Carlisle.

    ✻   ✻   ✻   ✻   ✻   ✻

HELPS

Belvoir. Belvoir Castle, near Grantham, the seat of the Duke of Rutland; pronounced Beaver.

QUESTIONS

(1) Lord Macaulay does not once use the word 'beacon', but he manages to insert nine substitutes. Hunt them out and write them down.

(2) Why were the beacons lit, and on what sort of heights, or eminences, besides hills? What hills are actually mentioned by name?

(3) What precautions in this country took the place of beacons after the collapse of France in 1940?

(4) Do you consider 'dusky' and 'purple' suitable adjectives to use of the 'beach' and 'sea'? If so, why?

(5) Why are the beacons described as 'twinkling'?

(6) Give other words with the same meaning as 'bounds', 'fane', 'courier', 'swarthy', 'burghers', 'embattled pile'.

(7) Make a list of suitable eminences for beacons along the south coast of England in addition to Beachy Head.

(8) In what counties are Eddystone, the Wrekin, St Michael's Mount, the Peak, Malvern Hills, Lynn, Milford Bay, Ely, Skiddaw?

(9) Name six of the twelve counties which saw the beacon burn on the Malvern Hills.

(10) Why were the beacons 'untired' and why did they 'bound'?

(11) What substitutes does Macaulay use for Lancaster, the North Downs, Derbyshire and Nottinghamshire?

(12) What phrase does Macaulay employ for 'night'?

FOR AN ESSAY

(1) 'Such night in England ne'er...again shall be.' Do you consider that this prophecy has been fulfilled or not?

(2) Describe how a bonfire is built up and fired, for example on 5th November.

THE DEFEAT OF THE ARMADA

THEN, on that same Sunday afternoon a memorable council of war was held in the *Ark's* main cabin. Howard, Drake, Seymour, Hawkins, Martin Frobisher, and two or three others met to consult, knowing that on them at that moment the liberties of England were depending. Their resolution was taken promptly. There was no time for talk. After nightfall a strong flood tide would be setting up along shore to the Spanish anchorage. They would try what could be done with fire-ships, and the excursion of the pinnace, which was taken for bravado, was probably for a survey of the Armada's exact position. Meantime eight useless vessels were coated with pitch—hulls, spars, and rigging. Pitch was poured on the decks and over the sides, and parties were told off to steer them to their destination and then fire and leave them.

The hours stole on, and twilight passed into dark. The night was without a moon. The Duke paced his deck late with uneasy sense of danger. He observed lights moving up and down the English lines, and imagining that the *endemoniada gente*—the infernal devils—might be up to mischief, ordered a sharp look-out. A faint westerly air was curling the water, and towards midnight the watchers on board the galleons made out dimly several ships which seemed to be drifting down upon them. Their experiences since the action of Plymouth had been so strange and unlooked for that anything unintelligible which the English did was alarming.

The phantom forms drew nearer, and were almost among them when they broke into a blaze from water-line to truck, and the two fleets were seen by the lurid light of the conflagration; the anchorage, the walls and windows of Calais, and the sea shining red as far as eye could reach, as if the ocean itself was burning. Among the dangers which they might have to encounter, English fireworks had been especially dreaded by the Spaniards. Fire-ships—a fit device of heretics—had worked havoc among the Spanish troops, when the bridge was blown up, at Antwerp. They imagined that similar infernal machines were approaching the Armada. A capable commander would have sent a few launches to grapple the burning hulks, which of course were now deserted, and tow them out of harm's way. Spanish sailors were not cowards, and would not have flinched from duty because it might be dangerous; but the Duke and Diego Florez lost their heads again. A signal gun from the *San Martin* ordered the whole fleet to slip their cables and stand out to sea.

Orders given in panic are doubly unwise, for they spread the terror in which they originate. The danger from the fire-ships was chiefly from the effect on the imagination, for they appear to have drifted by and done no real injury. And it speaks well for the seamanship and courage of the Spaniards that they were able, crowded together as they were, at midnight and in sudden alarm to set their canvas and clear out without running into one another. They buoyed their cables, expecting to return for them at day-light, and with only a single accident, to be mentioned directly, they executed successfully a really difficult manœuvre.

The Duke was delighted with himself. The fire-ships burnt harmlessly out. He had baffled the inventions of the *endemoniada gente*. He brought up a league outside the harbour, and supposed that the whole Armada had done the same. Unluckily for him-self, he found it at day-light divided into two bodies. The *San Martin* with forty of the best appointed of the galleons were riding together at their anchors. The rest, two-thirds of the whole, having no second anchors ready, and inexperienced in Channel tides and currents, had been lying-to. The west wind was blowing up. Without seeing where they were going, they had drifted to leeward, and were two leagues off, towards Gravelines, dan-gerously near the shore. The Duke was too ignorant to realise the full peril of his situation. He signalled to them to return and rejoin him. As the wind and tide stood it was impossible. He proposed to follow them. The pilots told him that, if he did, the whole fleet might be lost on the banks. Towards the land the look of things was not more encouraging.

One accident only had happened the night before. The *Capitana* galleass with Don Hugo de Moncada and eight hundred men on board, had fouled her helm in a cable in getting under way and had become unmanageable. The galley slaves disobeyed orders, or else Don Hugo was as incompetent as his commander-in-chief. The galleass had gone on the sands, and as the tide ebbed had fallen over on her side. Howard, seeing her condition, had followed her in the *Ark* with four or five other of the Queen's ships, and was furiously attacking her with his boats, careless of neutrality laws. Howard's theory was, as he said, to pluck the feathers one by one from the Spaniard's wing, and here was a feather worth picking up. The galleass was the most splendid vessel of her kind afloat, Don Hugo one of the greatest of Spanish grandees.

Howard was making a double mistake. He took the galleass at last, after three hours' fighting. Don Hugo was killed by a musket ball. The vessel was plundered, and Howard's men took possession, meaning to carry her away when the tide rose. The French authorities ordered him off, threatening to fire upon him; and after wasting the forenoon, he was obliged at last to leave her where she lay. Worse than this, he had lost three precious hours, and had lost along with them, in the opinion of the Prince of Parma, the honours of the great day.

Drake and Hawkins knew better than to waste time plucking single feathers. The fire-ships had been more effective than they could have dared to hope. The enemy was broken up. The Duke was shorn of half his strength, and the Lord had delivered him into their hand. He had got under way, still signalling wildly, and uncertain in which direction to turn. His uncertainties were ended for him by seeing Drake bearing down upon him with the whole English fleet, save those which were loitering about the galleass. The English had now the advantage of numbers. The superiority of their guns he knew already, and their greater speed allowed him no hope to escape a battle. Forty ships alone were left to him to defend the banner of the crusade and the honour of Castile; but those forty were the largest and the most powerfully armed and manned that he had, and on board them were Oquendo, De Leyva, Recalde, and Bretandona, the best officer in the Spanish navy next to the lost Don Pedro.

It was now or never for England. The scene of the action which was to decide the future of Europe was between Calais and Dunkirk, a few miles off shore, and within sight of Parma's camp. There was no more manœuvring for the weather-gauge, no more fighting at long range. Drake dashed straight upon his prey as the falcon stoops upon its quarry. A chance had fallen to him which might never return; not for the vain distinction of carrying prizes into English ports, not for the ray of honour which would fall on him if he could carry off the sacred banner itself and hang it in the Abbey at Westminster, but a chance so to handle the Armada that it should never be seen again in English waters, and deal such a blow on Philip that the Spanish Empire should reel with it. The English ships had the same superiority over the galleons which steamers have now over sailing vessels. They had twice the speed; they could lie two points nearer to the wind. Sweeping round them at cable's length, crowding them in one upon the other, yet never once giving them a chance to grapple, they hurled in their cataracts of round shot. Short as was the powder supply, there was no sparing it that morning. The hours went on, and still the battle raged, if battle it could be called where the blows were all dealt on one side and the suffering was all on the other. Never on sea or land did the Spaniards show themselves worthier of their great name than on that day. But from the first they could do nothing. It was said afterwards in Spain that the Duke showed the white feather, that he charged his pilot to keep him out of harm's way, that he shut himself up in his cabin, buried in woolpacks, and so on. The Duke had faults enough, but poltroonery was not one of them. He, who till he entered the English Channel had never been in action on sea or land, found himself, as he said, in the midst of the most furious engagement recorded in the history of the world. As to being out of harm's way, the standard at his masthead drew the hottest of the fire upon him. The *San Martin's* timbers were of oak and a foot thick, but the shot, he said, went through them enough to shatter a rock. Her deck was a slaughter-house; half his company were killed or wounded, and no more would have been heard or seen of the *San Martin* or her commander had not Oquendo and De Leyva pushed in to the rescue and enabled him to creep away under their cover. He himself saw nothing more of the action after this. The smoke, he said, was so thick that he could make out nothing, even from his masthead. But all round it was but a repetition of the same scene. The Spanish shot flew high, as before, above the low English hulls, and they were themselves helpless butts to the English guns. And it is noticeable and supremely creditable to them that not a single galleon struck her colours. One of them, after a long duel with an Englishman, was on the point of sinking. An English officer, admiring the courage which the Spaniards had shown, ran out upon his bowsprit, told them that they had done all which became men, and urged them to surrender and save their lives. For answer they cursed the English as cowards and chickens because they refused to close. The officer was shot. His fall brought a last broadside on them, which finished the work. They went down, and the water closed over them. Rather death to the soldiers of the Cross than surrender to a heretic.

The deadly hail rained on. In some ships blood was seen streaming out of the scupper-holes. Yet there was no yielding; all ranks showed equal heroism. The priests went up and down in the midst of the carnage, holding the crucifix before the eyes of the dying. At midday Howard came up to claim a second share in a victory which was no longer doubtful. Towards the afternoon the Spanish fire slackened. Their powder was gone, and they could make no return to the cannonade which was still overwhelming them. They admitted freely afterwards that if the attack had been continued but two hours more they must all have struck or gone ashore. But the English magazines were empty also; the last cartridge was shot away, and the battle ended from mere inability to keep it up. It had been fought on both sides with peculiar determination. In the English there was the accumulated resentment of thirty years of menace to their country and their creed, with the enemy in tangible shape at last to be caught and grappled with; in the Spanish, the sense that if their cause had not brought them the help they looked for from above, the honour and faith of Castile should not suffer in their hands.

English Seamen in the Sixteenth Century.

HELPS

The Duke. The Commander-in-Chief of the Spanish Armada, the Duke of Medina Sidonia. He represented King Philip II afloat and was more a Viceroy than a military expert. His flagship was the *San Martin*, and his naval adviser and chief of staff was Don Diego Florez.

Prince of Parma. Alexander Farnese, Duke of Parma, Commander-in-Chief of the expedition against England in 1588. The Duke was to hand over his command to Parma as soon as contact was established.

Don Pedro. Don Pedro Valdez, one of the most capable leaders under Medina Sidonia, had been captured by Drake in a previous battle off Plymouth.

Seymour. Lord Henry Seymour, Commander-in-Chief of a squadron keeping watch on Parma's army. His force combined with the main English fleet after the Armada had been driven from Calais.

Ark. An abbreviation of *Ark Royal*, flagship of Lord Howard of Effingham. Drake's flagship was the *Revenge*.

Galleon. Here used for the typical fighting-ship of the Spanish Armada. By contrast, the Galleasse was an oared battleship like the Galley, but with broadside guns on the deck above. Four of these formidable vessels were included in the Armada under the command of Don Hugo de Monçada.

QUESTIONS

(1) How was a fire-ship made? How was it used?

(2) Did the English fire-ships at Calais have the effect the English leaders desired? If not, why not?

(3) What was the immediate effect of the fire-ships on the Spaniards? And how did their employment affect the course of the fighting as a whole?

(4) Give another simpler word for 'conflagration', 'poltroonery', 'lurid', 'bravado', 'manœuvre', 'cataracts', 'menace', 'quarry', 'forenoon', 'weather gauge', 'phantom forms'.

(5) Give the names of four Spanish leaders whose bravery was conspicuous.

(6) Of what was the Duke accused when he got back to Spain? Was there any just cause for the accusation?

(7) To what is Drake's impetuous attack upon the enemy compared?

(8) How thick were the sides of the Spanish galleons?

(9) What is the difference between raising the anchor, slipping the cable, and cutting the cable?

(10) To what special peril were those galleons that cut their cables exposed off the coast near Dunkirk?

(11) 'Howard's plan was to pluck the feathers one by one from the Spaniard's wing.'

This is a 'metaphor', a figure of speech whereby (for the sake of clearness or picturesqueness) one thing is compared with another quite different thing. Here the Spanish fleet is likened to a bird. Continue with the explanation, showing what the feathers were and what would be the effect of their being plucked.

(12) What commanders were really responsible for the defeat of the Armada? What action did the Lord High Admiral take?

(13) 'Careless of neutrality laws.' What does this mean? Name any countries that have remained neutral in the second German war of aggression.

(14) What did the Spaniards mean when they talked of heretics?

(15) By what words does Froude translate the Spanish words 'endemoniada gente' (literally, a nation possessed)?

FOR A PRÉCIS

Make a précis of the passage beginning 'But from the first they could do nothing...' and ending '...not a single galleon struck her colours'.

FOR AN ESSAY

(1) Suppose that you are a Spanish officer who has survived the battle and that it is your duty to report on the action to King Philip of Spain.

Give an account of what you would say and what reasons you would give for the defeat.

(2) The description in this passage is very '*vivid*': that is, the writer brings a living picture before our eyes.

Describe as vividly as you can how the ships of England in these self-same waters brought away the Allied Army from Dunkirk, 26 May–3 June 1940.

THE REVENGE

A Ballad of the Fleet

[INTRODUCTORY NOTE. The defeat of the Spanish Armada did not bring the war with Spain to a close; and Queen Elizabeth persevered for some years in an attempt to cripple her opponents by raids upon the sources of their great wealth, the treasure fleets from the New World and the Orient. By way of counter measures, the Spaniards directed their treasure fleets, both from the West Indies and the East, to halt on their homeward way at the Azores, one thousand miles from the coasts of Europe, and wait there until a strong escort fleet could fetch them safely home.

In 1590, an expedition under Sir John Hawkins and Sir Martin Frobisher proceeded to the Azores, but Philip II's orders kept the West Indies fleet where it was, and the East Indies fleet by good fortune escaped from the English ambuscade. In 1591, accordingly, Lord Thomas Howard and Sir Richard Grenville, with a small fleet, reached the Azores (in what proved to be a very sickly season) and were waiting the Treasure Fleet, held up in the West Indies the previous year, when (as the following poem tells) an English pinnace, the *Moonshine*, from the coast of Spain, warned them just in time of the approach of the strong Spanish escort.]

I

At Flores in the Azores Sir Richard Grenville lay,
And a pinnace, like a flutter'd bird, came flying from far away:
'Spanish ships of war at sea! we have sighted fifty-three!'
Then sware Lord Thomas Howard: ''Fore God I am no coward;
But I cannot meet them here, for my ships are out of gear,
And the half my men are sick. I must fly, but follow quick.
We are six ships of the line; can we fight with fifty-three?'

II

Then spake Sir Richard Grenville: 'I know you are no coward;
You fly them for a moment to fight with them again.
But I've ninety men and more that are lying sick ashore.
I should count myself the coward if I left them, my Lord Howard,
To these Inquisition dogs, and the devildoms of Spain.'

III

So Lord Howard passed away with five ships of war that day,
Till he melted like a cloud in the silent summer heaven;
But Sir Richard bore in hand all his sick men from the land
Very carefully and slow,
Men of Bideford in Devon,
And we laid them on the ballast down below;
For we brought them all aboard,
And they blest him in their pain, that they were not left to Spain,
To the thumbscrew and the stake, for the glory of the Lord.

IV

He had only a hundred seamen to work the ship and to fight,
And he sailed away from Flores till the Spaniard came in sight,
With his huge sea-castles heaving upon the weather bow.
'Shall we fight or shall we fly?
Good Sir Richard, tell us now,
For to fight is but to die!
There'll be little of us left by the time this sun be set.'
And Sir Richard said again: 'We be all good English men.
Let us bang these dogs of Seville, the children of the devil,
For I never turn'd my back upon Don or devil yet.'

V

Sir Richard spoke and he laugh'd, and we roared a hurrah, and so
The little *Revenge* ran on sheer into the heart of the foe,
With her hundred fighters on deck, and her ninety sick below;
For half of their fleet to the right and half to the left were seen,
And the little *Revenge* ran on thro' the long sea-lane between.

VI

Thousands of their soldiers look'd down from their decks and
    laugh'd,
Thousands of their seamen made mock at the mad little craft

Running on and on, till delay'd
By their mountain-like *San Philip* that, of fifteen hundred tons,
And up-shadowing high above us with her yawning tiers of guns,
Took the breath from our sails, and we stay'd.

VII

And while now the great *San Philip* hung above us like a cloud
Whence the thunderbolt will fall
Long and loud,
Four galleons drew away
From the Spanish fleet that day,
And two upon the larboard and two upon the starboard lay,
And the battle thunder broke from them all.

VIII

But anon the great *San Philip*, she bethought herself and went
Having that within her womb that had left her ill content;
And the rest they came aboard us, and they fought us hand to
hand.
For a dozen times they came with their pikes and musqueteers,
And a dozen times we shook 'em off as a dog that shakes his ears
When he leaps from the water to the land.

IX

And the sun went down, and the stars came out far over the
summer sea,
But never a moment ceased the fight of the one and the fifty-three.
Ship after ship, the whole night long, their high-built galleons
came
Ship after ship, the whole night long, with her battle-thunder
and flame;
Ship after ship, the whole night long, drew back with her dead
and her shame.
For some were sunk and many were shatter'd, and so could fight
us no more—
God of battles, was ever a battle like this in the world before?

X

For he said 'Fight on! fight on!'
Tho' his vessel was all but a wreck;
And it chanced that when half of the short summer night was gone,
With a grisly wound to be drest he had left the deck,
But a bullet struck him that was dressing it suddenly dead,
And himself he was wounded again in the side and the head.
And he said 'Fïght on! fight on!'

XI

And the night went down, and the sun smiled out far over the
    summer sea.
And the Spanish fleet with broken sides lay round us all in a ring;
But they dared not touch us again, for they feared that we still
    could sting,
So they watch'd what the end would be.
And we had not fought them in vain,
But in perilous plight were we,
Seeing forty of our poor hundred were slain,
And half of the rest of us maim'd for life
In the crash of the cannonades and the desperate strife;
And the sick men down in the hold were most of them stark and
    cold,
And the pikes were all broken or bent, and the powder was all
    of it spent;
And the masts and the rigging were lying over the side;
But Sir Richard cried in his English pride,
'We have fought such a fight for a day and a night
As may never be fought again!
We have won great glory, my men!
And a day less or more
At sea or ashore,
We die,—does it matter when?
Sink me the ship, Master Gunner—sink her, split her in twain!
Fall into the hands of God, not into the hands of Spain!'

XII

And the gunner said 'Ay, ay,' but the seamen made reply:
'We have children, we have wives,
And the Lord hath spared our lives.
We will make the Spaniard promise, if we yield, to let us go;
We shall live to fight again and to strike another blow.'
And the lion there lay dying, and they yielded to the foe.

XIII

And the stately Spanish men to their flagship bore him then,
Where they laid him by the mast, old Sir Richard caught at last,
And they praised him to his face with their courtly foreign grace;
But he rose upon their decks, and he cried:
'I have fought for Queen and Faith like a valiant man and true;
I have only done my duty as a man is bound to do:
With a joyful spirit I Sir Richard Grenville die!'
And he fell upon their decks, and he died.

XIV

And they stared at the dead that had been so valiant and true,
And had holden the power and glory of Spain so cheap
That he dared her with one little ship and his English few;
Was he devil or man? He was devil for aught they knew.
But they sank his body with honour down into the deep,
And they mann'd the *Revenge* with a swarthier alien crew,
And away she sail'd with her loss and long'd for her own;
When a wind from the lands they had ruin'd awoke from sleep,
And the water began to heave and the weather to moan,
And or ever that evening ended a great gale blew,
And a wave like the wave that is raised by an earthquake grew,
Till it smote on their hulls and their sails and their masts and their
    flags
And the whole sea plunged and fell on the shot-shatter'd navy
    of Spain,
And the little *Revenge* herself went down by the island crags
To be lost evermore in the main.

HELPS

The two place-names in the opening words of the poem are pronounced 'Floor-ez' and 'Azoor-ez'.

Pinnace. A fast little ship like the gun-brig or schooner of Nelson's day; not to be confused with the boat of to-day. The pinnace which brought the news to Flores was the *Moonshine*.

Inquisition. A tribunal for the detection and punishment of heresy.

Revenge. Tennyson heightens the heroism of the English ship by reducing her size. Actually she had been Drake's flagship against the Armada; was one of the finest battleships afloat, and quite able to stand up to several opponents at once.

QUESTIONS

(1) Who was the English Commander-in-Chief and who the second in command?

(2) Mention two reproachful or opprobrious expressions applied by Grenville to his enemies.

(3) Where had the ship's company of the *Revenge* been recruited?

(4) What was the full complement of the *Revenge* and upon how many could Grenville rely in the hour of battle?

(5) Where were the wounded put for safety during the engagement?

(6) What is Tennyson's phrase to describe the bigness of the Spanish galleons?

(7) Which was the largest ship in the Spanish fleet and what was her tonnage?

(8) At the outset of the encounter how many galleons did the *Revenge* engage single-handed?

(9) How many men did the *Revenge* lose during the fight?

(10) Quote from memory Sir Richard Grenville's dying speech.

(11) How did it come about that Sir Richard's last command was not obeyed?

(12) Substitute other words for the following without change of sense: 'devildoms', 'grisly', 'sheer', 'perilous', 'stark', 'courtly', 'valiant', 'desperate', 'crags', 'main', 'shot-shattered'.

(13) What was, or is, a thumbscrew, a pike, a Don, a thunderbolt, a musketeer?

(14) Why does Tennyson describe the guns as 'yawning'? Would the word still be applicable if tompions were in place?

(15) How did the great battle at Flores in the Azores end?

COMPARISONS

To what does Tennyson by comparison liken

(a) the pinnace *Moonshine*;
(b) Howard's disappearance from the battlefield;
(c) the water interval between the two Spanish squadrons;
(d) the manner in which the *Revenge* shook off her opponents;
(e) the rush of water that sent the *Revenge* to the bottom?

QUOTATIONS

Attempt to complete from memory the following quotations:

(a) 'they were not left to Spain, to the...'
(b) 'the little *Revenge* ran on...'
(c) 'And the sun went down, and the stars...'
(d) 'And the Spanish fleet with broken sides...'
(e) 'And the sick men down in the hold...'
(f) 'Fall into the hands of God, not...'
(g) 'And they praised him to his face...'
(h) 'In the crash of the cannonades...'

FOR A PRÉCIS

(1) Make a précis of the passage beginning 'Then sware Lord Thomas...' and ending '...devildoms of Spain'.

(2) Make a précis of the passage beginning, 'Shall we fight...' and ending '...or devil yet'.

FOR AN ESSAY

(1) Imagine yourself to be a junior officer of the *Revenge* who eventually escaped to England in safety. Describe in simple language for the benefit of those at home what actually occurred off Flores in the Azores from the time Sir Richard gave the word for battle until the ship's company insisted on a capitulation.

(2) 'Shall we fight or shall we fly?...There'll be little of us left by the time this sun be set.'

This sentiment, though reasonable, did not influence Grenville's resolution. He knew that it was his duty to guard the rear of the defenceless English ships which Howard was endeavouring to deliver from the Spanish ambuscade.

The same action was taken by Captain Fegen of the *Jervis Bay* in November 1940. Collect details of the *Jervis Bay's* last fight and write an account of it, making use of any of Tennyson's words or phrases which you think suited to the occasion.

HOW THE FIRST DUTCH WAR BEGAN

[INTRODUCTORY NOTE. When Queen Elizabeth died, her successor drew out of the war, or, in other words, allowed the Spaniards to utilize the English Channel as they would. The Dutch were, therefore, compelled to fight their own battles alone, alike on land and sea; and in the long struggle, which did not end until 1648, they became not only the greatest naval power in Northern Europe, but the greatest naval power the world till then had ever seen. Dutch sea-power extended to the ends of the earth. The Spanish Empire had absorbed the Portuguese; and the Dutch navies preyed upon both.

The sea-power of England under the Commonwealth and Cromwell was not deliberately built up to challenge or oppose the Dutch, but as a necessary consequence of the Great Civil War between King and Parliament. After their defeat on land, the Cavaliers were still strong at sea and threatened the very existence of the Republican Government in London. When, however, Robert Blake had reversed this state of things and secured command of the English Channel, a collision with the Dutch became inevitable. They ordered 150 men-of-war to be mobilized; and their Admiral, Martin H. Tromp, had the arrogance to enter an English roadstead and anchor there, as if anxious to provoke hostilities.]

It was about the beginning of May* in the year 1652, that the Dutch fleet, consisting of about forty sail under the command of Van Tromp, rode at anchor in Dover Road, being driven by a strong wind [as they pretended] from the Flanders coast, when the English fleet, under the command of Blake, of a much less number, appeared in view; upon which the Dutch weighed anchor and put out to sea without striking their flag; which Blake, observing, caused three guns to be fired without any ball. It was then observed that there was an express ketch came at the very time from Holland on board the Admiral; and it was then conceived that he had by that express received more positive orders to fight; for, upon the arrival of that express, he tacked about, and bore directly towards the English fleet; and the three guns were no sooner fired, but, in contempt of the advertisement, he discharged one single gun from his poop, and hung out a red

* 19 May.

flag, and came up to the English admiral, and gave him a broadside, with which he killed many of his men, and hurt his ship. With which, though Blake was surprised, as not expecting such an assault, he deferred not to give him the same rude salutation; and so both fleets were forthwith engaged in a very fierce encounter; which continued for the space of four hours, and until the night parted them, after the loss of much blood on both sides.

On the part of the Dutch, they lost two ships, whereof one was sunk and the other taken, with both the captains, and near two hundred prisoners. On the English side there were many slain, and more wounded, but no ship lost, nor officer of name. When the morning appeared the Dutch were gone to their coast. And thus the war was entered into before it was suspected in England.

With what consideration soever the Dutch had embarked themselves in this sudden enterprise, it quickly appeared they had taken very ill measures of the people's affections. For the news of this conflict no sooner arrived in Holland, but there was the most general consternation amongst all sorts of men that can be imagined; and the States themselves were so much troubled at it, that with marvellous expedition they despatched two extraordinary ambassadors into England; by whom they protested that the late unhappy engagement between the fleets of the two commonwealths had happened without their knowledge, and contrary to the desire of the lords, the States General; that they had received the fatal tidings of so rash an attempt with amazement and astonishment; and that they had immediately entered into consultation how they might best close this fresh bleeding wound, and to avoid the farther effusion of Christian blood, so much desired by the enemies of both states: and therefore they most earnestly desired them, by their mutual concurrence in religion, and by their mutual love of liberty, that nothing might be done with passion and heat, which might widen the breach, but that they might speedily receive such an answer that there might be no farther obstruction to the trade of both common-wealths.

To which answer was presently returned to them: that the civility which they had always showed towards the States of the United Provinces was so notorious, that nothing was more strange than the ill return they had made to them; that the extra-ordinary preparation which they had made, of a hundred and fifty ships, without any apparent necessity, and the instructions which they had given to the seamen, had administered too much cause to believe that the lords the States General of the United Provinces had a purpose to usurp the known right which the English have to the seas, and to destroy their fleets, which, under the protection of the Almighty, are their walls and bulwarks, that so they might be exposed to the invasion of any powerful enemy: therefore they thought themselves obliged to endeavour, by God's assistance, to seek reparation for the injuries and damage they had already received, and to prevent the like for the future: however, they should never be without an intention and desire that some effectual means might be found to establish a good peace, union, and right understanding between the two nations.

With this haughty answer they vigorously prosecuted their revenge, and commanded Blake presently to sail to the north-ward; it being then the season of the year for their great fisheries upon the coasts of Scotland and the isles of Orkney, (by the benefit whereof they derive a great part of their trade over Europe;) and where he now found their multitude of fishing boats, guarded by twelve ships of war; all which, with the fish they had made ready, he brought away with him as good prize.

When Blake was sent to the north, Sir George Ayscue [being just returned from the West Indies] was sent with another part of the fleet to the south; who at his very going out met with thirty sail of their merchants between Dover and Calais: a good part whereof he took or sunk, and forced the rest to run on shore upon the French coast; which is very little better than being taken. And from thence he stood westward; and near Plymouth, in the middle of August, with thirty sail of men of war he engaged the whole Dutch fleet, consisting of sixty ships of war and thirty merchants. It was near four of the clock in the afternoon when both fleets began to engage, so that the night quickly parted them; yet not before two of the Holland ships of war were sunk and most of the men lost; the Dutch in that action applying themselves most to spoil the tackling and sails of the English; in which they had so good success, that the next morning they were not able to give them farther chase, till their sails and rigging could be repaired. But no day passed without the taking and bringing in many and valuable Dutch ships into the ports of England, which, having begun their voyages before any notice given to them of the war, were making haste home without any fear of their security: so that there being now no hope of a peace by the mediation of their ambassadors, who could not prevail in any thing they proposed, they returned; and the war was proclaimed on either side as well as prosecuted.

History of the Rebellion.

QUESTIONS

(1) How did Blake order Tromp to salute the English flag?

(2) How did Tromp signal to the rest of the Dutch fleet to engage?

(3) How long did the battle of Dover last?

(4) What was the result of the engagement?

(5) What brought the engagement to a close?

(6) What four different words or phrases does Lord Clarendon use when he speaks of England's enemies?

(7) How many men-of-war did the Dutch mobilize before Tromp dared to anchor in an English roadstead?

(8) In the battle of Dover, Blake had thirteen ships and Tromp two more than Lord Clarendon mentions; by how many sail was Blake outnumbered?

(9) What do you understand by an 'express ketch'?

(10) Find alternative and (if possible) simpler words for Lord Clarendon's 'advertisement', 'extraordinary [ambassadors]', 'notorious', 'reparation', 'vigorously', 'mediation', 'contention'.

(11) After the first clash at Dover, Tromp seems to fade out of the story. What do you think became of him?

(12) Complete from memory the following sentence as Lord Clarendon first wrote it: 'The known right which the English have to the seas... which, under the protection of the Almighty, are their × × × × × and × × × × × × × ×.'

(13) Rewrite the following, altering the words but retaining the meaning.

(a) 'He deferred not to give him the same rude salutation.'
(b) 'They had taken very ill measures of the people's affections.'
(c) 'Avoid the farther effusion of Christian blood, so much desired by the enemies of both states.'
(d) 'By their mutual concurrence in religion.'
(e) 'The war was proclaimed on both sides as well as prosecuted.'

(14) Who took charge of the Channel Fleet when Blake attacked the Dutch fisheries?

(15) The Dutch Ambassadors Extraordinary hoped that nothing would occur 'to widen the breach'. What is the military significance of this phrase?

FOR A PRÉCIS

Write a précis of the passage beginning, 'They protested that the late unhappy engagement...' and ending '...understanding between the two nations'.

FOR AN ESSAY

(1) In the battle of Dover, Tromp lost two ships. After the engagement he wrote a polite letter to Blake asking him to be so kind as to return them.

Blake began his reply as follows: 'Sir, It is not without great astonishment that I have read yours of the 23 May, wherein though representing yourself as a person of honour, you introduce many gross misstatements...', and ended as follows: '...follow up your former insults by your present letter: to which the only meet answer that I can return is that I presume Parliament will keenly resent this great insult and the spilling of the blood of their unoffending subjects, and that you will moreover find in the undersigned one ever ready to carry out their commands. Your humble servant Robert Blake.'

Make this reply more complete by adding fresh facts and arguments into the middle portion and copy out the whole letter afresh.

(2) In your capacity as Mayor of Dover, write a letter to the Council of State describing what occurred in the 'late sea-fight' according to the reports from eye-witnesses hourly coming in.

[You need not confine your narrative to the facts that Lord Clarendon describes. Begin your letter, 'Gentlemen'.]

(3) Describe the course of the First Dutch War at sea from the moment both parties to the struggle realized that hostilities were unavoidable; explaining why England, in spite of marked inferiority in ships and in warlike preparations, managed to secure so large a measure of success.

TWO LETTERS OF ROBERT BLAKE TO
MR SECRETARY THURLOE

THE CAMPAIGN IN TUNISIA

[INTRODUCTORY NOTE. When the Dutch had been decisively defeated, and English naval pre-eminence had recovered the prestige which it had enjoyed in the days of Drake, Cromwell sent a fleet under Blake to the Mediterranean to show the flag and to bring sea-power to bear upon the relations of his government with those of France, Spain, Portugal and the Italian states, not omitting (if time allowed) the four Mohammedan powers along the northern coasts of Africa—Morocco, Algiers, Tunis and Tripoli. Of these four, Tunis was by far the most important and formidable, in part on account of the number and excellence of its harbours, but in chief because it commanded the Channel where the two basins of the Mediterranean are constricted, like the two bulbs of an hour-glass, into a narrow defile. At this point the Dey of Tunis battened on passing ships; and, ignorant of political and other changes in England, made no exception where London merchants were concerned. Indeed, he not only devoured both ships and cargoes; but, against the laws of war, impressed English seamen to man his own vessels and serve against their countrymen afloat.]

Aboard the *George* in the bay of Cagliari.
14 March 1655.

Sir,—Yours of the 25th January, as also the former mentioned in that, I have received. In the latter you inform me of the dissolution of the Parliament, with the grounds and consequences of it. I was not much surprised with the intelligence; the slow proceedings and awkward motions of that assembly giving great cause to suspect it would come to some such period; and I cannot but exceedingly wonder, that there should yet remain so strong a spirit of prejudice and animosity in the minds of men, who profess themselves most affectionate patriots, as to postpone the necessary ways and means for preservation of the Commonwealth, especially in such a time of concurrence of the mischievous plots and designs both of old and new enemies, tending all to the destruction of the same. But blessed be the Lord, who hath hitherto delivered, and still doth deliver us; and I trust will continue so to do, although He be very much tempted by us.

Sir, in my last unto you I gave you notice of our intention to sail out of the road of Leghorn to Trapani, and thence to Tunis; but upon intelligence after given us of the sudden meeting of the *Algiers* and other men-of-war in Tunis Bay, bound into the Levant for the service of the Grand Seigneur (which intelligence proved to be untrue) we hasted away towards Tunis directly, and somewhat sooner than did well stand with the state of our provisions at that time.

After our arrival there, which was the 7th of February, I did forthwith send ashore to the Dey of Tunis a paper of demands for restitution of the ship *Princess*, with satisfaction for losses, and enlargement of captives, according to the particular instruction, which I received for that purpose. After some answers and replies, Commissioners of both sides were agreed upon to capitulate, which met aboard our ship; but the meeting proved altogether fruitless, they refusing to make a restitution of satisfaction for what was past, but pretending an earnest desire to conclude a firm peace for the future.

Hereupon we sailed away before Porto Farina, not far off, where their ships of war lay, being kept in by a party of our frigates sent thither before. At our coming before the place, we perceived their ships to be drawn up as near the shore as they could, lightened and unrigged; their guns planted upon divers batteries upon the land, and a kind of formed camp, consisting of some thousands of horse and foot, as if they feared some invasion. Some debate had amongst ourselves, whether we should sail into the port with our fleet, and attack their ships where they were: to which there seemed to be a willing inclination in all.

But entering upon consideration of the best ways how to effect it, we found the enterprise to have so much difficulty, in regard of a strong castle within, before which we must anchor with our great ships at half-musket shot, and the port too narrow for our fleet to turn in it, especially at that time: it was judged to be an attempt unreasonable and desperate, there not being in the fleet above five days' liquor, and a great scarcity of bread.

And here I hold it seasonable to let you know, that we are not fully satisfied as touching the power given in that particular instruction, authorising us, in case of refusal of right, to seize, surprise, sink, and destroy all ships and vessels belonging to the kingdom of Tunis, that we shall meet; which, as it doth not expressly forbid us to enter their ports to that end, so neither doth it expressly empower us, especially being compared with that part of the general instruction, concerning Turkish pirates, limiting us in such cases only to block up their harbours for some days. This I write, as wishing that the intent of this and other instructions of this nature might be more clear and explicit, and more plainly significant as to our duty; but upon the forementioned consideration we desisted from the enterprise at that present, and sailed directly for this place, leaving the *Plymouth*, *Kent*, *Newcastle*, *Mermaid*, *Taunton*, *Foresight* to attend that service.

At our arrival in this place, we found the *Langport* and other three frigates sent out of Leghorn Road to ply between Majorca and Cape Paul, which brought in with them a new French frigate of 15 guns, but one that will bear more; another ship of war, called the *Percy*, an English vessel, well known, of thirty guns, they forced ashore at Majorca, where not able to possess themselves of it, being also extremely battered and spoiled, they took 3000 dollars of the Governor of that place for it, who was likewise upon agreement to be at the charge of sending home all the French in her, which were 300 in number.

This morning I sent the *Langport* and *Diamond* to Majorca, to take in what bread they can get, and so to range as far as Alicante, and thence to go to Genoa, to meet with the *Maidstone*, and *Hampshire*, which I have ordered to sail thither to make clean, and also to get a supply of bread. We were also this morning under sail with the rest of the fleet, the *Hope* flyboat only excepted, which is to remain here to make provision of bread, till further order. But it proving first calm, and then the wind, which was contrary, we came again to anchor.

Our intention is to sail hence with the first opportunity to the Bay of Tunis, to put an end to the business there, which we shall endeavour to do with all the resolution and circumspection we can, as God shall direct us, it being a business of manifold concernments and interests, and subject to divers consequences and constructions. Of the issue thereof, with all the particular passages, I will hereafter (the Lord willing) give you an account.

Sir, the commands of his Highness the Lord Protector writ with his own hand, of which you gave me an intimation in yours, I have received, and here make bold to return an answer thereto in writing, which I desire you to present, together with my most humble and faithful acknowledgements of duty and service for all the favours, which for many years I have received in a very large measure from his Highness. You will hereby very much endear me, and continue to add, as you ever do, to the obligations of,

Sir, your affectionate friend and servant,

ROBERT BLAKE

Aboard the *George* in the Bay of Cagliari.

18th April, 1655.

Sir,—My last unto you was from this place of the 14th March, since which time I have not had any opportunity of sending unto you, by reason of our various motions, and stops which hath been put upon us in those places, where was no means of conveyance by contrary and stormy winds, such as have scarcely been known in those parts. In that letter I gave you some account of what had passed between us and those of Tunis, refusing to do us any justice in order to my demands, according to the particular instructions I received to that purpose. Also of our withdrawing from that place for a while, with an intention to return thither, which we did upon the 18th of that month.

After our arrival we found them more wilful and untractable than before, adding to their obstinacy much insolence and contumely, denying us all commerce of civility, and hindering all others as much as they could from the same. These barbarous provocations did so far work upon our spirits, that we judged it necessary for the honour of the fleet, our nation, and religion, seeing they would not deal with us as friends, to make them feel as enemies; and it was thereupon resolved at a Council of War to endeavour the firing their ships in Porto Farina.

The better to effect the same, we drew off again and sailed to Trapani, (our occasions likewise agreeing thereunto) that so they might be the more secure.

After the stay of some days there, we set sail back for Porto Farina, where we arrived the 3rd instant in the afternoon, and met again at a Council of War, at which it was resolved by the permission of God, to put in execution our former intentions. Accordingly the next morning very early, we entered with the fleet into the harbour, and anchored before their castles, the Lord being pleased to favour us with a gentle gale off the sea, which cast all the smoke upon them, and made our work the more easy; for after some hours' dispute, we set on fire all their ships, which were in number nine, and the same favourable gale still continuing, we retreated out again into the road. We had twenty-five men slain and about forty hurt, with very little other loss. It is also remarkable by us, that, shortly after our getting forth, the wind and weather changed and continued very stormy for many days, so that we could not have effected the business, had not the Lord afforded that nick of time in which it was done.

And now, seeing it hath pleased God so signally to justify us therein, I hope his Highness will not be offended at it, nor any who regard duly the honour of our nation, although I expect to hear of many complaints and clamours of interested men. I confess, that, in contemplation thereof, and some seeming ambiguity in my instructions (of which I gave you a hint in my last) I did awhile much hesitate myself, and was balanced in my thoughts until the barbarous carriage of those pirates did turn the scale.

I have sent a perfect account of the whole business unto Sir Thomas Bendish at Constantinople, by the commander of the *Merchant's Delight* of London, which was then by providence in the road of Goletta. You will also herewith receive copies of all the particular passages between us. We are even now setting sail to go to Algiers, that being the only place in the Straits, that can afford us a considerable supply of bread and flesh, if they will; otherwise we are likely to be brought into great necessity, being disappointed of the hope we had out of England, according to an offer made us long ago by the Commissioners at Whitehall. From Algiers we intend, if God enable us, to sail for Majorca, and from thence to range along the coast of Provence, to attend the French fleet in our way homeward, as long as our victuals will admit; they are now drawing very near expiration.

As touching the Neapolitan horses and mares, Mr Longland writes me that they are at high and excessive rates; howbeit I have sent the *Success* to Naples to attend there, for the transportation of them, in lieu of the *Elias*, which having in her a good quantity of beverage wine, and I hope some bread for the fleet, I have ordered to come to us at Majorca. Sir, I have no more at present to trouble you with, only desire you to present my humble service and duty to his Highness the Lord Protector.

Recommending you to the Lord,

I remain,

Your very affectionate friend and servant,

ROBERT BLAKE.

HELPS

Grand Seigneur (or Signior). The Sultan of Turkey.
To capitulate. To draw up terms of agreement.
Frigate. Not (as in Nelson's day) equivalent to a cruiser or light cruiser; but here used of men-of-war generally, more especially ships of the line.

QUESTIONS

[Before attempting to answer the following questions, draw a map of the Western Mediterranean and with the help of an atlas insert the following places: Algiers, Alicante, Cagliari, Cape Paul (Palos), Genoa, Goletta (La Goulette), Leghorn, Majorca, Naples, Porto Farina, Trapani, Tunis.]

(1) Who was John Thurloe?

(2) What is meant by the Levant?

(3) By what titles does Blake refer to (a) the Ruler of Tunis, (b) the Sultan?

(4) What did Blake do on his first arrival at Tunis on 7 February 1655?

(5) What does Blake imply when he speaks of making a ship 'clean'?

(6) What action did Blake take when negotiations with Tunis broke down?

(7) To whom does Blake refer as 'His Highness'? What other term is used in speaking of the same highly-placed person?

(8) What were the chief necessities of which Blake's fleet ran short? Why did he not obtain what he required from England? How did he make good the deficiency?

(9) How long an interval elapses between Blake's two dispatches?

(10) What does Blake mean by the dissolution of Parliament?

(11) Who was Sir Thomas Bendish?

(12) What is meant by 'in the Straits'?

(13) What did Blake propose to do after the battle of Porto Farina?

(14) Quote any words or sentences to illustrate the piety of Robert Blake.

(15) Sixteen English ships are mentioned by name in these two letters. Write down those you can remember.

(16) Supply alternative words, having the same meaning, as Blake's 'period', 'concurrence', 'intelligence', 'enlargement', 'restitution', 'inclination', 'desisted', 'circumspection', 'manifold', 'concernments', 'divers', 'motions', 'stops', 'contumely', 'commerce', 'provocations', 'ambiguity', 'carriage', 'flesh', 'victuals', 'beverage', 'expiration'.

(17) Rewrite the following sentences, using simple words of your own choice without alteration of the sense:

(a) 'I cannot but exceedingly wonder, that there should yet remain so strong a spirit of prejudice and animosity in the minds of men, who profess themselves most affectionate patriots.'

(b) 'I trust will continue so to do, although He be very much tempted by us.'

(c) 'We hasted away towards Tunis directly, and somewhat sooner than did well stand with the state of our provisions at the time.'

(d) 'Commissioners of both sides were agreed upon to capitulate, which met aboard our ship; but the meeting proved altogether fruitless, they refusing to make a restitution of satisfaction for what was past.'

(e) 'This and other instructions of this nature might be more clear and explicit, and more plainly significant as to our duty.'

(f) 'We found them more wilful and untractable than before, adding to their obstinacy much insolence and contumely, denying us all commerce of civility.'

FOR AN ESSAY

(1) When Blake finally left the Mediterranean, he prophesied that the time would come when the name of England would be held in greater awe and veneration in that sea than the names of Greece and Rome. Give your reasons for thinking that this prophecy has been fulfilled.

(2) In these letters, it has been said, Blake clearly shows his own character. What sort of a man do you think he must have been?

(3) It has been calculated that, in Blake's day, the Mediterranean was relatively farther from England than the South-West Pacific to-day. What were the chief difficulties encountered by Blake on this campaign and how did he overcome them?

(4) Write a full account of the destruction of the Navy of Tunis as if you had been present in person at the battle.

(5) Write a report as from the Captain of the *Langport*, giving Blake an account of your proceedings during his absence.

THOMAS CARLYLE

THE BATTLE OF SANTA CRUZ
1657

[INTRODUCTORY NOTE. When Blake returned from his victorious campaign in the Mediterranean, he found that Cromwell, anxious to distract attention from many grounds for uneasiness at home, had decided to intervene in the war then raging between France and Spain. With the latter power in particular, England had many unsettled disputes; and in majestic tones the Protector demanded of Spain the very terms which should have been exacted at the close of Elizabeth's reign. Receiving a haughty negative, and knowing what a thunderbolt he had at his disposal, Cromwell once more sent forth Robert Blake to do his worst.]

COURAGE, my Lord Protector! Blake even now, though as yet you know it not, is giving the Spaniards a terrible scorching for you, in the port of Santa Cruz!—worth noting:

In those very minutes while the Lord Protector is speaking as above, there goes on far off, on the Atlantic brine, under shadow of the Peak of Teneriffe, one of the fieriest actions ever fought by land or water; this action of the Sea King Blake at the Port of Santa Cruz. The case was this. Blake cruising on the coast of Spain, watching as usual for Plate Fleets, heard for certain that there was a Fleet actually come as far as the Canary Isles, and now lying in the Bay of Santa Cruz in Teneriffe there. Blake makes instant sail thither; arrives there still in Time this Monday morning* early; finds the Fleet fast moored in Santa Cruz Bay; rich silver-ships, strong war-ships, sixteen as we count them; stronger almost than himself, and moored here under defences unassailable apparently by any mortal.

Santa Cruz Bay is shaped as a horse-shoe: at the entrance are Castles, in the inner circuit are other Castles, eight of them in all, bristling with great guns; war-ships moored at the entrance, war-frigates moored all round the beach, and men and gunners at command: one great magazine of sleeping thunder and destruc-

* 20 April 1657.

tion: to appearance, if you wish for sure suicide to run into, this must be it. Blake, taking measure of the business, runs into it, defying its loud thunder; much out-thunders it,—mere whirlwinds of fire and iron hail, the old Peak never heard the like;—silences the Castles, sinks or burns every sail in the Harbour; annihilates the Spanish Fleet; and then, the wind veering round in his favour, sails out again, leaving Santa Cruz Bay much astonished at him. It is the last action of the brave Blake; who worn out with toil and sickness and a cruise of three years, makes homewards shortly after; dies within sight of Plymouth.

Oliver Cromwell's Letters and Speeches.

QUESTIONS

(1) Draw a map of the north-west shoulder of Africa and insert Casablanca, Dakar, the Madeira, and Canary Isles.

(2) Where is the harbour of Santa Cruz situated? Be exact.

(3) Why does Carlyle use the word 'scorching' of the punishment meted out to the Spaniards on this occasion? In what other connection has the same word been employed in a military sense?

(4) What is meant by 'Plate Fleet'?

(5) Where was Blake when he heard of the target at the Canary Isles?

(6) To whom do the Canary Isles belong to-day? What else do we associate with these Isles besides Canary Wine?

(7) What resemblance do you note between the attack on Santa Cruz and the attack on Porto Farina?

(8) How long had Blake been absent from England when he sighted its shores for the last time?

(9) What other British Admiral dared to attack Santa Cruz? What measure of success attended his onslaught?

(10) Mention any other famous English sea-commanders who died at sea.

(11) What was Oliver Cromwell doing while Blake was destroying the Spanish fleet?

(12) What did Carlyle mean by 'As we count them', 'Atlantic brine', 'the old Peak'?

(13) From Carlyle's description draw a plan to illustrate the defences of Santa Cruz.

(14) Substitute other words for the following: 'unassailable', 'circuit', 'whirlwinds', 'annihilates', 'veering'.

(15) To what does Carlyle compare the shape of Santa Cruz bay?

(16) Carlyle in this passage employs unusual forms:

(a) *Historic Present*: to make his narrative more vivid he changes the tense from Past to Present (a mannerism best avoided by ordinary writers).

(b) *Apostrophe*: he addresses one of the characters whom he has introduced into his narrative.

Quote from the preceding passage examples of the Historic Present and Apostrophe.

(17) Express in other words:

(a) 'Blake, taking measure of the business, runs into it.'

(b) 'One great magazine of sleeping thunder and destruction.'

(c) 'Leaving Santa Cruz Bay much astonished at him.'

FOR AN ESSAY

(1) The dictionary defines a 'King' as 'chief ruler' or 'one pre-eminent among his fellow-men'.

Bearing this definition in mind, give your reasons for thinking Carlyle right in describing Blake as a 'Sea King'.

(2) [Before attempting the following, read carefully the poem that follows, 'Robert Blake' by Gerald Massey; and collect from it suitable words and phrases in praise of the Admiral.]

When his flagship reached Plymouth, Blake's body was conveyed to Greenwich where it lay in state, then by river to London, and so to a magnificent funeral at Westminster. Compose a speech to be delivered in praise of the great sea ruler on this last solemn occasion.

THE PASSING OF ROBERT BLAKE

HOMEWARD the dying Sea-King turns
   From his last famous fight.
For England's dear green hills he yearns
   At heart, and strains his sight.
The old cliffs loom out grey and grand;
   The old war-ship glides on:
With one last wave life tries to land,
   Falls seaward and is gone.

With that last leap to touch the coast
   He passed into his rest,
And Blake's unwearying arms were crossed
   Upon his martial breast.
And while our England waits, and twines
   For him her latest wreath,
His is a crown of stars that shines
   From out the dusk of death.

For him no pleasant age of ease
   To wear what youth could win;
For him no children round his knees
   To gather his harvest in.
But with a soul serene he takes
   Whatever lot may come;
And such a life of labour makes
   A glorious coming home.

Famous old Trueheart, dead and gone!
   Long shall his glory grow,
Who never turned his back upon
   A friend, nor face from foe.

He made them fear old England's name
  Wherever it was heard.
He put her proudest foe to shame,
  And Peace smiled on his sword.

With lofty courage, loftier love,
  He died for England's sake;
And 'mid the loftiest lights above
  Shines our illustrious Blake.
And shall shine! Glory of the West
  And Beacon of the Seas;
While Britain bares its sailor breast
  To battle or to breeze.

Great sailor on the seas of strife
  Victor by land and wave;
Brave liver of a gallant life;
  Lord of a glorious grave;
True soldier set on earthly hill
  As sentinel of Heaven;
A king who keeps his kingdom till
  The last award be given.

Till she forget her old sea-fame
  Shall England honour him;
And keep the grave-grass from his name
  Till her old eyes be dim:
And long as free waves folding round,
  Brimful with blessing break,
At heart she holds him, calm and crowned,
  Immortal Robert Blake.

THE FOUR DAYS' BATTLE

Thursday, 1 June to Sunday, 4 June 1666

[INTRODUCTORY NOTE. There were three Dutch Wars, and in each there were several hotly contested actions. The battle of Dover (see p. 45–8) was the first engagement of the First Dutch War (1652–4) in the time of the Commonwealth. The 'Four Days' Battle' was the second engagement of the Second Dutch War in the reign of Charles II. An earlier battle in the previous year had proved an easy victory for the Royal Navy; but when the French joined the Dutch, the British Government made a sad mistake, sending half their fleet under Prince Rupert against the French, so leaving the other half (under the Duke of Albemarle) at a signal disadvantage in his struggle with the Dutch under de Ruyter.

The battle was the longest ever fought at sea and its phases were:
(1) Thursday, 1 June: Albemarle surprises the Dutch left wing and gains a temporary advantage: during the night the Dutch bring up reserves.
(2) Friday, 2 June: The initiative passes to de Ruyter and Albemarle is worsted, though offering a stout resistance.
(3) Saturday, 3 June: The British fleet retreats.
(4) Sunday, 4 June: Prince Rupert successfully brings up reinforcements and joins Albemarle. The battle is renewed, and the Dutch retire, Albemarle cursing them for running away.

PERSONS MENTIONED BY MR PEPYS

His name for them	*Our name for them*
ASHORE: 'The King'	Charles II
'The Duke'	The Duke of York, Lord High Admiral (afterwards James II)
Sir William Coventry	Sir William Coventry, Secretary to the Lord High Admiral
Sir William Penn Sir John Minnes I (Samuel Pepys)	The Navy Board
AFLOAT: 'The Duke'	George Monk, Duke of Albemarle, Commander-in-Chief, with his flag in the *Royal Charles*
'The Prince'	Prince Rupert
'Sir G. Ayscue'	Admiral Sir George Ayscue
'Mr Daniel'	Lieutenant Samuel Danerell, R.N., of the *Royal Charles*.

4 JUNE 1666. To White Hall, where, when we come, we find the Duke at St James's, whither he has lately gone to lodge. So, walking through the Park, we saw hundreds of people listening at the Gravel-pits, and to and again in the Park, to hear the guns. I saw a letter, dated last night, from Strowd, Governor of Dover Castle, which says that the Prince come thither the night before with his fleet; but that for the guns which we writ that we heard, it is only a mistake for thunder; and, so far as to yesterday, it is a miraculous thing that we all Friday, and Saturday, and yesterday, did hear everywhere most plainly the guns go off, and yet at Deal and Dover, to last night, they did not hear one word of a fight, nor think they heard one gun. This added to what I have set down before, the other day, about the *Catherine*, makes room for a great dispute in philosophy, how we should hear it, and they not, the same wind that brought it to us being the same that should bring it to them: but so it is. Major Halsey, however, who was sent down on purpose to hear the news, did bring news this morning that he did see the Prince and his fleet at nine of the clock yesterday morning, four or five leagues to sea behind the Goodwins, so that, by the hearing of the guns this morning, we conclude he is come to the fleet.

After waiting upon the Duke with Sir W. Penn, who was commanded to go to-night by water, down to Harwich, to dispatch away all the ships he can, I home; where no sooner come, but news is brought me of a couple of men come to speak with me from the fleet; so I down, and who should it be but Mr Daniel,* all muffled up, and his face as black as the chimney, and covered with dirt, pitch, and tar, and powder, and muffled with dirty clouts, and his right eye stopped with oakum. He is come last night, at five o'clock, from the fleet, with a comrade of his that hath endangered another eye. They were set on shore at Harwich this morning, and at two o'clock in a ketch with about twenty more wounded men from the *Royal Charles*. They being able to

---

* Mr Pepys has got the name wrong. The special messenger from the *Royal Charles* was Lieutenant Samuel Danerell.

ride, took post about three this morning, and were here between eleven and twelve. I went presently into the coach with them, and carried them to Somerset-House-stairs, and there took water, all the world gazing upon us, and concluding it to be news from the fleet, and everybody's face appeared expecting of news, to the Privy-stairs, and left them at Sir William Coventry's lodging, he, though, not being there; and so I into the Park to the King, and told him my Lord General was well the last night at five o'clock, and the Prince come with his fleet, and joined with his about seven. The King was mightily pleased with this news, and so took me by the hand and talked a little of it, I giving him the best account I could; and then he bid me to fetch the two seamen to him, he walking into the house. So I went and fetched the seamen into the Vane Room to him, and there he heard the whole account.

How we found the Dutch fleet at anchor on Friday, half seas over, between Dunkirk and Ostend, and made them slip their anchors. They about ninety, and we less than sixty. We fought them, and put them to the run, till they met with about sixteen sail of fresh ships, and so bore up again. The fight continued till night, and then again the next morning, from five till seven at night. And, so, too, yesterday morning they begun again, and continued till about four o'clock, they chasing us for the most part of Saturday, and yesterday we flying from them. The Duke himself, and then those people who were put into the ketch, by and by spied the Prince's fleet coming, upon which De Ruyter called a little council, being in chase at this time of us, and thereupon their fleet divided into two squadrons; forty in one, and about thirty in the other, the fleet being at first about ninety, but, by one accident or other, supposed to be lessened to about seventy; the bigger to follow the Duke, the less to meet the Prince. But the Prince come up with the General's fleet, and the Dutch come together again, and bore towards their own coast, and we with them; and now what the consequence of this day will be, we know not.

The Duke was forced to come to anchor on Friday, having lost his sails and rigging. No particular person spoken of to be hurt but Sir W. Clerke, who hath lost his leg, and bore it bravely. The Duke himself had a little hurt in his thigh, but signified little. The King did pull out of his pocket about twenty pieces in gold, and did give Daniel for himself and his companion; and so parted, mightily pleased with the account he did give him of the fight, and the success it aided with, of the Prince's coming, though it seems the Duke did give way again and again. The King did give order for care to be had of Mr Daniel and his companion; and so we parted from him, and then met the Duke of York, and gave him the same account: and so broke up, and I left them going to the surgeon's. So home, about four o'clock to dinner, and was followed by several people to be told the news, and good news it is.

God send we may hear a good issue of this day's business! To the Crown, behind the Change, and there supped at the club with my Lord Brouncker, Sir G. Ent, and others of Gresham College; and all our discourse is of this fight at sea, and all are doubtful of the success, and conclude all had been lost, if the Prince had not come in, they having chased us the greatest part of Saturday and Sunday. Thence with my Lord Brouncker, and Creed by coach to White Hall, where fresh letters are come from Harwich, where the *Gloucester*, Captain Clerke, is come in, and says that, on Sunday night upon the coming in of the Prince, the Duke did fly;* but all this day they have been fighting; therefore they did face again, to be sure. Captain Bacon of the *Bristol* is killed. They cry up Jennings of the *Ruby*, and Saunders of the *Sweepstake*. They condemn mightily Sir Thomas Tiddiman for a coward, but with what reason time must show.

5 JUNE. At noon though I should have dined with my Lord Mayor, and Aldermen at an entertainment of Commissioner Taylor's; yet, it being a time of expectation of the success of the

---

* At the time of Prince Rupert's arrival, the main British fleet was retreating.

fleet, I did not go. No manner of news this day, but of the *Rainbow's* being put in from the fleet, maimed as the other ships are.

6 JUNE. By water to St James's, it being a monthly fast-day for the plague. There we all met, and did our business as usual with the Duke. By and by walking a little further, Sir Philip Frowde did meet the Duke with an express to Sir W. Coventry, who was by, from Captain Taylor, the Storekeeper at Harwich, being the narration of Captain Hayward of the *Dunkirk*; who gives a very serious account, how upon Monday the two fleets fought all day, till seven at night, and then the whole fleet of Dutch did betake themselves to a very plain flight, and never looked back again. That Sir Christopher* is wounded in the leg; that the General is well. That it is conceived reasonably, that of all the Dutch fleet, which with what recruits they had, come to one hundred sail, there is not above fifty got home; and of them, few, if any, of their flags.† And that little Captain Bell, in one of the fire-ships, did at the end of the day fire a ship of 70 guns. We were also so overtaken with this good news, that the Duke ran with it to the King, who was gone to chapel, and there all the Court was in a hubbub, being rejoiced over head and ears in this good news.

Away I go by coach to the New Exchange, and there did spread this good news a little, though I find it had broke out before. And so home to our own church, it being the common Fast-day, and it was just before sermon; but Lord! how all the people in the church stared upon me to see me whisper to Sir John Minnes and my Lady Penn. Anon I saw people stirring and whispering below, and by and by comes up the sexton from my Lady Ford to tell me the news which I had brought, being now sent into the church by Sir W. Batten in writing and passed from pew to pew. But that which pleased me as much as the news, was, to have the fair Mrs Middleton at our church, who indeed is a very beautiful lady. My father to Hales's where my father is

---

* Sir Christopher Myngs.   † Flagships.

to begin to sit to-day for his picture, which I have a desire to have. At home, drawing up my vows for the rest of the year, to Christmas; but, Lord! to see in what a condition of happiness I am, if I would but keep myself so; but my love of pleasure is such, that my very soul is angry with itself for its vanity in so doing.

Home, and my father and wife not coming in, I proceeded with my coach to take a little air as far as Bow all alone, and there turned back; but, before I got home, the bonfires were lighted all the town over, and I going through Crutched Friars, seeing Mercer at her mother's gate, stopped, and alight, and into her mothers, the first time I ever was there, and find all my people, father and all, at a very fine supper at Mr Hewer's lodging, very neatly, and to my great pleasure. After supper, into his chamber, which is mighty fine, with pictures and everything else, very curious. Thence to the gate, with all the women about me, and Mrs Mercer's son had provided a great many serpents, and so I made the women all fire some serpents. By and by comes in our fair neighbour, Mrs Turner, and two neighbours' daughters, Mrs Tite—the eldest of which, a long red-nosed silly jade; the other a pretty black* girl, and the merriest sprightly jade that ever I saw. Idled away the whole night, till twelve at night, at the bonfire in the streets. Some of the people thereabouts going about with muskets and did give me two or three volleys of their muskets, I giving them a crown to drink; and so home.

Mightily pleased with this happy day's news, and the more, because confirmed by Sir Daniel Harvey, who was in the whole fight with the General, and tells me that there appear but thirty-six in all of the Dutch fleet left at the end of the voyage when they run home. The joy of the City was this night exceeding great.

7 JUNE. Up betimes, and to my office about business, Sir W. Coventry having sent me word that he is gone down to the fleet to see how matters stand, and to be back again speedily; and with the same expectation of congratulating ourselves with the victory

* Dark-haired.

that I had yesterday. But my Lord Brouncker and Sir T. H.*
that come from Court, tell me the contrary news, which astonishes
me: that is to say, that we are beaten, lost many ships and good
commanders; have not taken one ship of the enemy's; and so can
only report ourselves a victory; nor is it certain that we were left
masters of the field. But, above all, that the *Prince* run on shore
upon the Galloper, and there stuck; was endeavoured to be
fetched off by the Dutch, but could not; and so they burned her;
and Sir G. Ayscue is taken prisoner, and carried into Holland.

This news do much trouble me, and the thoughts of the ill
consequences of it, and the pride and presumption that brought
us to it. At noon to the Change, and there find the discourse of
town, and their countenances much changed; but yet not very
plain. By and by comes Mr Wayth to me; and discoursing of
our ill success, he tells me plainly, from Captain Page's own mouth,
who hath lost his arm in the fight, that the Dutch did pursue us
two hours before they left us, and then they suffered us to go on
homewards, and they retreated towards their coast; which is very
sad news. The Duke much damped in his discourse, touching the
late fight, and all the Court talk sadly of it. The Duke did give
me several letters he had received from the fleet, and Sir W.
Coventry, and Sir W. Penn, who are gone down thither, for me
to pick out some works to be done for the setting out the fleet
again; and so I took them home with me, and was drawing out
an abstract of them till midnight. And as to news, I do find great
reason to think that we are beaten in every respect, and that we
are the losers. The *Prince* upon the Galloper, where both the
Royal Charles and *Royal Catherine* had come twice aground, but
got off. The *Essex* carried into Holland; the *Swiftsure* missing
(Sir W. Berkeley) ever since the beginning of the fight. Captains
Bacon, Tearne, Wood, Mootham, Whitly, and Coppin slain.
The Duke of Albemarle writes, that he never fought with worse
officers in his life, not above twenty of them behaving themselves
like men. Sir William Clerke lost his leg; and in two days died.

* Sir Thomas Harvey.

The *Loyal George*, *Seven Oaks*, and *Swiftsure*, are still missing, and have never, as the General writes himself, engaged with them. It was as great an alteration to find myself required to write a sad letter, instead of a triumphant one, to my Lady Sandwich this night, as ever on any occasion I had in my life.

Diary.

QUESTIONS

(1) In what direction was Prince Rupert steering when Major Halsey saw him beyond the Goodwins?

(2) Where and what are the Goodwins?

(3) Describe the appearance of 'Mr Daniel' when he called at Mr Pepys's house. Whence had he come? from what ship? how did he reach London? how long did he take to do the journey?

(4) Give other words for the following without alteration of sense: 'half seas over', 'sprightly', 'discourse', 'hubbub', 'crown', 'abstract', 'presumption', 'jade'.

(5) What does Mr Pepys mean by 'ride post', 'take water', 'Change', 'ketch', 'great dispute in philosophy'?

(6) Where did Charles II receive 'Mr Daniel' to hear his account of the battle? Was it a complete account?

(7) Where was the battle first engaged?

(8) What did the Dutch do when they 'slipped their cables'? In what previous passage have we met the same expression?

(9) How many ships had the Dutch and the English on the second and third days of the fight?

(10) What did the Dutch proceed to do when Prince Rupert joined Albemarle? Was the manœuvre successful?

(11) How did Charles II receive the earlier news from the fleet and what particular tidings gave him special pleasure?

(12) What time did Mr Pepys have dinner? Where did he eat it and where did he resort for supper?

(13) What Captains were particularly praised for their gallantry in action?

(14) What treat did Mr Pepys miss on Monday, 5 June, owing to business connected with the battle?

(15) Why did Mr Pepys go to church on a Tuesday and how did he behave when he got there?

(16) What pleased him most about the service?

(17) How did he spend the rest of the day?

(18) Where did he go for a drive in his coach?

(19) What kind of fireworks interested him?

(20) How does he describe Mrs Tite and her sister?

(21) What happened to H.M.S. *Prince*? What Admiral flew his flag in her and what must have happened to him?

(22) What was the 'Galloper'?

FOR A PRÉCIS

Write a précis of Mr Pepys's Diary for 7 June 1666.

FOR AN ESSAY

(1) Mr Pepys was admitted to be the ideal secretary. He worked incessantly and tirelessly. Yet, as the Diary shows, he enjoyed what leisure came his way.

Imagine him on a public holiday; and from your own invention write a page or two as from his Diary describing a day in the country, or a round of gaieties in town.

(2) Describe any chapter of events, or special incident, during the war against Hitler when a seeming success turned out to be quite the opposite; or vice versa.

(3) Samuel Pepys kept a diary continuously for ten years and only gave it up to save his eyesight. What is your opinion of diary-keeping and what have your personal experiences been?

(4) The sailors described the battle as the 'Four Days' Bloody Blunder'. Do you consider this a fair criticism and if so why?

JOHN EVELYN

SAMUEL PEPYS

MAY 26, 1703. This day died Mr Samuel Pepys, a very worthy industrious and curious person, none in England exceeding him in knowledge of the Navy, in which he had passed through all the most considerable offices, Clerk of the Acts and Secretary of the Admiralty, all which he performed with great integrity. When King James II went out of England, he laid down his office and would serve no more; but withdrawing himself from all public affairs, he lived at Clapham with his partner, Mr Hewer, formerly his clerk, in a very noble and sweet place, where he enjoyed the fruit of his labours in great prosperity. He was universally beloved, hospitable, generous, learned in many things, skilled in music, a very great cherisher of learned men of whom he had the conversation.

His library and collection of other curiosities were of the most considerable, the models of ships especially. Besides what he published of an account of the Navy as he found and left it, he had for divers years under his hand the History of the Navy, or *Navalia* as he called it; but how far advanced and what will follow of his, is left, I suppose, to his sister's son, Mr Jackson, a young gentleman whom Mr Pepys had educated in all sorts of useful learning, sending him to travel abroad, from whence he returned with extraordinary accomplishments and worthy to be his heir. Mr Pepys had been for near forty years so much my particular friend that Mr Jackson sent me complete mourning, desiring me to be one to hold up the pall at his magnificent obsequies; but my indisposition hindered me from doing this last office.

Diary.

HELPS

Curious. Inquisitive, of an enquiring turn of mind.

Clerk of the Acts. In Mr Pepys's day the name given to the secretary of the Navy Board or Navy Office, that is, the institution responsible (under the Lord High Admiral) for the building of new ships, reconditioning of old, and supply of all materials requisite for fitting out a fleet.

Navalia. Though he collected much material, Mr Pepys never found time to write his 'History of the Navy'. His books and papers were bequeathed by him to Magdalene College, Cambridge.

QUESTIONS

(1) Mr Pepys began his Diary on 1 January 1660; on 29 June in the same year he became 'Clerk of the Acts'; and on 19 June 1673, Secretary of the Admiralty. What was the date of his retirement?

(2) Substitute other words for the following without alterations of the sense: 'industrious', 'prosperity', 'obsequies', 'accomplishments', 'integrity', 'offices', 'worthy', 'hospitable', 'pall', 'universally', 'considerable', 'divers', 'partner', 'cherisher', 'curiosities', 'indisposition'.

(3) Who was Mr Pepys's predecessor at the Admiralty when the 'Four Days' Battle' was in progress?

(4) What was the surname of Mr Pepys's secretary? Mr Pepys always called him 'Will'.

(5) Make a list of Mr Pepys's virtues, accomplishments and hobbies.

(6) Who was Mr Pepys's heir?

(7) How did he desire to mark the forty years of close friendship between his uncle and John Evelyn?

FOR AN ESSAY

(1) Select any character in History or Fiction, really well known to you; and write an appreciation or character-sketch of him or her in the manner of the foregoing passage.

(2) 'Home-keeping youths have ever homely wits', wrote Shakespeare. For this reason Mr Pepys insisted that his heir should travel abroad.

If some wealthy benefactor decided to give you the opportunity of travelling abroad, to which countries would you choose to go and why?

(3) Clapham to-day is famous for its railway junction. In Mr Pepys's day, John Evelyn, a lover of gardens and woods and forests and open country, called it a 'noble and sweet place'.

Explain why you would like to support, or perhaps to oppose, the work of the 'National Trust', an institution which endeavours to secure for national ownership tracts of open country and beautiful scenery, which might otherwise be disforested, disfigured, and built over.

JOSEPH ADDISON

OF MONUMENTS AND IN PARTICULAR OF SIR CLOWDISLEY SHOVEL'S

[INTRODUCTORY NOTE. The capture of Gibraltar in 1704 made it necessary for Great Britain to maintain a fleet in the Mediterranean as well as at home. This was really quite impracticable without a naval base; but the need for a naval base was not at first realized either by the Government or the people at large. For some years, therefore, a fleet was sent to the Mediterranean in the summer, and summoned home again in winter—at great risk: for by this method the ships were wearied with long service and foolishly exposed to wild and heavy weather. In 1707 a serious disaster occurred. Admiral Sir Clowdisley Shovel, Commander-in-Chief Mediterranean, suffered shipwreck at the mouth of the Channel, when his flagship, the *Association*, and other valuable ships and lives were lost.

The Admiral himself, being an exceptionally powerful swimmer, struck out bravely through the raging surges and was at last washed up ashore—alive but exhausted. Scilly islanders found him (perhaps unconscious), robbed him of his possessions, especially a magnificent emerald ring, and buried his body. Penitence for this shameful act led eventually to a confession, to the recovery of the Admiral's body, and to a funeral and imposing monument in Westminster Abbey.]

WHEN I am in a serious humour, I very often walk by myself in Westminster Abbey, where the gloominess of the place and the use to which it is applied, with the solemnity of the building, and the condition of the people who lie in it, are apt to fill the mind with a kind of melancholy, or rather thoughtfulness that is not disagreeable.

I yesterday passed a whole afternoon in the church-yard, the cloisters, and the church, amusing myself with the tombstones and inscriptions that I met with in those several regions of the dead. Most of them recorded nothing else of the buried person, but that he was born upon one day, and died upon another; the whole history of his life being comprehended in those two circumstances that are common to all mankind. I could not but look upon these registers of existence, whether of brass or marble, as a kind of satire upon the departed persons, who had left no other memorial of them, but that they were born, and that they died. They put me in mind of several persons mentioned in the battles of heroic poems, who have sounding names given them, for no other reason but that they may be killed, and are celebrated for nothing but being knocked on the head.

Glaucus and Medon and Thersilochus.

The life of these men is finely described in holy writ by 'the path of an arrow', which is immediately closed up and lost.*

Upon my going into the church, I entertained myself with the digging of a grave; and saw in every shovel-full of it that was thrown up, the fragment of a bone or skull intermixed with a kind of fresh mouldering earth that some time or other had a place in the composition of a human body. Upon this I began to consider with myself what innumerable multitudes of people lay confused together under the pavement of that ancient Cathedral; how men and women, friends and enemies, priests and soldiers, monks and prebendaries, were crumbled amongst one another, and blended together in the same common mass; how beauty, strength, and youth, with old age, weakness, and deformity, lay undistinguished in the same promiscuous heap of matter.

After having thus surveyed the great magazine of mortality, as it were, in the lump, I examined it more particularly by the accounts which I found on several of the monuments which are raised in every quarter of that ancient fabric. Some of them were covered with such extravagant epitaphs, that if it were possible for the dead person to be acquainted with them, he would blush at the praises which his friends have bestowed upon him. There are others so excessively modest, that they deliver the character of the person departed in Greek or Hebrew, and by that means are not understood once in a twelvemonth. In the poetical quarter, I found there were poets who had no monuments, and monuments which had no poets. I observed, indeed, that the present war has filled the church with many of these uninhabited monuments, which had been erected to the memory of persons

* *Wisdom of Solomon*, v. 12–13.

whose bodies were perhaps buried in the plains of Blenheim, or in the bosom of the ocean.

I could not but be very much delighted with several modern epitaphs, which are written with great elegance of expression and justness of thought, and therefore do honour to the living as well as the dead. As a foreigner is very apt to conceive an idea of the ignorance or politeness of a nation from the turn of their public monuments and inscriptions, they should be submitted to the perusal of men of learning and genius before they are put into execution.

Sir Clowdisley Shovel's monument has very often given me great offence. Instead of the brave rough English admiral, which was the distinguishing character of that plain gallant man, he is represented on his tomb by the figure of a beau, dressed in a long periwig, and reposing himself upon velvet cushions, under a canopy of state. The inscription is answerable to the monument; for instead of celebrating the many remarkable actions he had performed in the service of his country, it acquaints us only with the manner of his death, in which it was impossible for him to reap any honour.

The Dutch, whom we are apt to despise for want of genius, show an infinitely greater taste of antiquity and politeness in their buildings and works of this nature than what we meet with in those of our own country. The monuments of their admirals, which have been erected at the public expense, represent them like themselves, and are adorned with rostral crowns, and naval ornaments, with beautiful festoons of seaweed, shells, and coral.

But to return to our subject. I have left the repository of our English kings for the contemplation of another day, when I shall find my mind disposed for so serious an amusement. I know that entertainments of this nature are apt to raise dark and dismal thoughts in timorous minds and gloomy imaginations; but for my own part, though I am always serious, I do not know what it is to be melancholy; and can therefore take a view of nature in her deep and solemn scenes with the same pleasure as in her most gay and delightful ones. By this means I can improve myself with those objects which others consider with terror. When I look upon the tombs of the great, every motion of envy dies in me; when I read the epitaphs of the beautiful, every inordinate desire goes out; when I meet with the grief of parents upon a tombstone, my heart melts with compassion; when I see the tomb of the parents themselves, I consider the vanity of grieving for those whom we must quickly follow. When I see Kings lying by those who deposed them, when I consider rival wits placed side by side, or the holy men that divided the world with their contests and disputes, I reflect with sorrow and astonishment on the little competitions, factions, and debates of mankind. When I read the several dates of the tombs, of some that died yesterday, and some six hundred years ago, I consider that great day when we shall all of us be contemporaries, and make an appearance together.

HELPS

Amusing myself with the tombstones. Amusing is perhaps here used in its older sense, i.e. causing myself to muse or contemplate.

Glaucus and Medon and Thersilochus. Three names taken at random from Homer's *Iliad*, the story of the Siege of Troy.

QUESTIONS

(1) What are 'cloisters' and why were they built?

(2) What is the chief fault that Addison finds with sepulchral monuments as a class?

(3) Describe Sir Clowdisley Shovel's monument.

(4) What features does Addison specially admire in the monuments erected to famous Dutch Admirals?

(5) Recall the names of any two Dutch Admirals of whose battles you have read in this book.

(6) What comparison does Addison draw with 'the path of an arrow', a phrase drawn by him from the 'Wisdom' of Solomon?

(7) In contemplating the numberless dead buried in the Abbey Church Addison contrasts 'friends' with 'enemies'. What opposites does he supply for 'priests', 'monks', 'beauty', 'strength' and 'youth'?

(8) To what is Addison referring when he speaks of 'Holy Writ', 'Registers of Existence'?

(9) To avoid repetition of the words 'Westminster Abbey', Addison uses alternative expressions, e.g. 'Repository of our English Kings'. Supply two or more of such alternatives.

(10) Addison wittily remarks that some Memorials are so modest that they conceal their meaning in Greek or Hebrew. What was the real reason why these languages were used?

(11) What does Addison mean when he speaks of 'poets who had no monuments, and monuments which had no poets'?

(12) Write short sentences of your own invention, making use of the following words in the same sense as Addison: 'melancholy', 'compassion', 'promiscuous', 'vanity', 'satire'.

(13) What land battlefield is mentioned in this passage? In what foreign country must it be sought?

(14) What was a periwig? Are periwigs ever worn in England to-day?

(15) Give alternative words for the following without alteration of sense: 'solemnity', 'mouldering', 'timorous', 'comprehended', 'celebrated', 'innumerable', 'antiquity', 'gloomy', 'festoons', 'epitaphs', 'elegance', 'factions', 'humour', 'pavement', 'survey'.

(16) Complete the following sentence: 'Some of them were covered with such extravagant epitaphs, that if it were possible for the dead person to be acquainted with them, he would....'

(17) Write down from memory the concluding sentence of Addison's musings on Westminster Abbey.

FOR A PRÉCIS

Write a précis of the passage beginning 'When I am in serious...' and ending '...knocked on the head'.

FOR AN ESSAY

(1) Propose a scheme for a great national memorial to be erected to the memory of all the British heroes who died fighting against Hitler's Germany.

(2) Doctor Johnson maintained that a memorial to a famous man should always be expressed in Latin, so that foreigners, visiting this country, should pay homage to our greatness without the aid of a dictionary. How far do you think that he was right?

(3) Find out all you can about 'the many remarkable actions' which Sir Clowdisley Shovel 'performed in the service of his country', and write an appreciation of the Admiral after the manner of John Evelyn's eulogy of Samuel Pepys (see p. 72).

(4) Should you have any objections to sitting up alone in an empty church or in a churchyard from eleven o'clock at night till two o'clock in the morning? If so, say what they are. If not, explain the prevalent objection to undertaking such a watch.

[NOTE. The monument is to be found in the south aisle just west of the east cloister door. Addison does it less than justice in omitting all mention of the sea trophies and the sculpture in low relief of the shipwreck. The modern critic would probably call the monument good of its kind; but would condemn very vigorously, what Addison passes over, namely the removal of the lovely mediaeval work of Henry III's time to make room for a memorial which offends by reason of its excessive size.]

THE COCKPIT IN TIME OF BATTLE

[INTRODUCTORY NOTE. After the death of Queen Anne in 1714, Great Britain remained at peace for a quarter of a century. But in 1739 war with Spain broke out suddenly and found everyone quite unprepared. An expedition was sent against Porto Bello under Admiral Vernon, who took the place easily 'with six ships only'; and in 1741 proceeded to the assault of Carthagena. Among the ships then under him was H.M.S. *Cumberland*; and serving in the *Cumberland* as Surgeon's Mate was Tobias Smollett, afterwards a literary giant. But though he wrote a *History of England*, this serious work is not now consulted or even opened; and the following passage is taken from one of his great novels, *Roderick Random*. As a surgeon's mate, or Surgeon-Lieutenant (as he would be styled to-day), he could easily have given a truthful account of the navy's medical service; but his love of exaggeration and slander renders his picture untrustworthy as a whole; and in its concluding paragraphs reduces it to a caricature.]

OUR forces being landed and stationed as I have already mentioned, set about erecting a fascine battery to cannonade the principal fort of the enemy, and in something more than three weeks it was ready to open. That we might do the Spaniards as much honour as possible, it was determined in a Council of War, that five of our largest ships should attack the fort on one side, while the battery, strengthened by two mortars and twenty-four coehorns, should ply it on the other.

Accordingly, the signal for our ship to engage, among others, was hoisted, we being advertised the night before, to make everything clear for that purpose; and in so doing a difference happened between Captain Oakum and his well-beloved cousin and counsellor, Mackshane, which had well nigh terminated in an open rupture.

The doctor, who had imagined there was no more danger of being hurt by the enemy's shot in the cockpit than in the centre of the earth, was lately informed that a surgeon's mate had been killed in that part of the ship by a cannon-ball from two small redoubts that were destroyed before the disembarkation of our soldiers; and therefore insisted upon having a platform raised for the convenience of the sick and wounded, in the after-hold, where he deemed himself more secure than on the deck above.

The Captain, offended at this extraordinary proposal, accused him of pusillanimity, and told him there was no room in the hold for such an occasion; or if there was, he could not expect to be indulged more than the rest of the surgeons of the navy who used the cockpit for that purpose. Fear rendered Mackshane obstinate: he persisted in his demand, and showed his instructions by which it was authorized.

The Captain swore these instructions were dictated by a parcel of lazy poltroons who were never at sea; nevertheless, he was obliged to comply, and sent for the carpenter to give him orders about it: but before any such measure could be taken, our signal was thrown out, and the doctor compelled to trust his carcase in the cockpit, where Morgan and I were busy in putting our instruments and dressings in order.

Our ship, with others destined for this service, immediately weighed, and in less than half an hour came to an anchor before the castle of Boca Chica, with a spring upon our cable; and the cannonading, which indeed was terrible, began.

The surgeon, after having crossed himself, fell flat on the deck; and the Chaplain and purser, who were stationed with us in the quality of assistants, followed his example, while the Welshman and I sat upon a chest, looking at one another with great discomposure, scarce able to restrain from the like prostration. And that the reader may know it was not a common occasion that alarmed us thus, I must inform him of the particulars of this dreadful din that astonished us. The fire of the Spaniards proceeded from eighty-four great guns, besides a mortar and small arms, in Boca Chica, thirty-six in Fort St Joseph, twenty in two fascine batteries, and four men-of-war, mounting sixty-four guns each. This was answered by our land battery, mounted with twenty-one cannon, two mortars, and twenty-four coehorns, and five great ships of seventy or eighty guns, that fired without intermission.

We had not been many minutes engaged, when one of the sailors brought another on his back to the cockpit, where he tossed him down like a bag of oats, and pulling out his pouch, put a large chew of tobacco in his mouth, without speaking a word.

Morgan immediately examined the condition of the wounded man, and cried out—

'As I shall answer now, the man is as tead as my great grand-father.'

'Dead!' said his comrade. 'He may be dead now, for ought I know, but I'll be damned if he was not alive when I took him up.'

So saying, he was about to return to his quarters, when I bade him carry the body along with him, and throw it overboard.

'Damn the body!' said he. 'I think it's fair enough if I take care of my own.'

My fellow-mate snatching up the amputation knife, pursued him half-way up the cockpit ladder, crying—

'You louzy rascal, is this the churchyard, or the charnel house, or the sepulchre, or the Golgotha of the ship'—but was stopped in his career by one calling—

'Yo, ho, avast there—scaldings!'

'Scaldings!' answered Morgan. 'God knows 'tis hot enough indeed. Who are yon?'

'Here's one,' replied the voice.

And I immediately knew it to be that of my honest friend, Jack Rattlin, who, coming towards me, told me, with great deliberation, he was come to be docked at last, and discovered the remains of one hand, which had been shattered to pieces with grape shot.

I lamented with unfeigned sorrow his misfortune, which he bore with heroic courage, observing that every shot had its commission. It was well it did not take him in the head; or if it had, what then?—he should have died bravely, fighting for his King and country. Death was a debt which every man owed, and must pay; and that now was as well as another time.

I was much pleased and edified with the maxims of this sea-philosopher, who endured the amputation of his left hand without shrinking; the operation being performed, at his request, by me, after Mackshane, who was with difficulty prevailed to lift his head from the deck, had declared there was a necessity for his losing the limb.

While I was employed in dressing the stump, I asked Jack's opinion of the battle. He, shaking his head, frankly told me he believed we should do no good.

For why, because instead of dropping anchor close under shore, where we should have had to deal with one corner of Boca Chica only, we had opened the harbour, and exposed ourselves to the whole fire of the enemy from their shipping and Fort St Joseph, as well as from the castle we intended to cannonade; that, besides, we lay at too great a distance to damage the walls, and three parts in four of our shot did not take place; for there was scarce anybody on board who understood the pointing of a gun. Ah! God help us!' continued he, 'if your kinsman, Lieutenant Bowling, had been here, we should have had other guess-work.'

By this time our patients had increased to such a number that we did not know which to begin with; and the first mate plainly told the surgeon that if he did not get up immediately, and perform his duty, he would complain of his behaviour to the Admiral, and make application for his warrant.

This remonstrance effectually roused Mackshane, who was never deaf to an argument in which he thought his interest was concerned. He therefore rose up, and, in order to strengthen his resolution, had recourse more than once to a case-bottle of rum, which he freely communicated to the chaplain and purser, who had as much need of such extraordinary inspiration as himself. Being thus supported, he went to work, and arms and legs were hewed down without mercy.

The fumes of the liquor mounting into the parson's brain, conspired, with his former agitation of spirits, to make him quite delirious. He stripped himself to the skin, and, besmearing his body with blood, could scarce be withheld from running up on deck in that condition. Jack Rattlin, scandalized at this deportment, endeavoured to allay his transports with reason; but finding all he said ineffectual, and great confusion occasioned by his frolics, he knocked him down with his right hand, and by threats kept him quiet in that state of humiliation.

But it was not in the power of rum to elevate the purser, who sat on the floor wringing his hands, and cursing the hour in which he left his peaceable profession of a brewer in Rochester to engage in such a life of terror and disquiet.

Roderick Random.

HELPS

Fascine battery. Gun positions constructed with bundles of brushwood bound together with rope or withes.

Coehorn. A small and handy mortar made of brass and christened after the Dutch engineer who invented it.

Boca Chica. Literally 'the little mouth'; a narrow entrance into Carthagena harbour, in 1741 heavily defended by fortresses on the land and on the adjacent island of St Joseph.

QUESTIONS

(1) How long did it take to build the fascine battery?

(2) On what measure did the Chief Surgeon insist when the hour of battle approached?

(3) What were his reasons for recommending this measure?

(4) How was the proposal greeted by the Captain of the ship?

(5) It is clear that the Captain of the ship did not like his chief surgeon. Yet Dr Smollett refers to that officer as 'his well-beloved cousin and counsellor'.

This is of course intentional sarcasm. Read the passage afresh with a view to picking out other samples of Smollett's indulgence in this sort of satire.

(6) There were three surgeons allotted to this ship. Give their names in order of seniority.

(7) What other officers were detailed to assist them with ministrations to the wounded?

(8) When the ship was ordered to the attack, where did she anchor? and why with a spring on her cable?

(9) Describe the behaviour of the five inmates of the cockpit when the bombardment began.

(10) Describe the arrival in the cockpit of the first casualty. How was the casualty brought below and treated on arrival?

(11) What was the assistant surgeon's verdict after examination of the case?

(12) What alternative expressions did the assistant surgeon use when he enquired if the bearer-party had mistaken the cockpit for the churchyard?

(13) Why did Jack Rattlin cry 'Scaldings'?

(14) What was the nature of his injury and how had it been inflicted?

(15) What did Jack Rattlin say when he realized that he must lose a limb?

(16) By what flattering description did Dr Smollett refer to him?

(17) What was Jack Rattlin's opinion of the way in which the battle was going?

(18) What threat did the chief assistant surgeon utter to his superior officer when the number of casualties multiplied?

(19) Write sentences of your own invention introducing the following words in the same sense as in the passage above: 'prostration', 'allay', 'frolics', 'remonstrance', 'advertised'.

(20) Substitute other words for the following without change of sense: 'cannonade', 'terminated', 'rupture', 'poltroons', 'comply', 'discomposure', 'deliberation', 'deportment', 'ineffectual', 'humiliation', 'platform', 'offended', 'pusillanimity', 'indulged', 'intermission', 'lamented', 'edified', 'scandalized'.

FOR A PRÉCIS

Write a précis of the passage beginning 'We had not been many minutes...' and ending '...replied the voice'.

FOR AN ESSAY

(1) Describe in your own words one or more examples of outstanding heroism of men or boys wounded either in actual battle or as the result of enemy action.

(2) Read again the introductory notes to this passage, and then give your carefully considered opinion as to which parts of Smollett's narrative are substantially true and which parts false or grossly exaggerated.

(3) In no branch of science has progress been more remarkable since Smollett's day than in medicine and surgery. Imagine yourself to be a naval surgeon during the assault on Carthagena in 1741, and (with your knowledge of more modern methods and equipment) write to the Medical Director-General pointing out existing defects and making recommendations for improvements and reform.

WILLIAM COWPER

THE CASTAWAY

OBSCUREST night involved the sky
  Th' Atlantic billows roared,
When such a destin'd wretch as I
  Washed headlong from on board,
Of friends, of hope, of all bereft,
His floating home for ever left.

No braver chief could Albion boast
  Than he with whom he went
Nor ever ship left Albion's coast
  With warmer wishes sent.
He loved them both, but both in vain,
Nor him beheld, nor her again.

Not long beneath the whelming brine,
  Expert to swim he lay;
Nor soon he felt his strength decline,
  Or courage die away;
But waged with death a lasting strife
Supported by despair of life.

He shouted; nor his friends had failed
  To check the vessel's course,
But so the furious blast prevailed,
  That pitiless perforce,
They left their outcast mate behind,
And scudded still before the wind.

     *   *   *   *

He long survives, who lives an hour
  In ocean, self upheld;
And so long he, with unspent power

His destiny repelled;
And ever, as the minutes flew,
Entreated 'Help!' or breathed—'Adieu!'

At length, his transient respite past,
 His comrades, who before
Had heard his voice in every blast,
 Could catch the sound no more.
For then, by toil subdued, he drank
The stifling wave, and then—he sank.

No poet wept him: but the page
 Of narrative sincere,
That tells his name, his worth, his age,
 Is wet with Anson's tear.
And tears by bards or heroes shed
Alike immortalize the dead.

[NOTE. '23 MARCH 1741. As our ship kept the wind better than any of the rest, we were obliged, in the afternoon, to wear...and as we dared not venture any sail abroad, we were obliged to make use of an expedient which answered our purpose. This was, putting the helm a-weather and manning the fore shrouds. But though this method proved successful for the end intended, yet in the execution of it one of our ablest seamen was canted overboard. We perceived that, notwithstanding the prodigious agitation of the waves, he swam very strong, and it was with the utmost concern that we found ourselves incapable of helping him. Indeed, we were the more grieved at his unhappy fate, as we lost sight of him struggling with the waves, and conceived from the manner in which he swam that he might continue sensible, for a considerable time longer, of the horror attending his irretrievable situation.'

Reverend RICHARD WALTER,
Chaplain to Commodore Anson in H.M.S. *Centurion*.]

THE REVEREND RICHARD WALTER

Chaplain of H.M.S. *Centurion*

HOW ANSON TOOK THE GREAT GALLEON

[INTRODUCTORY NOTE. When war broke out with Spain in 1739 (see above, p. 79), Commodore George Anson was sent with a small squadron to the South Pacific to vex the Spanish provinces in South America. Ill fortune dogged his path and eventually robbed him of all his ships except that bearing his own broad pendant, the thrice famous *Centurion*. In her he encompassed the whole world; and, returning with a group of young officers trained in his own exemplary discipline, gladdened the hearts of his countrymen with treasure which reminded them of the wondrous days of Drake.]

ON the 20th of June, o.s., being just a month after their gaining their station, they were relieved out of this state of uncertainty; for at sunrise they discovered a sail from the mast-head, in the S.E. quarter. On this, a general joy spread through the whole ship, for they had no doubt but this was one of the galleons, and they expected soon to descry the other. The Commodore instantly stood towards her, and at half an hour after seven they were near enough to see her from the *Centurion's* deck, at which time the galleon fired a gun, and took in her top-gallant sails. This was supposed to be a signal to her consort to hasten her up, and therefore the *Centurion* fired a gun to leeward to amuse her. The Commodore was surprised to find that during all this interval the galleon did not change her course, but continued to bear down upon him; for he hardly believed, what afterwards appeared to be the case, that she knew his ship to be the *Centurion*, and resolved to fight him.

About noon the Commodore was little more than a league distant from the galleon, and could fetch her wake, so that she could not now escape; and, no second ship appearing, it was concluded that she had been separated from her consort. Soon after, the galleon hauled up her fore-sail and brought it under top-sails, with her head to the northward, hoisting Spanish colours, and having the standard of Spain flying at the top-gallant mast-head. Mr Anson in the meantime had prepared all things for an engagement on board the *Centurion*, and had taken every possible measure, both for the most effectual exertion of his small strength, and for the avoiding confusion and tumult too frequent in actions of this kind. He picked out about thirty of his choicest hands and best marksmen, whom he distributed into his tops, and who fully answered his expectation by the signal services they performed. As he had not hands enough remaining to quarter a sufficient number to each great gun in the customary manner, he therefore, on his lower tier, fixed only two men to each gun, who were to be solely employed in loading it, whilst the rest of his people were divided into different gangs of ten or twelve men each, who were continually moving about the decks to run out and fire such guns as were loaded. By this management he was enabled to make use of all his guns, and instead of whole broadsides, with intervals between them, he kept up a constant fire without intermission, whence he doubted not to procure very signal advantages. For it is common with the Spaniards to fall down upon the decks when they see a broadside preparing, and to continue in that posture till it is given, after which they rise again, and, presuming the danger to be for some time over, work their guns, and fire with great briskness, till another broadside is ready. But the firing gun by gun, in the manner directed by the Commodore, rendered this practice of theirs impossible.

The *Centurion* being thus prepared, and nearing the galleon apace, there happened, a little after noon, several squalls of wind and rain, which often obscured the galleon from their sight; but whenever it cleared up they observed her resolutely lying to. Towards one o'clock, the *Centurion* hoisted her broad pendant and colours, she being then within gun-shot of the enemy, and the Commodore perceiving the Spaniards to have neglected clearing their ship till that time, as he saw them throwing overboard cable and lumber, he gave orders to fire upon them with the chase guns, to disturb them in their work, and prevent them from completing it, though his general directions had been not to engage before they were within pistol-shot. The galleon returned the fire with two of her stern chase; and the *Centurion* getting her sprit-sail yard fore and aft, that, if necessary, she might be ready for boarding, the Spaniards, in a bravado, rigged their sprit-sail yard fore and aft likewise. Soon after, the *Centurion* came abreast of the enemy within pistol-shot, keeping to the leeward of them, with a view of preventing their pulling before the wind and gaining the port of Jalakay, from which they were about seven leagues distant.

And now the engagement began in earnest, and for the first half-hour Mr Anson over-reached the galleon and lay on her bow, where, by the great wideness of his ports, he could traverse almost all his guns upon the enemy, whilst the galleon could only bring a part of hers to bear. Immediately on the commencement of the action, the mats with which the galleon had stuffed her netting took fire and burnt violently, blazing up half as high as the mizzen-top. This accident, supposed to be caused by the *Centurion's* wads, threw the enemy into the utmost terror, and also alarmed the Commodore; for he feared lest the galleon should be burnt, and lest he himself too might suffer by her driving on board him. However, the Spaniards at last freed themselves from the fire, by cutting away the netting and tumbling the whole mass, which was in flames, into the sea.

All this interval the *Centurion* kept her first advantageous position, firing her cannon with great regularity and briskness, whilst at the same time the galleon's decks lay open to her top-men, who, having at their first volley driven the Spaniards from their tops, made prodigious havoc with their small arms, killing or wounding every officer but one that appeared on the quarter-deck, and wounding in particular the general of the galleon himself.

Thus the action proceeded for at least half an hour; but then the *Centurion* lost the superiority arising from her original situation, and was close alongside the galleon, and the enemy continued to fire briskly for near an hour longer; yet even in this posture the Commodore's grape-shot swept their decks so effectually, and the number of their slain and wounded became so considerable, that they began to fall into great disorder, especially as the General, who was the life of the action, was no longer capable of exerting himself. Their confusion was visible from on board the Commodore, for the ships were so near that some of the Spanish officers were seen running about with much assiduity, to prevent the desertion of their men from their quarters. But all their endeavours were in vain; for after having, as a last effort, fired five or six guns, with more judgment than usual, they yielded up the contest, and, the galleon's colours being singed off the ensign staff in the beginning of the engagement, she struck the standard at her main top-gallant mast-head; the person who was employed to perform this office having been in imminent peril of being killed, had not the Commodore, who perceived what he was about, given express orders to his people to desist from firing.

Thus was the *Centurion* possessed of this rich prize, amounting in value to near a million and a half of dollars. She was called the *Nuestra Señora de Cabadonga*, and was commanded by General Don Jeronimo de Mentero, a Portuguese, who was the most approved officer for skill and courage of any employed in that service. The galleon was much larger than the *Centurion*, and had five hundred and fifty men, and thirty-six guns mounted for action, besides twenty-eight pedreroes in her gunwale, quarters, and tops, each of which carried a four-pound ball. She was very well furnished with small arms, and was particularly provided against boarding,—both by her close quarters, and by a strong network of two-inch rope which was laced over her waist, and was defended by half-pikes. She had sixty-seven killed in the action, and eighty-four wounded, whilst the *Centurion* had only two killed, and a lieutenant and sixteen wounded, all of whom but one recovered: of so little consequence are the most destructive arms in untutored and unpractised hands.

The treasure thus taken by the *Centurion* having been, for at least eighteen months, the great object of their hopes, it is impossible to describe the transport on board where, after all their reiterated disappointments, they at last saw their wishes accomplished. But their joy was near being suddenly damped by a most tremendous incident, for no sooner had the galleon struck, than one of the lieutenants coming to Mr Anson to congratulate him on his prize, whispered him at the same time that the *Centurion* was dangerously on fire near the powder-room. The Commodore received this dreadful news without any apparent emotion, and taking care not to alarm his people, gave the necessary orders for extinguishing the fire, which was happily done in a short time, though its appearance at first was extremely terrible. It seems some cartridges had been blown up by accident between decks, and the blast had communicated its flame to a quantity of oakum in the after hatchway, near the after powder-room, where the great smother and smoke of the oakum occasioned the apprehension of a more extended and mischievous conflagration. All hopes too of avoiding its fury by escaping on board the prize had instantly vanished, for at the same moment the galleon fell on board the *Centurion* on the starboard quarter, though she was fortunately cleared without doing or receiving any considerable damage.

The Commodore appointed the Manila vessel to be a post ship in his Majesty's service, and gave the command of her to Mr Saumarez, his first lieutenant, who before night sent on board the *Centurion* all the Spanish prisoners, except such as were thought the most proper to be retained to assist in navigating the galleon. And now the Commodore learnt from some of these prisoners that the other ship, which he had kept in the port of Acapulco the preceding year, instead of returning in company with the present prize, as was expected, had set sail from Acapulco alone much sooner than usual, and had, in all probability, got into the port of Manila long before the *Centurion* arrived off Cape Espiritū Santo, so that Mr Anson, notwithstanding his present success, had great reason to regret his loss of time at Macao, which prevented him from taking two rich prizes instead of one.

The Commodore, when the action was ended, resolved to make the best of his way with his prize for the river of Canton, being the meantime fully employed in securing his prisoners, and in removing the treasure from on board the galleon into the *Centurion*. The last of these operations was too important to be postponed, for as the navigation to Canton was through seas but little known, and where, from the season of the year, very tempestuous weather might be expected, it was of great consequence that the treasure should be sent on board the *Centurion*, which ship, by the presence of the commander-in-chief, the larger number of her hands, and her other advantages, was doubtless better provided against all the casualties of winds and seas than the galleon. And the securing the prisoners was a matter of still more consequence, as not only the possession of the treasure but the lives of the captors depended thereon. This was indeed an article which gave the Commodore much trouble and disquietude, for they were above double the number of his own people, and some of them, when they were brought on board the *Centurion*, and had observed how slenderly she was manned, and the large proportion which the striplings bore to the rest, could not help expressing themselves with great indignation to be thus beaten by a handful of boys. The method which was taken to hinder them from rising was by placing all but the officers and the wounded in the hold, where, to give them as much air as possible, two hatchways were left open; but then (to avoid any danger that might happen whilst the *Centurion's* people should be employed upon deck) there was a square partition of thick planks, made in the shape of a funnel, which enclosed each hatchway on the lower deck, and reached to that directly over it on the upper deck. These funnels served to communicate the air to the hold better than could have been done without them, and, at the same time, added greatly to the security of the ship, for they being seven or eight feet high, it would have been extremely difficult for the Spaniards to have clambered up; and still to augment that difficulty, four swivel guns, loaded with musket-bullets, were planted at the mouth of each funnel, and a sentinel with a lighted match was posted there ready to fire into the hold amongst them, in case of any disturbance.

Their officers, who amounted to seventeen or eighteen, were all lodged in the first lieutenant's cabin, under a guard of six men; and the general, as he was wounded, lay in the Commodore's cabin with a sentinel always with him; every prisoner, too, was sufficiently apprised that any violence or disturbance would be punished with instant death. And, that the *Centurion's* people might be at all times prepared, if, notwithstanding these regulations, any tumult should arise, the small arms were constantly kept loaded in a proper place, whilst all the men went armed with cutlasses and pistols; and no officer ever pulled off his clothes where he slept, or, where he lay down, omitted to have his arms always ready by him.

These measures were obviously necessary, considering the hazards to which the Commodore and his people would have been exposed had they been less careful. Indeed, the sufferings of the poor prisoners, though impossible to be alleviated, were much to be commiserated; for the weather was extremely hot, the stench of the hold loathsome beyond all conception, and their allowance of water but just sufficient to keep them alive, it not being practicable to spare them more than at the rate of a pint a day for each, the crew themselves having only an allowance of a pint and a half. All this considered, it was wonderful that not a man of them died during their long confinement, except three of the wounded, who expired the same night they were taken, though it must be confessed that the greatest part of them were strangely metamorphosed by the heat of the hold; for when they were first brought on board, they were sightly robust fellows, but when, after above a month's imprisonment, they were discharged in the river Canton, they were reduced to mere skeletons, and their air and looks corresponded much more to the conception formed of ghosts and spectres than to the figure and appearance of real men.

A Voyage round the World.

HELPS

The treasure galleon was sailing from Acapulco in Mexico to Manila in the Philippines. Anson lay in wait for her off Cape Espiritu Santo in the island of Samar.

QUESTIONS

(1) How did the galleon behave when she was first sighted?

(2) What colours did she hoist?

(3) What special steps did Anson take against his immense adversary?

(4) What was the customary procedure of the Spaniards when they saw their adversary run out his guns for a broadside?

(5) How did Anson cure them of this habit?

(6) What colours did the *Centurion* hoist in addition to Anson's broad pendant?

(7) At what range had Anson decided to open fire?

(8) What are chase guns?

(9) What steps did Anson take to make boarding possible?

(10) On what side did Anson engage the galleon and why?

(11) What gunnery advantage did Anson secure before opening fire?

(12) How was the conflagration started on board the galleon, and how high were the flames?

(13) What was the cause of Anson's anxiety as the flames took firmer hold?

(14) How did the Spaniards eventually extinguish the fire?

(15) How did the loss of morale on board the galleon first declare itself?

(16) What became of the galleon's ensign? and how did she signify her willingness to surrender?

(17) What was the value of the prize in the money of that day; and what would be her approximate value to-day?

(18) The *Centurion* had 60 guns and 400 men. How many guns and how many men had the *Nuestra Señora de Cabadonga*?

(19) What were pedereroes? Give them another name.

(20) What casualties were sustained by the *Centurion* and her adversary?

(21) How did Anson receive the news that the *Centurion* was dangerously on fire near the magazine?

(22) To which of his Lieutenants did Anson give command of the Prize?

(23) What most annoyed the Spanish prisoners when they came on board the *Centurion*?

(24) Where were the prisoners stowed and how were they prevented from making their escape?

(25) Where were the Spanish officers lodged, and how came it that this accommodation was available?

(26) How were the ship's company of the *Centurion* armed while the Spanish prisoners were on board?

(27) On the passage to Canton how much water was allowed per man per day to the ship's company of the *Centurion* and to the Spanish prisoners?

(28) Make a sketch-map showing the Philippine Islands, Luzon, Cape Espiritu Santo, Manila, Canton River, Canton, and Macao.

(29) Write sentences of your own invention to illustrate the meaning of the following words as used in the narrative above: 'traverse', 'havoc', 'transports', 'hazards', 'alleviated', 'desist'.

(30) Substitute other words for the following without change of meaning: 'marksmen', 'bravado', 'robust', 'assiduity', 'briskness', 'obscured', 'signal', 'reiterated', 'imminent', 'overreached', 'meta-morphosed', 'emotion', 'apace', 'prodigious', 'posture', 'commiserated'.

FOR A PRÉCIS

Write a précis of the passage beginning 'The Commodore when the action was ended...' and ending '...appearance of real men'.

FOR AN ESSAY

(1) Imagine yourself to be a Lieutenant in charge of four guns on the lower deck of the *Centurion*. Write a description to a friend of yours describing all the measures taken by the Commodore to ensure success in battle with his much greater antagonist.

(2) When the *Centurion* reached home, the treasure was brought ashore at Plymouth and carried up to London by road so that the people of England might enjoy the spectacle.

Imagine yourself to be a citizen of Salisbury. Write a letter to a friend in Norwich, describing the excitement in your native city as the carefully guarded cavalcade came through; not forgetting to recount the handsome compliments paid everywhere to Commodore Anson, and the officers and men who had sailed round the world with him.

(3) Imagine yourself to be a midshipman of the *Centurion* at the time she dropped anchor at Canton. Write a letter to your father describing the manners and customs, the appearance and dress of the Chinese.

[N.B. Do not forget that in Anson's day Englishmen were content to eat off wooden platters, and to drink out of pewter mugs and tankards.]

(4) Anson is regarded as one of the greatest of England's sea commanders. From his Chaplain's narrative pick out evidence of the qualities and virtues which in your opinion helped to make him great.

HAWKE

In seventeen hundred and fifty-nine,
   When Hawke came swooping from the West,
The French King's Admiral with twenty of the line,
   Was sailing forth, to sack us, out of Brest.
The ports of France were crowded, the quays of France a-hum
With thirty thousand soldiers marching to the drum,
For bragging time was over and fighting time was come
   When Hawke came swooping from the West.

'Twas long past noon of a wild November day
   When Hawke came swooping from the West;
He heard the breakers thundering in Quiberon Bay
   But he flew the flag for battle, line abreast.
Down upon the quicksands roaring out of sight
Fiercely beat the storm-wind, darkly fell the night,
But they took the foe for pilot and the cannon's glare for light
   When Hawke came swooping from the West.

The Frenchmen turned like a covey down the wind
   When Hawke came swooping from the West;
One he sank with all hands, one he caught and pinned,
   And the shallows and the storm took the rest.
The guns that should have conquered us they rusted on the shore,
The men that would have mastered us they drummed and
     marched no more,
For England was England, and a mighty brood she bore
   When Hawke came swooping from the West.

THE BATTLE OF QUIBERON BAY

20 NOVEMBER 1759

Lord Hawke's Dispatch

[INTRODUCTORY NOTE. Lord Hawke's dispatch, describing one of the greatest battles ever won at sea, is so modestly worded as to be almost apologetic. For this reason Sir Henry Newbolt's poem, *Hawke* (see p. 96), should first be committed to memory, or studied with the most careful attention, because in three inspiring stanzas it brings before the mind's eye not only the extreme gravity of the peril confronting this country, but the impetuosity of the great Admiral's attack, the tremendous risks attaching to it, and the paralysing completeness of his victory.]

Royal George, off Penris Point,
November 24th, 1759.

SIR,

In my letter of the 17th by express, I desired you would acquaint their Lordships with my having received intelligence of eighteen sail of the line, and three frigates of the Brest squadron being discovered about twenty-four leagues to the north-west of Belleisle, steering to the eastward. All the prisoners, however, agree that on the day we chased them, their squadron consisted, according to the accompanying list, of four ships of eighty, six of seventy-four, three of seventy, eight of sixty-four, one frigate of thirty-six, one of thirty-four, and one of sixteen guns, with a small vessel to look out. They sailed from Brest the 14th instant, the same day I sailed from Torbay. Concluding that their first rendezvous would be Quiberon, the instant I received the intelligence I directed my course thither with a pressed sail. At first the wind blowing hard at S. b. E. & S. drove us considerably to the westward. But on the 18th and 19th, though variable, it proved more favourable. In the meantime, having been joined by the *Maidstone* and *Coventry* frigates, I directed their commanders to keep ahead of the squadron, one on the starboard, and the other on the larboard bow.

At half-past eight o'clock on the morning of the 20th, Belleisle,

4

by our reckoning, bearing E. b. N. ¼ N. about thirteen leagues, the *Maidstone* made the signal for seeing a fleet. I immediately spread abroad the signal for the line abreast, in order to draw all the ships of the squadron up with me. I had before sent the *Magnanime* ahead to make the land. At three-quarters past nine she made the signal for seeing an enemy. Observing, on my discovering them, that they made off, I threw out the signal for the seven ships nearest them to chase, and draw into a line of battle ahead of me, and endeavour to stop them till the rest of the squadron should come up, who were also to form as they chased, that no time might be lost in the pursuit. That morning they were in chase* of the *Rochester*, *Chatham*, *Portland*, *Falkland*, *Minerva*, *Vengeance*, and *Venus*, all which joined me about eleven o'clock, and in the evening the *Sapphire* from Quiberon Bay.

All the day we had very fresh gales at N.W. and W.N.W. with heavy squalls. Monsieur Conflans kept going off under such sail as all his squadron could carry, and at the same time keep together; while we crowded after him with every sail our ships could bear. At half-past two p.m. the fire beginning ahead, I made the signal for engaging. We were then to the southward of Belleisle, and the French Admiral headmost, soon after led round the Cardinals, while his rear was in action. About four o'clock the *Formidable* struck, and a little after, the *Thésée* and *Superbe* were sunk. About five, the *Héros* struck, and came to an anchor, but it blowing hard, no boat could be sent on board her.

Night was now come, and being on a part of the coast, among islands and shoals, of which we were totally ignorant, without a pilot, as was the greatest part of the squadron, and blowing hard on a lee shore, I made the signal to anchor, and came-to in fifteen fathom water, the Island of Dumet bearing E. b. N. between two and three miles, the Cardinals W. ½ S., and the steeples of Croisic S.E., as we found next morning.

In the night we heard many guns of distress fired, but, blowing

* The enemy had been chasing these seven small ships which consequently were the nearest to him.

hard, want of knowledge of the coast, and whether they were fired by a friend or an enemy, prevented all means of relief.

By daybreak of the 21st we discovered one of our ships (the *Resolution*) dismasted, ashore on the Four. The French *Héros* also, and the *Soleil Royal*, which under cover of the night had anchored among us, cut and run ashore to the westward of Croisic. On the latter's moving I made the *Essex's* signal to slip and pursue her; but she unfortunately got upon the Four, and both she and the *Resolution* are irrevocably lost, notwithstanding that we sent them all the assistance that the weather would permit. About fourscore of the *Resolution's* company, in spite of the strongest remonstrances of their captain, made rafts, and with several French prisoners belonging to the *Formidable*, put off, and I am afraid drove out to sea. All the *Essex's* are safe, with as many of the stores as possible, except one lieutenant and a boat's crew, who were drove on the French shore, and have not since been heard of. The remains of both ships are set on fire. We found the *Dorsetshire*, *Revenge*, and *Defiance*, in the night of the 20th, put out to sea, as I hope the *Swiftsure* did, for she is still missing. The *Dorsetshire* and *Defiance* returned the next day, and the latter saw the *Revenge* without. Thus what loss we have sustained has been owing to the weather, not the enemy, seven or eight of whose line-of-battle ships got to sea, I believe, the night of the action.

As soon as it was broad daylight, in the morning of the 21st, I discovered seven or eight of the enemy's line-of-battle ships at anchor between Point Penris and the river Vilaine, on which I made the signal to weigh in order to work up and attack them. But it blowed so hard from the N.W. that instead of daring to cast the squadron loose, I was obliged to strike topgallant masts. Most of those ships appeared to be aground at low water. But on the flood, by lightening them, and the advantage of the wind under the land, all, except two, got that night into the river Vilaine.

The weather being moderate on the 22nd, I sent the *Portland*, *Chatham*, and *Vengeance*, to destroy the *Soleil Royal* and *Héros*.

The French, on the approach of our ships, set the first on fire; and soon after, the latter met the same fate from our people. In the meantime I got under way, and worked up with Penris Point, as well for the sake of its being a safer road as to destroy, if possible, the two ships of the enemy which still lay without the river Vilaine. But before the ships I sent ahead for that purpose could get near them, being quite light, and with the tide of flood, they got in.

All the 23rd we were occupied in reconnoitring the entrance of that river, which is very narrow, and only twelve foot water on the bar at low water. We discovered seven if not eight line-of-battle ships, about half a mile within, quite light, and two large frigates moored across to defend the mouth of the river. Only the frigates appeared to have guns in. By evening I had twelve long boats fitted as fireships ready to attempt burning them under cover of the *Sapphire* and *Coventry*. But the weather being bad, and the wind contrary, obliged me to defer it till at least the latter should be favourable. If they can by any means be destroyed, it shall be done.

In attacking a flying enemy, it was impossible in the space of a short winter's day that all our ships should be able to get into action, or all those of the enemy brought to it. The commanders and companies of such as did come up with the rear of the French on the 20th behaved with the greatest intrepidity, and gave the strongest proofs of a true British spirit. In the same manner I am satisfied would those have acquitted themselves whom bad-going ships, or the distance they were at in the morning, prevented from getting up.

Our loss by the enemy is not considerable. For in the ships which are now with me, I find only one lieutenant and fifty seamen and marines killed, and about two hundred and twenty wounded.

When I consider the season of the year, the hard gales on the day of action, a flying enemy, the shortness of the day, and the coast they were on, I can boldly affirm that all that could possibly be done has been done. As to the loss we have sustained, let it be placed to the account of the necessity I was under of running all risks to break this strong force of the enemy. Had we had but two hours more daylight, the whole had been totally destroyed or taken; for we were almost up with their van when night overtook us.

Yesterday came in here the *Pallas*, *Fortune* sloop, and the *Proserpine* fireship. On the 16th I had dispatched the *Fortune* to Quiberon, with directions to Captain Duff to keep strictly on his guard. In her way thither she fell in with the *Hebe*, a French frigate of forty guns, under jury masts and fought her several hours. During the engagement Lieutenant Stuart, second of the *Ramillies*, whom I had appointed to command her was unfortunately killed. The surviving officers, on consulting together, resolved to leave her, as she proved too strong for them. I have detached Captain Young to Quiberon Bay, with five ships, and am making up a flying squadron to scour the coast to the southward, as far as the Isle of Aix; and if practicable, to attempt any of the enemy's ships that may be there.

I am, &c.,

EDWARD HAWKE.

P.S. The manœuvres of the enemy crowding away on the 20th, prevented our being able to reckon their number exactly. Now I can with certainty assure their lordships that their squadron consisted of twenty-one sail of the line, with more seamen and soldiers than I gave in the list which accompanied my last. To the number destroyed I can also add the *Juste* of seventy guns (wrecked on the Charpentier); and I am in hopes, too, to find the *Magnifique* run ashore or lost, for she was terribly shattered.

HELPS

The typical battleship, or 'ship of the line', of this period was the 'Seventy-Four' gun ship. That standard of measurement will enable you to estimate the size of the French battleships mentioned in Hawke's dispatch: *Soleil Royal*, 80; *Formidable*, 80; *Thésée*, 74; *Héros*, 74; *Magnifique*, 74; *Superbe*, 70; *Juste*, 70.

QUESTIONS

[Before studying Hawke's dispatch, make a map of Brittany and the adjacent coasts and insert as many of the following names as possible: L'Orient, St Nazaire, Brest, Belle Isle, Quiberon Bay, Croisic, Dumet Isle, The Cardinals, The Four, River Vilaine, Penris Point, Mouth of River Loire.]

(1) On what day did the French fleet leave harbour and where was it first sighted?

(2) How many sail of the line [battleships] and how many frigates had the French Commander-in-Chief? And how did Hawke obtain this information?

(3) How did Hawke dispose the two frigates that joined him just before the battle—the *Maidstone* and *Coventry*?

(4) Which of Hawke's ships first sighted the enemy?

(5) What signal did Hawke then make, and what does he give as his reason?

(6) What readjustment did Hawke make when he had convinced himself that the enemy was trying to escape?

(7) Which ships were to chase and form line ahead as they did so?

(8) How does Hawke describe the weather on 20 November?

[N.B. Material for the answer should be gathered from all parts of the dispatch.]

(9) What was the name of the French Commander-in-Chief?

(10) In what polite words does Hawke describe the enemy's headlong flight?

(11) At what hour did Hawke signal to his leading ships to open fire?

(12) Which were the first two enemy battleships to surrender?

(13) Which were the first two sent to the bottom?

(14) In what words does Hawke describe his position when night descended?

(15) What was the fate of the French flagship?

(16) Which two English ships were lost and how?

(17) How did their ships' companies fare?

(18) What did Hawke do when the force of the gale increased on 21 November?

(19) What happened to the French battleships that came to an anchor off Penris Point?

(20) What happened to the *Héros*?

(21) How did Hawke spend 23 November, when the weather moderated?

(22) How much water was there on the bar of the River Vilaine and how did the French ships get over it?

(23) How did Hawke plan to destroy them?

(24) Which English ship rescued Frenchmen from the *Formidable*?

(25) The enemy had twenty-one battleships in all. How many, according to Hawke's dispatch, did they lose?

FOR A PRÉCIS

Write a précis of the passage beginning 'As soon as it was broad daylight...'
and ending '...if they can be destroyed, it shall be done'.

FOR AN ESSAY

(1) Imagine that you have been privileged to attend a session of the
House of Commons and heard the Rt Hon. William Pitt deliver a speech
in appreciation of the naval victory off the coast of Brittany and in praise
of Admiral Hawke, his officers and men.

Write down the speech or as much of it as you can remember.

(2) Imagine yourself to be a midshipman of H.M.S. *Essex* (64) and give
an account of the adventures undergone by your shipmates and yourself
from the beginning of the action to the end.

(3) Give your reasons for considering the battle of Quiberon unique in
the sea-annals even of Great Britain.

(4)   'Ere Hawke did bang
                       Monsieur Conflans,
                  You sent us beef and beer;
                      But now he's beat
                     We've naught to eat
                  For you have naught to fear!'

You can imagine what a festive Christmas England enjoyed in 1759.
Write a letter from Mrs Fothergill to her husband, Lieutenant Fothergill,
describing the all-prevailing jollity; and his reply, contrasting the hardships
of H.M.S. *Wideawake* still ploughing the winter seas.

THE WONDERFUL YEAR

[INTRODUCTORY NOTE. In addition to Quiberon Bay and its twin event, the victory of Lagos Bay, won by Admiral Boscawen in the previous August, the year 1759 witnessed the conquest of Quebec by a combined expedition under Admiral Sir Charles Saunders and General Wolfe, which laid securely the foundations of the Dominion of Canada. Good news came also from other quarters, notably from the Far East. Little wonder, then, that contemporary Britons christened 1759 'The Wonderful Year'. 'You shall hear from me again', wrote Horace Walpole to a friend, 'if we take Mexico or China before Christmas.' The following verses to celebrate 1759 were composed for the occasion by its greatest actor, David Garrick.]

COME cheer up, my lads, 'tis to glory we steer,
To add something new to this wonderful year,
To honour we call you, not press you like slaves,
For who are so free as the sons of the waves?

 Hearts of oak are our ships,
 Jolly tars are our men;
  We always are ready:
  Steady, boys, steady!
We'll fight and we'll conquer again and again.

We ne'er see our foes but we wish them to stay,
They never see us but they wish us away,
If they run, why we follow, and run them a-shore,
And if they won't fight us, we cannot do more.

 Hearts of oak are our ships,
 Jolly tars are our men;
  We always are ready:
  Steady, boys, steady!
We'll fight and we'll conquer again and again.

They swear they'll invade us, these terrible foes;
They frighten our women, our children and beaux;
But should their flat bottoms in darkness get o'er,
Still Britons they'll find to receive them on shore.

    Hearts of oak are our ships,
    Jolly tars are our men;
        We always are ready:
        Steady, boys, steady!
We'll fight and we'll conquer again and again.

Britannia triumphant, her ships sweep the sea;
Her standard is justice, her watchword 'Be free!'
Then cheer up, my lads! with one heart let us sing,
'Our soldiers, our sailors, our statesmen and king'.

    Hearts of oak are our ships,
    Jolly tars are our men;
        We always are ready:
        Steady, boys, steady!
We'll fight and we'll conquer again and again.

THE LIFE OF THE SHIP

THERE may have been lack of space in the Midshipmen's berth, there may have been deficiency of wholesome food, but at least there was always a fine superfluity of noise. Argument was incessant, and debates were conducted in the most vociferous manner. Those who had a mind to sing did not wait for a pause in the conversation. And the clamour was aggravated by the angry expostulations of those who were interrupted in their enjoyment of a game of cards or backgammon by an avalanche of beer down their necks.

One topic of perennial interest with the seniors was the possibility of promotion. Every midshipman longed for the time when he should earn his commission. Not till then could he exchange his hanger for a sword. Not till then could he wear his hat athwartships instead of fore and aft. Not till then could he escape from the Midshipmen's berth to the more seemly decorum of the Ward-Room. Not till then, whatever his age might be, could he count himself a man.

Every 'young gentleman', therefore, devoted himself with more or less keenness to the pursuit of professional knowledge. There were certain things that had to be done. All midshipmen were expected to keep a journal of the cruise, and their day's work went to the Captain for inspection. In harbour they took charge of the boats. At night they mustered the watch. At quarters they mustered the guns' crews. At noon they attended the Master on the quarter-deck and took the altitude of the sun. With varying degrees of accuracy they worked out the ship's position by dead reckoning. They qualified as able seamen by reefing and furling the main topsail, heaving the lead, and taking their trick at the wheel. They used to pull an oar from time to time, and listen attentively to the bos'n's instructions as he taught them to knot and splice. Some midshipmen grew tired of waiting for promotion and qualified as Master's Mate. This status entitled them to considerable increase of pay, and pay to a poor man often meant everything. But the rank of Master's Mate, unlike the rank of Sub-Lieutenant to-day, carried with it no succession rights to a lieutenancy. There was a recognized distinction between the 'Mate' with his professional knowledge and the petty officer, or Master's assistant. But the proper line of progress was from Master's Mate to Master, and, therefore, the exercise of patience was commendable in those who wished to rise above a warrant.

However hard a midshipman might toil, his labours bore the same relation to his life's work as those of a university student. At their best they were a little out of touch with reality. A reefer, like an undergraduate, might slave from early morn to dewy eve; he might accomplish as much or more than a full-blown lieutenant. But for all that, he was a student. He was not professed; he was a novice. He was not independent; he was under tutelage. His position was not authoritative. And therefore, like his fellow students all the world over, he liked to accentuate his irresponsibility. He loved mad romps and wild escapades. Skylarking was as the breath of life to him. Ragging alone made existence tolerable. His spirits were ever bubbling. His pranks were boyish. He was irrepressible.

When dinner was served in the Ward-Room; when the Lieutenants, the Captain of Marines, the Master, the Purser, the Surgeon, and the Chaplain sat round their table enjoying perhaps a brace of roast fowl, and dallying over their wine, then was the joyous time for midshipmen. The First Lieutenant was their ogre and their bugbear. He was like a dean or proctor. He set down on the tablets of his memory all the sins of a midshipman, all his shortcomings and deficiencies. But the First Lieutenant was president of the officers' mess. And the Ward-Room was situated aft of the middle deck, immediately under the Admiral's cabin, and immediately over the Gun-Room. In other words, it was well removed from the upper deck and the orlop. The midshipmen did not linger over their meal. There was little reason perhaps for doing so. Salt junk, lobscouse, dog's body, sea pie, pea coffee, hurry hush, and chowder were the standing dishes. By these you are to understand various messes and hashes made up in equal parts of meat, fish, biscuit, dried peas, potatoes and onions. They were washed down with water that tasted strongly of gunpowder. Grog was to be had. But more often than not it was used by midshipmen as a medium of exchange, the purchase price of more esteemed commodities or hush money to a bos'n's mate.

The table being cleared, the fun began. Sometimes resort was had to the poop, which served as an admirable castle. Sides were picked. One side defended and one attacked. Crows and pike-staffs formed splendid weapons of offence. Mops, brooms, and half-ports served to repel them. Sometimes the game was 'follow-my-leader', up the lee mizzen shrouds, over the futtocks, down the weather shrouds, up the main, down the backstay, into the waist—a breathless dance. Sometimes a sleeper was discovered, and molasses were gently poured under him, that his form might be glued to the deck. But if the victim was a reveller who had been splicing the mainbrace and was three sheets in the wind, then the tormentors painted his face with red ochre, added black eyebrows, and a fierce moustache, dressed him in a flaxen wig made from the fag ends of the tiller rope, crammed a cocked hat over his head, and completed the picture by removing his shirt and painting him blue like an ancient Briton.

Unpopular members of the Midshipmen's berth and even deserving inmates of the orlop had often enough a terrible time. One night the gay young sparks of the *Victory* caught the purser's steward, against whom they bore a grudge. Some cattle had recently been slaughtered, and they sewed him up in a bullock's skin. A bull-fight after the true Spanish fashion then followed. The toreadors flung cloaks over his head and brought him to the ground. The picadors prodded him with marling spikes. And the matador put him out of his misery by knocking him over the head with a wooden sword. The idea of an animal running amok was always a source of boundless amusement. One night they insisted that a clerk whose name was Newnham was the admiral's cow got adrift. It was no use for the wretched fellow to protest. After hunting him from side to side, and flying in simulated fear at his approach, they suddenly clapped a selvagee round him with a hauling-line made fast, and roused him up the hatchway in a minute, terrified almost to death.

Sometimes considerable diversion was obtained by personating ghosts and goblins. The darkness of the tier and of the hold and the superstition of seamen afforded ample opportunity, and the midshipmen gave rein to their fantasy. Dear, too, were the joys obtained in moments stolen from duty. In the middle watch, when the night was as dark as pitch, when the wind was blowing half a gale and the rain descending in torrents, the mids on duty would steal down to their berth to stew beef steaks. This was done by lighting several pieces of candle in the bottom of a lantern and sticking forks into the table round it, with a plate resting on them over the flame, the head of the lantern being off. The mess thus concocted was always voted delicious. But the sauce that gave such a tasty seasoning was, doubtless, the knowledge that the First Lieutenant imagined them at the post of duty on the upper deck.

There was always the keenest rivalry between the midshipmen of the *Victory*, and the midshipmen of other vessels in the fleet. Disputes raged hotly between them over the comparative merits of their respective ships. Things which were voted a nuisance in the privacy of one's own berth were condoned and often vehemently supported in conversation with visitors. The First Lieutenant was unanimously voted an officer and a gentleman, and the bos'n a worthy fellow. The laws of hospitality were scrupulously observed. But if strangers had the best of an argument, or carried a debate in their own favour, the unanswerable question, 'Are you still on boiled parrot and monkey soup?' sent them home in a chastened frame of mind. Play-acting was a favourite amusement with the young people. They would compose the play, make the dresses and wigs, rig up a stage and screen, and act with remarkable vigour and success. The great Napoleon himself, when a prisoner on board the *Bellerophon,** condescended to be present at such a performance, and to judge by the smile on his face, must have enjoyed himself immensely. In these amateur theatricals there was always a keen competition for the honour of 'playing the woman'. When forced to stay below in the berth the midshipmen preferred before other games either backgammon or 'able whackets'. This last was a game with cards, wherein the loser was beaten over the palms with a handkerchief tightly twisted like a rope. 'Bait the bear' was a recreation of which no one grew tired except the unfortunate actor who was cast for the bear.

But to tell the truth, the happiest and merriest hours were spent in teasing a really gullible green-horn. If this was unkind or undeserved, it is to be feared that all the midshipmen alike were to blame. They gave Johnny Raw or Johnny Newcombe a terrible time. No sooner was he in his hammock than they cut the clew and let him down with a bump. Or they fixed a fish-hook in the rim of his mattress and dragged it from under him; or they reefed his blanket—that is, they made the ends fast, and by numerous turns formed the blanket itself into a ring like a horse's collar, which an hour's work would not undo. While the wretched gulpin was asleep they stole his uniform, and, hiding it in the cook's oven, left him no alternative but to perambulate the ship in his blanket, making polite enquiries of whomsoever he met. When he yielded to the rigours of sea-sickness, they dosed him with a quart of sea water, or persuaded him that the symptoms would yield at once if he would swallow a piece of salt pork attached to a string, and draw it backwards and forwards. When he expressed inability even to move, they performed the kind office themselves. When he recovered, they sent him to find

* See below, p. 161–6.

'Cheeks' the Marine, a quest that occasioned interminable research, for 'Cheeks' was first cousin to Sairey Gamp's 'Mrs Harris', a creature that never existed. They sent him at dusk to hear the dog-fish bark. As he listened intently some of the youngsters yelped in the mizzen chains. He hastened, of course, to investigate and was promptly doused with bucketfuls of water. They assured him that this sprinkled spray was the breath that the grampus blew. And if at any of their information he looked incredulous, they triced him half-way to the mizzen peak, with signal halliards lashed round his legs.

Occasionally, however, the tables were turned. Occasionally the tormentors were tormented. Occasionally the mischief-making midshipman was brought before a judge equally merciless. Then it was his turn to 'buy goose' or suffer punishment. The commonest award meted out by the First Lieutenant was one of banishment. The wretched delinquent was sent to the main top-mast cross-trees. At this dizzy eminence above the deck he was condemned to cool his heels sometimes for one hour, sometimes for two, sometimes for four, and sometimes for eight. Exposed to the weather, deprived of food and drink, robbed of the society of the berth, placed in a position where comfort was out of the question, the most wayward of malefactors became a penitent, and was glad to descend on any conditions. It might happen that his sentence was passed just as his hammock was slung below. In that case, if his term of exile were unduly prolonged, the bos'n was free to confiscate his sleeping accommodation and return it to his store. The midshipman was, in nine cases out of ten, unable at the moment to redeem the lost articles, and would have to content himself for a fortnight (or perhaps a month) with what rest he could snatch from the bare boards, or at best from a coiled-up cable.

A very contumacious and refractory fellow was sometimes spread-eagled—that is, he was lashed to the weather shrouds with arms and legs drawn in opposite directions. But if by chance the ship was in home waters or visiting home ports, a far more efficacious penalty was the denial of all permission to go ashore. Occasion sometimes arose when it was necessary to confine a young officer to his ship for three months together. This was a very heavy penalty indeed. And confinement was a punishment equally applicable at sea. For visiting as between ship and ship was usually possible on Sundays. If a midshipman really failed to behave himself, if he turned out a thoroughly bad character and displayed no desire or intention to reform, then he was dismissed his ship. This chastisement may be compared to the 'sending down' of a university student. The midshipman so treated not only lost touch with his messmates, not only brought disgrace upon his friends and family, but cut himself off from all chance of obtaining the one thing which the ship could give him —namely, the chance of quick promotion in the service. Transferred to another ship, he had to begin life over again and endeavour as best he might to live down a bad reputation.

Happily such cases were very rare. The midshipmen, alike in the *Victory* and in other ships, were keen and alert to a sense of duty, anxious above all to rise in their profession and most amenable to discipline. High spirits might lead them for occasional airings to the cross-trees, but no one thought the worse of them for that. They were the life and soul of the ship. However freely the bos'n may have cursed them, however soundly the Master may have rated them, there was no one aboard who did not relish their pranks, so long as they were not directed against himself. It is enough that Nelson loved his 'children' dearly, took them about with him when he went ashore, introduced them to his friends, and tried to make the ship a happier place for them. They repaid, of course, his indulgence with idolatry, and a midshipman it was that avenged his death.

The Story of H.M.S. Victory.

QUESTIONS

(1) What sort of a scene did the Midshipmen's berth present?
(2) Make a list of the items of professional knowledge which the midshipman was obliged to learn in order to earn his promotion.

(3) What were the chief attractions offered by promotion?

(4) Enumerate the advantages and disadvantages of becoming a Master's Mate.

(5) How did it happen that midshipmen were able to carry on their pranks without being noticed by a senior officer?

(6) Where was the Ward-Room and who were its occupants?

(7) How did the midshipmen cook a beef steak?

(8) What names did they give to their regular dishes?

(9) Use simpler words or phrases for the following: 'superfluity', 'seemly decorum', 'under tutelage', 'more esteemed commodities', 'simulated fear', 'perambulate', 'gullible green-horn'.

(10) In a Spanish bull-fight the following take part: toreadors, picadors, and a matador. What is the special task of each?

(11) 'First Cousin to Sairey Gamp's "Mrs Harris".' Do you know what profession Sairey Gamp followed and in what book by Dickens she appears'?

(12) What names were given in the Midshipmen's berth to the shipmate who was easily imposed upon?

(13) What do you learn from this passage about the character of Nelson?

(14) 'Run "amok"' is a Malay expression signifying 'excited to madness'. In what connection is it used in this passage?

(15) What other names have been given to midshipmen as a class?

FOR A PRÉCIS

Make a précis of the passage beginning 'The commonest award meted out by the First Lieutenant...' and ending '...live down a bad reputation'.

FOR AN ESSAY

(1) You are a midshipman. Write to a friend who is still at school and describe to him an evening on board ship, when you have been enjoying yourself with your friends.

(2) Write, as if in a diary which you are keeping, your experiences on board ship during your first week there.

(3) Describe as fully as you can

    (a) a football match in which you have taken part;

    (b) an exciting race in the school sports.

(4) 'The First Lieutenant was their ogre.' Describe any person who seemed an Ogre to you when you were very young.

(5) Narrate any fairy story or tale of adventure in which an Ogre appears.

(6) Describe a meal cooked by yourself out of doors.

PRINCE HOARE

THE ARETHUSA

[INTRODUCTORY NOTE. While the Americans were asserting their independence of Great Britain and supporting that assertion by force of arms, the French took up the cudgels for them; and in 1778 the struggle, till then colonial in character, developed into a world war, in which the British fleet [long neglected] was hard put to protect Britain's world-wide interests until the victories of Kempenfelt, Howe and Rodney restored the situation.

The single-ship action commemorated in the following ballad, took place at the time of the French intervention, the *Arethusa* being a frigate attached to the Channel fleet under Admiral Keppel, the friend of Reynolds (see above, p. 18-9). The *Belle Poule* had 40 guns to the *Arethusa's* 32 and more than double the number of men. The *Arethusa*, firing to kill, had the best of the encounter; but the *Belle Poule*, firing to destroy masts and sails, did so much damage to her adversary up aloft that the *Arethusa* was unable to 'lug' her to the 'Admiral's lee'; and the *Belle Poule* ran under her own coastal batteries, although, through the rather inefficient telescopes of that day, it appeared to the British officers that she had run herself aground like Hawke's victims in the River Vilaine.]

> COME, all ye jolly sailors bold,
> Whose hearts are cast in honour's mould,
> While England's glory I unfold—
>   Huzza for the *Arethusa*!
> She is a frigate tight and brave
> As ever stemmed the dashing wave;
>   Her men are staunch
>   To their fav'rite launch;
> And when the foe shall meet our fire,
> Sooner than strike we'll all expire
>   On board of the *Arethusa*.
>
> 'Twas with the spring fleet she went out
> The English Channel to cruise about,
> When four French sail, in show so stout,
>   Bore down on the *Arethusa*.*

* This remarkable frigate could make sixteen knots.

The famed *Belle Poule* straight ahead did lie.
The *Arethusa* seemed to fly.
   Not a sheet, or a tack,
   Or a brace, did she slack—
Though the Frenchmen laughed and thought it stuff.
But they knew not the handful of men, how tough,
   On board of the *Arethusa*.

On deck five hundred men did dance,
The stoutest they could find in France;
We, with two hundred, did advance
   On board of the *Arethusa*.
Our captain hailed the Frenchman, 'Ho!'
The Frenchman then cried out 'Hallo!'
   'Bear down, d'ye see,
   To our Admiral's lee!'
'No, no,' says the Frenchman, 'that can't be!'
'Then I must lug you along with me!'
   Says the saucy *Arethusa*.

The fight was off the Frenchman's land.
We forced them back upon their strand;
For we fought till not a stick would stand
   Of the gallant *Arethusa*.
And now we've driven the foe ashore
Never to fight with Britons more,
   Let each fill a glass
   To his favourite lass!
A health to our captain, and officers true,
And all that belong to the jovial crew,
   On board of the *Arethusa*!

QUESTIONS

(1) Arethusa in the Greek myth, or fairy tale, was a nymph who was turned into a fountain. What other ship-names have you already come across derived, like *Arethusa*, from Greek legends or tales?

(2) What exactly was a frigate?

(3) How does this ballad help us to understand why frigates eventually changed their generic name to 'cruisers'?

(4) As the *Arethusa* was outnumbered, why did not the spring fleet send assistance to her?

(5) What do you understand by 'spring fleet'?

(6) By whom is the ballad supposed to be recited?

(7) *Belle Poule* is French for 'Plump Chicken' or 'Weel tappit hen'. What induced them to christen the ship by such an odd title?

(8) What was the *Arethusa* actually doing when she seemed to fly?

(9) Why did the Frenchmen laugh?

(10) Express differently in your own words:
   (a) 'Hearts are cast in honour's mould.'
   (b) 'Stemmed the dashing wave.'
   (c) 'Thought it stuff.'

(11) Substitute other words for the following without change of sense: 'staunch', 'strike', 'stout', 'fly', 'slack', 'tough', 'strand', 'bold', 'tight', 'dance', 'lug', 'stick', 'glass', 'true'.

(12) What do you notice about all the words in the previous question?

FOR A PRÉCIS

Write a précis of the passage beginning ''Twas with the spring fleet...' and ending '...to fight with Britons more'. [N.B. No rhymes admissible.]

FOR AN ESSAY

(1) British naval history has numberless examples of single-ship duels. This particular instance is remembered because the *Arethusa* was so saucy.

Give other examples of sauciness on the part of our fighting ships either in past wars or the present.

(2) The French in 1778 considered that they had won a victory and 'Belle Poule' became to them an honoured name. Ladies' fashions were *à la Belle Poule*; cafés dressed their dishes *à la Belle Poule*; and gardeners christened new hybrids after the ship.

Imagine yourself to be a naval attaché at the British embassy in Paris; and write a letter to be conveyed to England in the Foreign Office bag, showing how the French were celebrating their 'success', explaining their probable reasons for thinking that they had won, and pointing out the differences between French methods of fighting at sea and our own.

(3) Write a dispatch as from Admiral The Hon. Augustus Keppel, Commander-in-Chief, Home Fleet, describing the action between the two frigates and recommending Captain Samuel Marshall of H.M.S. *Arethusa* for another ship.

EXAMINATION FOR LIEUTENANT

Midshipman Peter Simple, R.N., is examined for Promotion to Lieutenant

I HAD only brought one suit of clothes with me: they were in very good condition when I arrived, but salt water plays the devil with a uniform. I laid in bed until they were dry; but when I put them on again, not being before too large for me, for I grew very fast, they were now shrunk and shrivelled up, so as to be much too small. My wrists appeared below the sleeves of my coat—my trousers had shrunk half way up to my knees—the buttons were all tarnished, and altogether I certainly did not wear the appearance of a gentlemanly, smart midshipman. I would have ordered another suit, but the examination was to take place at ten o'clock the next morning, and there was no time. I was therefore obliged to appear as I was, on the quarter-deck of the line-of-battle ship, on board of which the passing was to take place. Many others were there to undergo the same ordeal, all strangers to me, and as I perceived by their nods and winks to each other, as they walked up and down in their smart clothes, not at all inclined to make my acquaintance.

There were many before me on the list, and our hearts beat every time that a name was called, and the owner of it walked aft into the cabin. Some returned with jocund faces, and our hopes mounted with the anticipation of similar good fortune; others came out melancholy and crest-fallen, and then the expression of their countenances was communicated to our own, and we quailed with fear and apprehension. I have no hesitation in asserting, that although 'passing' may be a proof of being qualified; 'not passing' is certainly no proof to the contrary. I have known many of the cleverest young men turned back (while others of inferior abilities have succeeded), merely from the feeling of awe occasioned by the peculiarity of the situation:

and it is not to be wondered at, when it is considered that all the labour and exertion of six years are at stake at this appalling moment. At last my name was called, and almost breathless from anxiety, I entered the cabin, where I found myself in presence of the three Captains who were to decide whether I were fit to hold a commission in His Majesty's service. My logs and certificates were examined and approved; my time calculated and allowed to be correct. The questions in navigation which were put to me were very few, for the best of all possible reasons, that most Captains in His Majesty's service know little or nothing of navigation. During their servitude as midshipmen, they learn it by *rote*, without being aware of the principles upon which the calculations they use are founded. As lieutenants, their services as to navigation are seldom required, and they rapidly forget all about it. As Captains, their whole remnant of mathematical knowledge consists in being able to set down the ship's position on the chart. As for navigating the ship, the Master is answerable; and the Captains not being responsible themselves, they trust entirely to his reckoning.…

As soon as I had answered several questions satisfactorily, I was desired to stand up. The Captain who had interrogated me on navigation, was very grave in his demeanour towards me, but at the same time not uncivil. During his examination, he was not interfered with by the other two, who only undertook the examination in 'seamanship'. The Captain, who now desired me to stand up, spoke in a very harsh tone, and quite frightened me. I stood up pale and trembling, for I augured no good from this commencement. Several questions in seamanship were put to me, which I have no doubt I answered in a very lame way, for I cannot even now recollect what I said.

'I thought so,' observed the Captain; 'I judged as much from your appearance. An officer who is so careless of his dress, as not even to put on a decent coat when he appears at his examination, generally turns out an idle fellow, and no seaman. One would think you had served all your time in a cutter, or a ten-gun brig, instead of dashing frigates. Come, sir, I'll give you one more chance.'

I was so hurt at what the Captain said, that I could not control my feelings. I replied, with a quivering lip, 'that I had had no time to order another uniform,'—and I burst into tears.

'Indeed, Burrows, you are rather too harsh,' said the third Captain; 'the lad is frightened. Let him sit down and compose himself for a little while. Sit down, Mr Simple, and we will try you again directly.'

I sat down, checking my grief and trying to recall my scattered senses. The Captains, in the meantime, turning over the logs to pass away the time; the one who had questioned me in navigation reading the Plymouth newspaper, which had a few minutes before been brought on board and sent into the cabin. 'Heh! What's this? I say Burrows—Keats, look here,' and he pointed to a paragraph. 'Mr Simple, may I ask whether it was you who saved the soldier who leaped off the wharf yesterday?'

'Yes, sir,' replied I; 'and that's the reason why my uniforms are so shabby. I spoilt them then, and had no time to order others. I did not like to say why they were spoilt.' I saw a change in the countenances of all three, and it gave me courage. Indeed, now that my feelings had found vent, I was no longer under any apprehension.

'Come, Mr Simple, stand up again,' said the Captain, kindly, 'that is, if you feel sufficiently composed; if not, we will wait a little longer. Don't be afraid, we *wish* to pass you.'

I was not afraid, and stood up immediately. I answered every question satisfactorily; and finding that I did so, they put more difficult ones. 'Very good, very good indeed, Mr Simple; now let me ask you one more; it's seldom done in the service, and perhaps you may not be able to answer it. Do you know how to *club-haul* a ship?'

'Yes, Sir,' replied I, having as the reader may recollect, witnessed the manœuvre when serving under poor Captain Savage, and I immediately stated how it was to be done.

'That is sufficient, Mr Simple. I wish to ask you no more questions. I thought at first you were a careless officer and no seaman: I now find that you are a good seaman and a gallant young man. Do you wish to ask any more questions?' continued he, turning to the two others.

They replied in the negative; my passing certificate was signed, and the Captains did me the honour to shake hands with me, and wish me speedy promotion. Thus ended happily this severe trial to my poor nerves; and, as I came out of the cabin, no one could have imagined that I had been in such distress within, when they beheld the joy that irradiated my countenance.

Peter Simple.

QUESTIONS

(1) Describe the state of Peter's uniform when he appeared for his examination.

(2) To what was his slovenly appearance due?

(3) Where did the examination take place and who were the examiners?

(4) How did the other examination candidates betray their contempt for Midshipman Simple?

(5) To what cause does Captain Marryat ascribe the failure of candidates to qualify, apart from lack of proficiency in Navigation and Seamanship?

(6) Define Navigation and Seamanship and show clearly the difference between them.

(7) How many years' work had Peter devoted to these subjects when he came up for examination?

(8) Name any Captain under whom Peter had served as Midshipman.

(9) Supply alternative words of similar meaning to replace Captain Marryat's 'jocund', 'melancholy', 'augured', 'apprehension', 'crestfallen', 'servitude', 'rote', 'demeanour', 'quailed', 'interrogated', 'vent', 'countenances', 'irradiated'.

(10) What were the first steps taken by the examiners to test Peter's qualifications?

(11) Why did Peter come off so easily in Navigation?

(12) Why was Peter required to stand up during his examination?

(13) Captain Burrows found it difficult to believe that Peter had served in smart frigates. What vessels did he suggest as more probable?

(14) What did the Board of Examiners do while Peter wept?

(15) What was the most difficult question on seamanship that Peter was asked?

FOR A PRÉCIS

Write a précis on the passage beginning '"I thought so," observed the Captain...' and ending '...my passing certificate was signed'.

FOR AN ESSAY

(1) Write a letter from Peter to his father describing how he saved the soldier's life and what effect this had on his chances of promotion.

(2) Peter Simple had studied Navigation for several years and at his examination was asked only a few unimportant questions. Describe in detail the explanation which Captain Marryat gives for this strange omission.

(3) Which do you consider the more satisfactory of the two—written examinations or oral? Give reasons for your choice.

(4) Describe as vividly as possible an outstanding deed of heroism, witnessed by yourself, described to you by others, or read about in a book.

ROBERT SOUTHEY

THE BATTLE OF COPENHAGEN*

2 APRIL 1801

[INTRODUCTORY NOTE. Of all the schemes formed by Napoleon for the overthrow of Great Britain, none was more perilous for the Island Race than his alliance with the Baltic powers—Denmark (which then included Norway), Sweden, and Russia. At the moment Napoleon was supreme upon the Continent and England on the sea. But the Royal Navy depended on masts and sails and rigging, not to mention pitch and tar: and for all these commodities, Great Britain depended on the Baltic powers, with whom she had for many years cultivated a policy of friendship and close accord. If Great Britain was to survive Napoleon's threat, the Northern Confederation had at once to be hewn in pieces. A strong fleet was, therefore, sent under Admiral Sir Hyde Parker to reason with Great Britain's old friends; and in case diplomatic negotiations should break down (which they did), Nelson was appointed second-in-command to repeat at Copenhagen—and elsewhere, if necessary—the lightning stroke which he had delivered at the Nile.]

AT five minutes after ten the action began. The first half of our fleet was engaged in about half-an-hour; and, by half-past eleven, the battle became general. The plan of the attack had been complete: but seldom has any plan been more disconcerted by untoward accidents. Of twelve ships of the line, one was entirely useless, and two others in a situation where they could not render half the service which was required of them.† Of the squadron of gun-brigs, only one could get into action; the rest were prevented by baffling currents from weathering the eastern end of the shoal; and only two of the bomb-vessels could reach their station on the Middle Ground, and open their mortars on the arsenal, firing over both fleets. Riou took the vacant station against the Crown Battery with his frigates; attempting with

---

* Also called the Battle of the Baltic.

† During the difficult navigation preceding the battle three of Nelson's battleships ran aground: Nelson's own *Agamemnon*, at too great a distance from the enemy to be of any service; the *Bellona* and *Russell*, within practicable range, but hampered by the shoals that held them captive.

that unequal force a service in which three sail of the line had been directed to assist.

Nelson's agitation had been extreme when he saw himself, before the action began, deprived of a fourth part of his ships of the line; but no sooner was he in battle, where his squadron was received with the fire of more than a thousand guns, than, as if that artillery like music had driven away all care and painful thoughts, his countenance brightened; and, as a bystander describes him, his conversation became joyous, animated, elevated, and delightful. The commander-in-chief, meantime, near enough to the scene of action to know the unfavourable accidents which had so materially weakened Nelson, and yet too distant to know the real state of the contending parties, suffered the most dreadful anxiety. To get to his assistance was impossible; both wind and current were against him. Fear for the event, in such circumstances, would naturally preponderate in the bravest mind; and at one o'clock, perceiving that, after three hours' endurance, the enemy's fire was unslackened, he began to despair of success.

'I will make the signal of recall,' said he to his captain, 'for Nelson's sake. If he is in a condition to continue the action successfully, he will disregard it; if he is not, it will be an excuse for his retreat, and no blame can be imputed to him.' Captain Domett urged him at least to delay the signal, till he could communicate with Nelson; but, in Sir Hyde's opinion, the danger was too pressing for delay. The fire, he said, was too hot for Nelson to oppose. A retreat he thought must be made. He was aware of the consequences to his own personal reputation, but it would be cowardly in him to leave Nelson to bear the whole shame of the failure, if shame it should be deemed. Under a mistaken judgment, therefore, but with this disinterested and generous feeling, he made the signal for retreat.

Nelson was at this time, in all the excitement of action, pacing the quarter-deck. A shot through the mainmast knocked the splinters about; and he observed to one of his officers, with a smile, 'It is warm work; and this day may be the last to any of us at a moment': and then stopping short at the gangway, added, with emotion, 'But mark you! I would not be elsewhere for thousands.' About this time the signal lieutenant called out, that Number Thirty-nine (the signal for discontinuing the action) was thrown out by the commander-in-chief. He continued to walk the deck, and appeared to take no notice of it. The signal officer met him at the next turn, and asked if he should repeat it. 'No,' he replied; 'acknowledge it.' Presently he called after him to know if the signal for close action was still hoisted; and being answered in the affirmative, said, 'Mind you keep it so.' He now paced the deck, moving the stump of his lost arm in a manner which always indicated great emotion. 'Do you know,' said he to Mr Ferguson, 'what is shown on board the commander-in-chief? Number Thirty-nine!' Mr Ferguson* asked what that meant. 'Why, to leave off action!' Then, shrugging up his shoulders, he repeated the words. 'Leave off action! Now, damn me if I do! You know, Foley,' turning to the captain, 'I have only one eye,—I have a right to be blind sometimes':—and then putting the glass to his blind eye, in that mood of mind which sports with bitterness, he exclaimed, 'I really do not see the signal!' Presently he exclaimed, 'Damn the signal! Keep mine for closer battle flying! That's the way I answer such signals! Nail mine to the mast!'

Admiral Graves, who was so situated that he could not discern what was done on board the *Elephant*, disobeyed Sir Hyde's signal in like manner; whether by fortunate mistake, or by a like brave intention, has not been made known.

The other ships of the line, looking only to Nelson, continued the action. The signal, however, saved Riou's little squadron, but did not save its heroic leader. This squadron, which was nearest the commander-in-chief obeyed, and hauled off. It had suffered severely in its most unequal contest. For a long time the *Amazon* had been firing, enveloped in smoke, when Riou desired his men to stand fast, and let the smoke clear off, that they might see what

* More properly 'Dr' Ferguson, surgeon of the *Elephant*.

they were about. A fatal order; for the Danes then got clear sight of her from the batteries, and pointed their guns with such tremendous effect, that nothing but the signal for retreat saved this frigate from destruction. 'What will Nelson think of us?' was Riou's mournful exclamation, when he unwillingly drew off. He had been wounded in the head by a splinter, and was sitting on a gun, encouraging his men, when, just as the *Amazon* showed her stern to the Trekroner Battery, his clerk was killed by his side; and another shot swept away several marines, who were hauling in the main-brace. 'Come, then, my boys!' cried Riou; 'let us die all together!' The words had scarcely been uttered, before a raking shot cut him in two. Except it had been Nelson himself, the British navy could not have suffered a severer loss.

The action continued along the line with unabated vigour on our side, and with the most determined resolution on the part of the Danes. They fought to great advantage, because most of the vessels in their line of defence were without masts. The few which had any standing had their topmasts struck, and the hulls could not be seen at intervals. The *Isis* must have been destroyed by the superior weight of her enemy's fire if Captain Inman, in the *Desirée* frigate, had not judiciously taken a situation which enabled him to rake the Dane, and if the *Polyphemus* had not also relieved her. Both in the *Bellona* and the *Isis* many men were lost by the bursting of their guns.

The former ship was about forty years old, and these guns were believed to be the same which she had first taken to sea. They were, probably, originally faulty, for the fragments were full of little air-holes.

The *Bellona* lost seventy-five men; the *Isis*, one hundred and ten; the *Monarch*, two hundred and ten. She was, more than any other line-of-battle ship, exposed to the great battery: and supporting at the same time the united fire of the *Holstein* and the *Zealand*, her loss this day exceeded that of any single ship during the whole war. Amid the tremendous carnage of this vessel, some of the men displayed a singular instance of coolness:

the pork and peas happened to be in the kettle; a shot knocked its contents about; they picked up the pieces, and ate and fought at the same time....

By half-past two the action had ceased along that part of the line which was astern of the *Elephant*, but not with the ships ahead and the Crown Batteries.

Nelson, seeing the manner in which his boats were fired upon, when they went to take possession of the prizes, became angry, and said he must either send on shore to have this irregular proceeding stopped, or send a fire-ship and burn them.

Half the shot from the Trekroner, and from the batteries at Amag, at this time, struck the surrendered ships, four of which had got close together; and the fire of the English, in return, was equally or even more destructive to these poor devoted Danes. Nelson, who was as humane as he was brave, was shocked at this massacre, for such he called it; and with a presence of mind peculiar to himself, and never more signally displayed than now, he retired into the stern-gallery and wrote thus to the Crown Prince. 'Vice-Admiral Lord Nelson has been commanded to spare Denmark when she no longer resists. The line of defence which covered her shores has struck to the British flag: but if the firing is continued on the part of Denmark, he must set on fire all the prizes that he has taken, without having the power of saving the men who have so nobly defended them. The brave Danes are the brothers, and should never be the enemies of the English.' A wafer was given him; but he ordered a candle to be brought from the cockpit, and sealed the letter with wax, affixing a larger seal than he ordinarily used. 'This,' said he, 'is no time to appear hurried and informal.' Captain Sir Frederick Thesiger, who acted as his aide-de-camp, carried this letter with a flag of truce. Meantime the fire of the ships ahead, and the approach of the *Ramillies* and *Defence* from Sir Hyde's division, which had now worked near enough to alarm the enemy, though not to injure them, silenced the remainder of the Danish line to the eastward of the Trekroner. That battery, however, continued its fire. This formidable work, owing to the want of the ships which had been destined to attack it and the inadequate force of Riou's little squadron, was comparatively uninjured. Towards the close of the action it had been manned with nearly fifteen hundred men; and the intention of storming it, for which every preparation had been made, was abandoned as impracticable.

During Thesiger's absence, Nelson sent for Fremantle from the *Ganges*, and consulted with him and Foley, whether it was advisable to advance, with those ships which had sustained least damage, against the yet uninjured part of the Danish line. They were decidedly of opinion, that the best thing that could be done was, while the wind continued fair, to remove the fleet out of the intricate channel, from which it had to retreat. In somewhat more than half an hour after Thesiger had been dispatched, the Danish Adjutant-General Lindholm came, bearing a flag of truce, upon which the Trekroner ceased to fire, and the action closed, after four hours' continuance. He brought an inquiry from the Prince, 'What was the object of Nelson's note?' The British Admiral wrote in reply, 'Lord Nelson's object in sending the flag of truce was humanity: he therefore consents that hostilities shall cease, and that the wounded Danes may be taken on shore. And Lord Nelson will take his prisoners out of the vessels, and burn or carry off his prizes as he shall think fit. Lord Nelson, with humble duty to his Royal Highness the Prince, will consider this the greatest victory he has ever gained, if it may be the cause of a happy reconciliation and union between his own most gracious sovereign and his Majesty the King of Denmark.'

Life of Nelson.

QUESTIONS

[Before beginning your study of the foregoing passage, draw a rough plan of the sea approaches to Copenhagen, showing the city walls and the shoals adjoining them; the Middle Ground; the King's Channel or Deep; and the Trekroner or Crown Batteries defending the direct approach to the city from the north. Nelson 'turned' the enemy's position by approaching from the south, and attacking the Danish fleet anchored in the King's Deep.]

(1) What was the name of Nelson's Commander-in-Chief and what ship bore his flag?

(2) What was the name of his Flag Captain?

(3) What was the name of Nelson's flagship?

(4) Who was his Flag Captain?

(5) Who was second-in-command to Nelson?

(6) Who was in command of Nelson's frigates? What was the name of his ship? What part in the battle did Nelson assign to him? What were his last words?

(7) How many of our bomb-vessels took up their position on the Middle Ground to bombard the city over the heads of the British sail of the line?

(8) By what epithet did a bystander describe Nelson's conversation when the guns began to fire?

(9) What were the feelings of the British Commander-in-Chief when he saw a quarter of Nelson's squadron run aground? What signal did he hoist and why?

(10) Why did not the Commander-in-Chief come to Nelson's rescue?

(11) Quote Nelson's remark when a shot in the mainmast sent the splinters flying.

(12) What was the difference between 'repeating a signal' and acknowledging it?

(13) 'Mind you keep it so', said Nelson. To what was he referring?

(14) How did his officers know when Nelson experienced great emotion?

(15) Did any of Nelson's squadron obey the Commander-in-Chief's signal?

(16) How was it that the Danes sustained so long the force of Nelson's attack?

(17) Which English ships suffered most in the battle?

(18) Which English ship suffered heavier casualties than any other ship during the whole war?

(19) And what did her ship's company have for dinner?

(20) What stirred Nelson's righteous anger during the later stages of the action?

(21) In what part of his flagship did Nelson write his letter to the Crown Prince of Denmark?

(22) What did he say in his letter?

(23) What were then the two methods of fastening a letter? Which did Nelson prefer and why?

(24) Who took Nelson's letter under a flag of truce ashore? Whom did the Crown Prince send back to negotiate?

(25) Substitute other words for the following without alteration of sense: 'disconcerted', 'resolution', 'carnage', 'untoward', 'animated', 'joyous', 'mournful', 'faulty', 'unslackened', 'preponderate', 'materially', 'reconciliation', 'humanity', 'unabated', 'fragments', 'inadequate'.

FOR A PRÉCIS

Write a précis of the passage beginning 'Nelson was at this time...' and ending '...severer loss'.

FOR AN ESSAY

(1) With the aid of your imagination, describe in detail the scene on board the *Elephant*:

    (a) When Nelson was writing his letter to the Crown Prince; *or*

    (b) When the Commander-in-Chief hoisted the signal of recall.

(2) Write a letter, supposedly from Nelson, enclosing a contribution to the cost of Riou's monument, and drawing the attention of the public to the splendour of the frigate-captain's services.

(3) Read Campbell's *Battle of the Baltic* and then criticize it as a 'picture' of the battle.

(4) Collect facts from Southey's *Nelson*, or elsewhere, and then write an account of the Baltic campaign prior to the entry of the British ships into the King's Deep; *or*, of Nelson's career prior to his departure for the Baltic.

ROBERT BROWNING

IN MEMORY OF NELSON

HERE'S to Nelson's memory!
'Tis the second time that I, at sea,
Right off Cape Trafalgar here,
Have drunk it deep in British beer.
'Nelson for ever!'—any time
Am I his to command in prose or rhyme!
Give of Nelson only a touch,
And I save it, be it little or much:
Here's one our Captain gives, and so
Down at the word, by George, shall it go!
He says that at Greenwich they point the beholder
To Nelson's coat, 'still with tar on the shoulder:
For he used to lean with one shoulder digging,
Jigging, as it were, and zig-zag-zigging
Up against the mizzen-rigging!'

THOMAS HARDY, O.M.

OUTWARD BOUND

[INTRODUCTORY NOTE. The annual visit to the seaside, with bathing, boating and other delights, first became popular when King George III set the fashion by his visits to Weymouth. Such a visit is supposed to have taken place when the following passage begins.]

ANNE lay awake that night thinking of the *Victory*, and of those who floated in her. To the best of Anne's calculation that ship of war would, during the next twenty-four hours, pass within a few miles of where she herself then lay. Next to seeing Bob,* the thing that would give her more pleasure than any other in the world was to see the vessel that contained him—his floating city—his sole dependence in battle and storm—upon whose safety from winds and enemies hung all her hope.

The morrow was market-day at the seaport,† and in this she saw her opportunity. A carrier went from Overcombe at six o'clock thither, and having to do a little shopping for herself she gave it as a reason for her intended day's absence, and took a place in the van. When she reached the town it was still early morning, but the borough was already in the zenith of its daily bustle and show. The King was always out-of-doors by six o'clock, and such cock-crow hours at Gloucester Lodge produced an equally forward stir among the population. She alighted, and passed down the esplanade, as fully thronged by persons of fashion at this time of mist and level sunlight as a watering-place in the present day is at four in the afternoon. Dashing bucks and beaux in cocked hats, black feathers, ruffles, and frills, stared at her as she hurried along; the beach was swarming with bathing women, wearing waistbands that bore the national refrain, 'God save the King', in gilt letters; the shops were all open, and Sergeant Stanner, with his sword-stuck bank-notes and heroic

---

* Robert Loveday, her sweetheart.   † Weymouth.

gaze, was beating up at two guineas and a crown, the crown to drink his Majesty's health.

She soon finished her shopping, and then, crossing over into the old town, pursued her way along the coast-road to Portland. At the end of an hour she had been rowed across the Fleet (which then lacked the convenience of a bridge), and reached the base of Portland Hill. The steep incline before her was dotted with houses, showing the pleasant peculiarity of one man's doorstep being behind his neighbour's chimney, and slabs of stone as the common material for walls, roof, floor, pig-sty, stable-manger, door-scraper, and garden-stile. Anne gained the summit, and followed along the central track over the huge lump of freestone which forms the peninsula, the wide sea prospect extending as she went on. Weary with her journey, she approached the extreme southerly peak of rock, and gazed from the cliff at Portland Bill, or Beal, as it was in those days more correctly called.

The wild, herbless, weather-worn promontory was quite a solitude, and, saving the one old lighthouse about fifty yards up the slope, scarce a mark was visible to show that humanity had ever been near the spot. Anne found herself a seat on a stone, and swept with her eyes the tremulous expanse of water around her that seemed to utter a ceaseless unintelligible incantation. Out of the three hundred and sixty degrees of her complete horizon two hundred and fifty were covered by waves, the *coup d'œil* including the area of troubled waters known as the Race, where two seas met to effect the destruction of such vessels as could not be mastered by one. She counted the craft within her view: there were five; no, there were only four; no, there were seven, some of the specks having resolved themselves into two. They were all small coasters, and kept well within sight of land.

Anne sank into a reverie. Then she heard a slight noise on her left hand, and turning beheld an old sailor, who had approached with a glass. He was levelling it over the sea in a direction to the south-east, and somewhat removed from that in which her own eyes had been wandering. Anne moved a few steps thitherward, so as to unclose to her view a deeper sweep on that side, and by this discovered a ship of far larger size than any which had yet dotted the main before her. Its sails were for the most part new and clean, and in comparison with its rapid progress before the wind the small brigs and ketches seemed standing still. Upon this striking object the old man's glass was bent.

'What do you see, sailor?' she asked.

'Almost nothing,' he answered. 'My sight is so gone off lately that things, one and all, be but a November mist to me. And yet I fain would see to-day. I am looking for the *Victory.*'

'Why?' she said quickly.

'I have a son aboard her. He's one of three from these parts. There's the captain, there's my son Ned, and there's young Loveday of Overcombe—he that lately joined.'

'Shall I look for you?' said Anne after a pause.

'Certainly, mis'ess, if so be you please.'

Anne took the glass, and he supported it by his arm. 'It is a large ship,' she said, 'with three masts, three rows of guns along the side, and all her sails set.'

'I guessed as much.'

'There is a little flag in front—over her bowsprit.'

'The jack.'

'And there's a large one flying at her stern.'

'The ensign.'

'And a white one on her foretopmast.'

'That's the admiral's flag, the flag of my Lord Nelson. What is her figure-head, my dear?'

'A coat-of-arms, supported on this side by a sailor.'

Her companion nodded with satisfaction. 'On the other side of that figure-head is a marine.'

'She is twisting round in a curious way, and her sails sink in like old cheeks, and she shivers like a leaf upon a tree.'

'She is in stays, for the larboard tack. I can see what she's been doing. She's been re'ching close in to avoid the flood tide, as the

wind is to the sou'-west, and she's bound down; but as soon as
the ebb made, d'ye see, they made sail to the west'ard. Captain
Hardy may be depended upon for that; he knows every current
about here, being a native.'

'And now I can see the other side; it is a soldier where a sailor
was before. You are *sure* it is the *Victory*?'

'I am sure.'

After this a frigate came into view—the *Euryalus*—sailing in
the same direction. Anne sat down, and her eyes never left the
ships. 'Tell me more about the *Victory*,' she said.

'She is the best sailer in the service, and she carries a hundred
guns. The heaviest be on the lower deck, the next size on the
middle deck, the next on the main and upper decks. My son
Ned's place is on the lower deck, because he's short, and they put
the short men below.'

Bob, though not tall, was not likely to be specially selected for
shortness. She pictured him on the upper deck, in his snow-white
trousers and jacket of navy blue, looking perhaps towards the
very point of land where she then was.

The great silent ship, with her population of blue-jackets,
marines, officers, captain, and the admiral who was not to return
alive, passed like a phantom the meridian of the Bill. Sometimes
her aspect was that of a large white bat, sometimes that of a grey
one. In the course of time the watching girl saw that the ship
had passed her nearest point; the breadth of her sails diminished
by foreshortening, till she assumed the form of an egg on end.
After this something seemed to twinkle, and Anne, who had
previously withdrawn from the old sailor, went back to him,
and looked again through the glass. The twinkling was the light
falling upon the cabin windows of the ship's stern. She explained
it to the old man.

'Then we see now what the enemy have seen but once. That
was in seventy-nine, when she sighted the French and Spanish
fleet off Scilly, and she retreated because she feared a landing.
Well, 'tis a brave ship and she carries brave men!'

Anne's tender bosom heaved, but she said nothing, and again became absorbed in contemplation.

The *Victory* was fast dropping away. She was on the horizon, and soon appeared hull down. That seemed to be like the beginning of a greater end than her present vanishing. Anne Garland could not stay by the sailor any longer, and went about a stone's throw off, where she was hidden by the inequality of the cliff from his view. The vessel was now exactly end on, and stood out in the direction of the Start, her width having contracted to the proportion of a feather. She sat down again, and mechanically took out some biscuits that she had brought, foreseeing that her waiting might be long. But she could not eat one of them; eating seemed to jar with the mental tenseness of the moment; and her undeviating gaze continued to follow the lessened ship with the fidelity of a balanced needle to a magnetic stone, all else in her being motionless.

The courses of the *Victory* were absorbed into the main, then her top sails went, and then her top-gallants. She was now no more than a dead fly's wing on a sheet of spider's web; and even this fragment diminished. Anne could hardly bear to see the end, and yet she resolved not to flinch. The admiral's flag sank behind the watery line, and in a minute the very truck of the last topmast stole away. The *Victory* was gone.

Anne's lip quivered as she murmured, without removing her wet eyes from the vacant and solemn horizon, '"They that go down to the sea in ships that do business in great waters..."'.

'"These see the works of the Lord, and His wonders in the deep,"' was returned by a man's voice from behind her.

Looking round quickly, she saw a soldier standing there; and the grave eyes of John Loveday* bent on her.

''Tis what I was thinking,' she said, trying to be composed.

'You were saying it,' he answered gently.

'Was I?—I did not know it....How came you here?' she presently added.

* Bob's brother, the Trumpet-Major.

'I have been behind you a good while; but you never turned round.'

'I was deeply occupied,' she said in an undertone.

'Yes—I too came to see him pass. I heard this morning that Lord Nelson had embarked, and I knew at once that they would sail immediately. The *Victory* and *Euryalus* are to join the rest of the fleet at Plymouth. There was a great crowd of people assembled to see the admiral off; they cheered him and the ship as she dropped down. He took his coffin on board with him, they say.'

'His coffin!' said Anne, turning deadly pale. 'Something terrible, then, is meant by that! O, why *would* Bob go in that ship? doomed to destruction from the very beginning like this!'

'It was his determination to sail under Captain Hardy, and under no one else,' said John. 'There may be hot work; but we must hope for the best.' And observing how wretched she looked, he added, 'But won't you let me help you back? If you can walk as far as Hope Cove it will be enough. A lerret is going from there across the bay homeward to the harbour in the course of an hour; it belongs to a man I know, and they can take one passenger, I am sure.'

She turned her back upon the Channel, and by his help soon reached the place indicated. The boat was lying there as he had said. She found it to belong to the old man who had been with her at the Bill, and was in charge of his two younger sons. The trumpet-major helped her into it over the slippery blocks of stone, one of the young men spread his jacket for her to sit on, and as soon as they pulled from shore John climbed up the blue-grey cliff, and disappeared over the top, to return to the mainland by road.

The Trumpet-Major.

HELP

Coup d'œil (French). A general view of a scene or subject taken in at a glance.

QUESTIONS

(1) Where did Anne Garland live?

(2) What time did she reach Weymouth?

(3) What time did George III get up in the morning?

(4) Where was he staying?

(5) How did the bathing-women show their loyalty?

(6) How was Sergeant Stanner employed?

(7) What was Anne's route after she had finished her shopping?

(8) What was the Fleet and how did she negotiate it?

(9) For what various purposes did the stone of Portland Bill do duty?

(10) What was the Bill called in 1805?

(11) How many degrees does the horizon embrace and how many were merely 'waves' when viewed from the Bill?

(12) How many coasters did Anne count? What sailing precautions were they taking and how were they rigged?

(13) In which direction did the old sailor first level his telescope?

(14) What did Anne see when she moved nearer to the old sailor?

(15) In addition to Robert Loveday and the old sailor's son, what other Dorset man was on board the *Victory*?

(16) What colours was the *Victory* flying? Describe them accurately.

(17) What was the figurehead of the *Victory* as described by Anne?

(18) What frigate was in attendance on the *Victory*?

(19) How did the old sailor explain the movement of the *Victory* which had puzzled Anne?

(20) How many guns had the *Victory* and how were they placed according to decks?

(21) What was the twinkling light on the *Victory* which Anne explained to the old sailor?

(22) When did the *Victory* show her stern to the enemy? and why?

(23) In what direction was the *Victory* sailing when Anne lost sight of her?

(24) What alarmed Anne in the news which Robert Loveday's brother brought with him?

(25) By what different route did Anne find her way home?

(26) To what is Thomas Hardy referring in the following? Write your answers down.

    (a) 'Time of mist and level sunlight.'

    (b) 'Area of troubled waters.'

    (c) 'Huge lump of freestone.'

    (d) 'With his sword-stuck bank-notes and heroic gaze.'

    (e) 'Seemed to utter a ceaseless unintelligible incantation.'

    (f) 'Dashing bucks and beaux.'

    (g) 'One man's doorstep being behind his neighbour's chimney.'

    (h) 'Tremulous expanse.'

    (i) 'No more than a dead fly's wing on a sheet of spider's web.'

(27) Substitute other words for the following without alteration of sense: 'promontory', 'inequality', 'tenseness', 'calculation', 'solitude',

'contemplation', 'incline', 'motionless', 'determination', 'dependence', 'alighted', 'reverie', 'phantom'.

(28) Explain 'zenith', 'meridian'.

(29) Take your written answers to question 26, and write down from memory Hardy's phrases for your words.

(30) To what does Hardy compare the appearance of the *Victory* as she came into, and passed out of, view? Supply as many comparisons as you can.

(31) 'They that go down to the sea in ships....' Where does this quotation come from?

FOR A PRÉCIS

Make a précis of the passage beginning 'The great silent ship...' and ending '...The *Victory* was gone'.

FOR AN ESSAY

(1) Describe in as much detail as possible any view you have seen from a hill or mountain top, or from any high tower or roof in a town or city.

(2) Why did the old ships have figureheads? Mention any figureheads that you have seen either in a picture or in reality; and account as well as you can for the almost total disappearance of this very distinctive feature.

(3) Describe accurately a land journey undertaken by you, during which a change has been necessary in the mode of transit before the destination has been reached.

(4) Read Part I of Coleridge's *Ancient Mariner* and then attempt to describe the feelings of a shipwrecked sailor on a desert island as he sees a ship that might have rescued him fade slowly out of sight.

NELSON

As earth has but one England, crown and head
Of all her glories till the sun be dead,
   Supreme in peace and war, supreme in song,
Supreme in freedom, since her rede was read,

Since first the soul that gave her speech grew strong
To help the right and heal the wild world's wrong,
   So she hath but one Nelson, born
To reign on time above the years that throng.

The music of his name puts fear to scorn,
And thrills our twilight through with sense of morn:
   As England was, how should not England be?
No tempest yet has left her banner torn.

TRAFALGAR: THE OPENING MOVES

NELSON was at work by six o'clock. Mounting the poop, he had a good look at the foe, and gave the necessary orders. For a time he watched his own ships anxiously, noting their obedience to his signals. As he did so, the formation which he desired began slowly but surely to disclose itself. Collingwood's ship drew alongside of his own, and over the starboard bulwarks loomed large through the morning haze. The wind was light, with flaws from the land, and there was a heavy ground-swell. The enemy for the most part were under top-sails and top-gallants. The *Victory* had been carrying her fore course and top-sails. But now she shook out all her reefs, and set royals and studding-sails. There being still twelve miles of sea to be crossed, Nelson retired to his cabin again, and occupied the short interval of leisure with business and private prayers.

Meanwhile the drums rolled, the bos'n and his mates piped the call at every hatchway, and the ship was made ready to engage. In addition to the usual arrangements, the boats on the quarters, lest they should interfere with the guns, were lowered and towed astern. All was quickly set in train. But the *Victory* moved slowly through the water. In pursuit of Villeneuve she had made on occasion her ten knots, but now the wind was so light that with stunsails out she made less than three. This slow progress promised a heavy casualty-list when the enemy opened fire. At eight o'clock the weather looked dull and cloudy and there were still nine miles to be gone. Presently Nelson came forth from his cabin again and went the rounds of the ship. He was accompanied by Captain Hardy, by Captain Blackwood of the *Euryalus* (who had come aboard for final orders), by Dr Beatty (surgeon of the *Victory*), and by others. As he proceeded from gun-deck to gun-deck, he often stopped and spoke, exhorting the gunners not to waste a shot, but to take careful aim and make sure of hitting. He also expressed himself to the officers as highly pleased with all their arrangements.

Rounds finished, Nelson repaired again to the poop, where he kept a watchful eye upon the enemy. Villeneuve's ships on the horizon still looked no larger than a row of model yachts, but through a glass it was becoming increasingly possible to distinguish one from another. Nelson walked about the poop in company with Hardy and Blackwood. The marines stood on either side with small-arms ready, while Pasco and his signalmen were busy with vocabulary and flags. Suddenly, in his eager way, Nelson turned to Blackwood with an exclamation. 'Now,' said he, 'I'll amuse the fleet with a signal. Mr Pasco, I wish to say to the fleet, "England confides that every man will do his duty".' The signal-lieutenant asked if he might substitute 'expects' for 'confides', because 'confides' was not in the vocabulary. Nelson readily agreed, and at 11.40 the flags began to ascend. They were hoisted by signalman John Roome, and we have it on the authority of Captain Blackwood that as ship after ship of both squadrons received the *Victory's* message, the thunder of enthusiastic cheering rolled in echoes down the line.

Nelson next bade Pasco hoist signal No. 16, 'Engage the enemy more closely'. The *Victory*, it must be understood, was not yet in action. But this signal with Nelson was no ordinary signal. It was to him a mascot and a talisman; a remedy for evils, an exhortation to waverers. He liked to have it ready in good time, and gave Pasco strict orders to keep it flying. So the flags were lashed to the main top-gallant, and there they remained until the spar was shot away.

The *Victory*, of course, carried her admiral's flag, white at the fore. But in the disposition of her other colours Nelson made certain changes. That in the ensign was inevitable. The fleet was not divided into van, centre, and rear, but into two independent squadrons. The use of three colours had lost significance, and Nelson ordered all ships of the fleet to wear the white ensign only; thereby anticipating—and in a manner dictating—the usage of to-day. The *Victory* was properly entitled to the red ensign; but Nelson chose the white to match his flag. As to Union Jacks, he had two of them, and hoisted in conspicuous places, one at the main topmast stay, the other at the fore top-gallant stay, so that the *Victory* in respect of her nationality was not likely to be mistaken.

It was at ten minutes to twelve that the actual fighting began, the wind being light, the sea smooth, and the sun shining on the freshly painted sides of the combined fleet. The *Fougueux* fired the first shot, and the *Royal Sovereign* was not long in answering. As soon as Collingwood found his range, Nelson ordered all who were not on duty on the *Victory's* upper deck to leave the poop and forecastle and repair to their proper quarters. About the same time Captain Blackwood took his leave, after a vain attempt to persuade the Admiral to come and conduct the fight in safety from the *Euryalus*.

About ten minutes past twelve one of the ships of the combined fleet, in a favourable position for doing so, fired a single shot at the *Victory* to try the range. The *Victory* was just moving, no more, making, perhaps, one and a half knots, and the shot fell short. After two or three minutes the trial was repeated. The *Victory* was by this time a mile and a quarter distant, and the second shot fell alongside. The third flew over the ship. The fourth and fifth did the same: But the sixth shot made a gash in the main top-gallant sail, showing that the range at last was found. There was a moment or two of intense silence, and then seven or eight of the enemy's ships opened fire, pouring in their broadsides. The *Victory*, ignoring them, still moved forward; solemn, stately, silent, and alone. A round-shot, flying across the deck, killed Nelson's secretary, John Scott, as he conversed with Captain Hardy. Aided by a seaman, Captain Adair of the marines tried to move the body before Nelson could see it. But the Admiral did not need to be told that a friend was gone.

'Is that poor Scott?' he said.

As firing became general the wind died away to a mere breath; but the *Victory* was carried along by her impetus and the swell.

How long she continued on the same course after the enemy had opened fire cannot be stated with exactitude; perhaps fifteen minutes, perhaps more, perhaps less. But Nelson, about twenty-five minutes past twelve, gave orders to port the helm. He had not yet finished his tactical manœuvre. He had one more surprise for the enemy, one more trump card to throw down. He had been steering well to the north of east, threatening the enemy's van. But the entire movement was a feint. He did not intend to engage the van at all. He now curved about on an entirely new course.

The enemy were no better able than before to gauge the depth of his cunning. Some flattered themselves their line was so closely knit that he despaired of breaking through the van and was looking elsewhere for a gap. But Nelson's business was with the·Franco-Spanish centre. And though he had concealed his purpose with masterly completeness, that had been his objective all along. After keeping the hostile van in a fever of suspense, he left them out of the battle altogether. That was one of his motives. By leaving them out of the battle altogether, he gained a local superiority, and matched his twenty-seven ships with twenty-three of the foe. He had other motives. By attacking the enemy's centre he joined hands with Collingwood, seconding his endeavours and receiving his support. And last, but not least, he struck his blow home where he hoped and expected to find Villeneuve himself.

Oddly enough, although less than half a mile separated him from the enemy's line, there was absolutely nothing to show which was Villeneuve's ship. Every glass on the *Victory's* quarter-deck was busily employed, but in answer to Nelson's repeated questions there was no information forthcoming. It was clear, however, that the French and Spanish had mixed their ships, not kept them separate. The Spaniards were distinguished not only by their ensigns but by enormous wooden crosses that swung from the end of each spanker boom. Prominent among them, and easily identified by her four decks, was Nelson's old enemy of St Vincent days, the *Santissima Trinidad*. She at least was bound to be a flagship. Astern of her there was a slight interval, and then came two French ships, the first large and the second something smaller. Towards the interval between the *Trinidad* and the two Frenchmen Nelson gave orders for the *Victory* to steer. The smaller French ship was the *Redoutable*, and the larger was Villeneuve's own *Bucentaure*, which Nelson by instinct was singling out in spite of her efforts to conceal herself. The *Trinidad*, the *Bucentaure*, and the *Redoutable* continued to pour in broadsides which the *Victory* sustained as she could. To have hauled her wind on the larboard tack would have brought her relief at once. But there was still much to be done before she could hope to engage on equal terms.

In spite of the enemy's heavy raking fire, Nelson and Hardy continued to walk the quarter-deck, engaged in earnest conversation. The position was one of considerable danger. For the Frenchmen, as usual, were firing at masts and rigging; and when their aim was too low, their shot swept the *Victory's* upper deck from bowsprit to taffrail. Five hundred yards from the larboard beam of the *Bucentaure* a well-aimed broadside from that vessel brought down the *Victory's* mizzen top-mast. This almost checked her career. A moment later a shot smashed the wheel to pieces. Without the loss of a moment the tiller was manned, and the ship steered from the gun-room; Lieutenant Quilliam and Mr Atkinson, the master, taking turns to direct operations. Two minutes afterwards a bar-shot killed eight marines on the poop and wounded others. At this Nelson ordered Captain Adair to take his men from the poop and distribute them about the ship. As he did so, a round-shot, that had come through four hammocks in the nettings on the larboard bow, and had carried away part of the larboard quarter of the Admiral's barge upon the booms, struck the fore brace bitts on the quarter-deck and passed between Nelson and Hardy. A splinter from the bitts brushed

Hardy's left foot and tore the buckle from his shoe. Both instantly stopped and surveyed each other with inquiring looks, each supposing the other to be wounded. Then Nelson smiled and said to Hardy, 'This is too warm work to last long.'

The truth is—for Nelson did not state it in full—that the *Victory* was undergoing an ordeal for which it would be vain to seek a comparison. Never had vessel endured what she was enduring—the long-drawn agony of silent torture. It was one thing to fight in the thick of foes, selling your life dearly, lashing out with all your batteries. But the *Victory* until now had been an almost stationary target, drawing the fire of all who could train their guns on her. Her sails were torn and tattered. Her studding-sails had all of them disappeared as if some giant had shorn them with a pair of shears. The enemy were trying until the very last moment to stop her altogether. They wasted not a thought on the men within her. And the gunners below were happy enough; busy, too, since the turn to starboard enabled them to work their guns. But on the fore-castle and on the quarter-deck, in the waist and on the poop, no less than fifty men had fallen: not in the heat of action, and with the flush of anger upon them; but by accident, by mischance, because the *Bucentaure*, or one of her consorts, had tried for a stay or a shroud and aimed too low for the mark. Those who remained alive were sorely tried. Yet they rose heroically to the situation. Nelson declared that he had never asked seamen to endure so much, or seen them endure with such unflinching courage.

At last! At last they reached the enemy's line. To Hardy it appeared a close-knit chain, an impenetrable wall. With disappointment for once in his cheery voice, he informed Nelson that they could proceed no farther without collision. But Nelson replied sharply, almost testily, 'I can't help it. Doesn't signify which we run aboard of. Go on board which you please. Take your choice.' He spoke rapidly. Yet the words were hardly out of his mouth when the *Victory*, responsive to his voice, shouldered a way for herself between the *Redoutable* and the *Bucentaure*. The

Redoutable was to starboard, and the *Bucentaure* to larboard. So close was Villeneuve's ship that the main yardarm of the *Victory* brushed the vangs of her gaff, and had there been wind enough to spread the *Bucentaure's* ensign, the *Victory's* men could have clutched it and torn it from the mizzen peak.

It was a quarter to one. The moment had come that was to decide the fate of nations. The sixty-eight-pounder carronade on the larboard side of the *Victory's* forecastle had the honour of beginning. She was loaded with a single round-shot and a keg of five hundred musket bullets, and these she delivered with unerring accuracy through the stern windows of the *Bucentaure*, where there was nothing to stop them, where there was nothing to shield the hundreds of men that crowded the long fighting-decks. The carronade began it, and the big guns took up the refrain. There were fifty of them on the *Victory's* larboard side, and they were manned by those who until now had been unmolested by the enemy's fire; lusty fellows, and stout and strong, the pick of England's gunners, the pick of England's fleet, gunners who at all times were true of aim, and who had received the Admiral's special injunctions to be steady and not waste a shot. The fifty guns of the *Victory's* side were double-shotted or treble-shotted, and as the *Victory* passed slowly under the *Bucentaure's* stern, they poured their charges one by one into the Frenchman's vitals. The British crew were nearly choked by the clouds of black smoke that entered the port-holes; and Nelson and Hardy were covered with dust from the crumbling ruins of the rich giltwork that had adorned the *Bucentaure's* stern.

This was the crowning moment of Trafalgar! This was the moment for which the *Victory* had been born! This was the moment for which she had lived! It was not so much that in a minute or two of time she had slain or wounded four hundred men and dismounted twenty guns, though this was a pitch of destructiveness without precedent, without example. It was not so much that she had broken the enemy's back, though that by itself might have conquered them; it was something more and something greater. The *Victory* had monopolized Villeneuve's attention until it was too late. For an hour she had drawn upon herself the eyes of twenty-one ships, the allied centre and van. They had waited for Villeneuve's commands, and received none. They had looked for Villeneuve's signal flags, and he had hoisted none. He too had been watching the *Victory*, watching and waiting (though delay was dangerous) for the *Victory* to reveal her design. And the *Victory* had revealed no design; and he had striven with all his strength to hold her off and push her back. And failed in that too. He had seen nothing else. He had not looked at his own left wing, which Collingwood had been shattering for nearly an hour past. He had not looked at his own right wing, which was standing by inactive. His eyes were riveted on the *Victory*, until the *Victory* ran under his very stern and blotted him out of existence; or still worse, reduced his vessel to a hulk and left him in the wreckage, powerless now to say a thing to his fleet, powerless to rectify any mistake—the least or the most egregious.

When the *Victory* burst through the enemy's line, the Battle of Trafalgar was won. It remained to convert a signal conquest into the completest ever gained at sea.

The Story of H.M.S. Victory.

QUESTIONS

(1) At what hour did Nelson come on deck?
(2) How did he first employ his time?
(3) What was the state of the weather?
(4) What was the position of Collingwood's squadron in relation to Nelson's?
(5) What special sails were set in light airs?
(6) Under what sail were the English ships and those of the 'Combined Fleet' (the enemy)?
(7) Describe briefly the preparations for battle.
(8) How were commands conveyed from deck to deck and through the length and breadth of the ship?
(9) What was the slow progress of the *Victory* likely to entail?
(10) Who accompanied Nelson during his rounds of the ship?
(11) What special injunction did Nelson impress upon his ship's company?
(12) Describe the company present on the poop when Nelson returned there after rounds.

(13) Who was the Captain of H.M.S. *Victory*?

(14) Who was her First Lieutenant?

(15) Who was her Signal Lieutenant?

(16) Who was her Master?

(17) Who was the Captain of Marines?

(18) Who was Nelson's secretary?

(19) Why was not Nelson's most famous signal hoisted in the form in which the Admiral first worded it?

(20) Who hoisted the flags?

(21) How was the signal received?

(22) What signal followed the famous one? and where was it hoisted?

(23) What change in the use of ensigns did Nelson's attack necessitate?

(24) Where was the Jack usually hoisted? and where did Nelson display it?

(25) At what hour did serious fighting begin?

(26) Which ship fired the first shot?

(27) Who was Captain Henry Blackwood, and how did he employ his last minutes on board the *Victory*?

(28) At what speed was the *Victory* moving through the water?

(29) At what distance from the enemy was any part of the *Victory* hit?

(30) Who was the first casualty?

(31) What important order did Nelson give at 12.25?

(32) What were his intentions in respect of the enemy's van?

(33) Who was the Commander-in-Chief of the Combined Fleet?

(34) How were the Spanish ships distinguished from the French?

(35) Which was the biggest ship in the Combined Fleet?

(36) Name the next two ships astern of her.

(37) Where was Nelson himself at this critical stage in the battle?

(38) What was the first serious damage suffered by the *Victory*?

(39) How was the *Victory* steered after her wheel had been knocked to pieces?

(40) What damage was done on board the *Victory* by a single bar shot?

(41) What made Nelson say, 'This is too warm work to last long'? And what did he mean by these words?

(42) What were the *Victory*'s losses by the time she herself opened fire?

(43) Which of the *Victory*'s guns was the first to do execution?

(44) What damage did the *Victory* inflict as she passed through the enemy's line?

(45) Substitute other words for the following without alteration of sense: 'mascot', 'manœuvre', 'gauge', 'ordeal', 'agony', 'waist', 'talisman', 'consort', 'vitals', 'monopolized', 'riveted'.

FOR A PRÉCIS

Write a précis of the passage beginning 'Oddly enough...' and ending '...equal terms'.

FOR AN ESSAY

(1) With the help of a diagram (or diagrams), explain carefully Nelson's plan of attack at Trafalgar; and show how and why it succeeded.

(2) Compose a dialogue between Nelson and Captain Blackwood of the *Euryalus* frigate during the last hours that these friends were together.

(3) The passage above gives the opening moves only; collect all the information you can concerning what followed and then write a continuation showing how the great battle ended.

(4) From the information which you have gleaned from this battle, describe how a ship was got ready for an engagement, and carried into battle, in 1805.

THOMAS HARDY, O.M.

THE STORM

Song of the South Wessex Boatmen

IN the wild October night-time, when the wind raved round the
land,

And the Back-sea met the Front-sea, and our doors were blocked
with sand,

And we heard the drub of Dead-man's Bay, where bones of
thousands are,

We knew not what the day had done for us at Trafalgár.

[*All*]   Had done,

Had done,

For us at Trafalgár!

'Pull hard, and make the Nothe, or down we go!' one says,
says he.

We pulled; and bedtime brought the storm; but snug at home
slept we.

Yet all the while our gallants after fighting through the day,

Were beating up and down the dark, sou' west of Cadiz Bay.

The dark,

The dark,

Sou' west of Cadiz Bay!

The victors and the vanquished then the storm it tossed and tore,

As hard they strove, those worn-out men, upon that surly shore;

Dead Nelson and his half-dead crews, his foes from near and far,

Were rolled together on the deep that night at Trafalgár!

The deep,

The deep,

That night at Trafalgár!

SIR ARTHUR QUILLER-COUCH

HOW THE NEWS OF TRAFALGAR REACHED ENGLAND

EVIDENTLY the Board Room had been but a few hours ago the scene of a large dinner-party. Glasses, dessert-plates, dishes of fruit, decanters empty and half empty, cumbered the great mahogany table as dead and wounded, guns and tumbrils, might a battlefield. Chairs stood askew; crumpled napkins lay as they had been dropped or tossed, some on the floor, others across the table between the dishes.

'Looks cosy, eh?' commented the First Lord. 'Maggs, set a screen around the fire, and look about for a decanter and some clean glasses.'

He drew a chair close to the reviving fire, and glanced at the cover of the dispatch before breaking its seal.

'Nelson's handwriting?' he asked. It was plain that his old eyes, unaided by spectacles, saw the superscription only as a blur.

'No, my lord: Admiral Collingwood's,' said Lieutenant Lapenotière, inclining his head.

Old Lord Barham looked up sharply. His wig set awry, he made a ridiculous figure in his hastily donned garments. Yet he did not lack dignity.

'Why Collingwood?' he asked, his fingers breaking the seal. 'God! you don't tell me—'

'Lord Nelson is dead, sir.'

'Dead—dead?...Here, Tylney—you read what it says. Dead? ...No, damme, let the captain tell his tale. Briefly, sir.'

'Briefly, sir—Lord Nelson had word of Admiral Villeneuve coming out of the Straits, and engaged the Combined Fleets off Cape Trafalgaro. They were in single line, roughly; and he bore down in two columns, and cut off their van under Dumanoir.

This was at dawn or thereabouts, and by five o'clock the enemy was destroyed.'

'How many prizes?'

'I cannot say precisely, my lord. The word went, when I was signalled aboard the Vice-Admiral's flagship, that either fifteen or sixteen had struck. My own men were engaged, at the time, in rescuing the crew of a French seventy-four that had blown up; and I was too busy to count, had counting been possible. One or two of my officers maintain to me that our gains were higher. But the dispatch will tell doubtless.'

'Aye, to be sure....Read, Tylney. Don't sit there clearing your throat, but read, man alive!' And yet it appeared that while the Secretary was willing enough to read, the First Lord had no capacity, as yet, to listen. Into the very first sentence he broke with—

'No, wait a minute. "Dead," d'ye say?...My God!... Lieutenant, pour yourself a glass of wine and tell us first how it happened.'

Lieutenant Lapenotière could not tell very clearly. He had twice been summoned to board the *Royal Sovereign*—the first time to receive the command to hold himself ready. It was then that, coming alongside the great ship, he had read in all the officers' faces an anxiety hard to reconcile with the evident tokens of victory around them. At once it had occurred to him that the Admiral had fallen, and he put the question to one of the lieutenants—to be told that Lord Nelson had indeed been mortally wounded and could not live long; but that he must be alive yet, and conscious, since the *Victory* was still signalling orders to the Fleet.

'I think, my lord,' said he, 'that Admiral Collingwood must have been doubtful, just then, what responsibility had fallen upon him, or how soon it might fall. He had sent for me to "stand by" so to speak. He was good enough to tell me the news as it had reached him—'

Here Lieutenant Lapenotière, obeying the order to fill his glass,

let spill some of the wine on the table. The sight of the dark
trickle on the mahogany touched some nerve of the brain: he
saw it widen into a pool of blood, from which, as they picked
up a shattered seaman and bore him below, a lazy stream crept
across the deck of the flag-ship towards the scuppers. He moved
his feet, as he had moved them then, to be out of the way of it:
but recovered himself in another moment and went on—

'He told me, my lord, that the *Victory* after passing under the
Bucentaure's stern, and so raking her that she was put out of action,
or almost, fell alongside the *Redoutable*. There was a long swell
running, with next to no wind, and the two ships could hardly
have cleared had they tried. At any rate, they hooked, and it was
then a question which could hammer the harder. The Frenchman
had filled his tops with sharp-shooters, and from one of these—
the mizzen-top, I believe—a musket-ball struck down the
Admiral. He was walking at the time to and fro on a sort of
gangway he had caused to be planked over his cabin sky-light,
between the wheel and the ladder-way....Admiral Collingwood
believed it had happened about half-past one....'

'Sit down, man, and drink your wine,' commanded the First
Lord as the dispatch-bearer swayed with a sudden faintness.

'It is nothing, my lord—'

But it must have been a real swoon, or something very like it:
for he recovered to find himself lying in an arm-chair. He heard
the Secretary's voice reading steadily on and on....Also they
must have given him wine, for he awoke to feel the warmth of it
in his veins and coursing about his heart. But he was weak yet,
and for the moment well content to lie still and listen.

Resting there and listening, he was aware of two sensations
that alternated within him, chasing each other in and out of his
consciousness. He felt all the while that he, John Richards
Lapenotière, a junior officer in His Majesty's service, was assisting
in one of the most momentous events in his country's history;
and alone in the room with these two men, he felt it as he had
never begun to feel it amid the smoke and roar of the actual

battle. He had seen the dead hero but half a dozen times in his life: he had never been honoured by a word from him: but like every other naval officer, he had come to look up to Nelson as to the splendid particular star among commanders. *There* was greatness: *there* was that which lifted men to such deeds as write man's name across the firmament! And, strange to say, Lieutenant Lapenotière recognised something of it in this queer old man, in dressing-gown and ill-fitting wig, who took snuff and interrupted now with a curse and anon with a 'bravo!' as the Secretary read. He was absurd: but he was no common man, this Lord Barham. He had something of the ineffable aura of greatness.

But in the Lieutenant's brain, across this serious, even awful sense of the moment and of its meaning, there played a curious secondary sense that the moment was not—that what was happening before his eyes had either happened before or was happening in some vacuum in which past, present, future and the ordinary divisions of time had lost their bearings. The great twenty-four-hour clock at the end of the Board Room, ticking on and on while the Secretary read, wore an unfamiliar face.

...Yes, time had gone wrong, somehow: and the events of the passage home to Falmouth, of the journey up to the doors of the Admiralty, though they ran on a chain, had no intervals to be measured by a clock, but followed one another like pictures on a wall. He saw the long, indigo-coloured swell thrusting the broken ships shoreward. He felt the wind freshening as it southered and he left the Fleet behind: he watched their many lanterns as they sank out of sight, then the glow of flares by the light of which dead-tired men were repairing damages, cutting away wreckage. His ship was wallowing heavily now, with the gale after her,—and now dawn was breaking clean and glorious on the swell off Lizard Point. A Mount's Bay lugger had spied them, and lying in wait, had sheered up close alongside, her crew bawling for news. He had not forbidden his men to call it back, and he could see the fellows' faces now, as it reached them from

the speaking-trumpet: 'Great victory—twenty taken or sunk—
Admiral Nelson killed!' They had guessed something, noting
the *Pickle's* ensign at half-mast: yet as they took in the purport of
the last three words, these honest fishermen had turned and stared
at one another; and without one answering word, the lugger had
been headed straight back to the mainland.

So it had been at Falmouth. A ship entering port has a thousand
eyes upon her, and the *Pickle's* errand could not be hidden. The
news seemed in some mysterious way to have spread even before
he stepped ashore there on the Market Strand. A small crowd
had collected, and, as he passed through it, many doffed their
hats. There was no cheering at all—no, not for this the most
glorious victory of the war—outshining even the Nile or Howe's
First of June.

He had set his face as he walked to the inn. But the news had
flown before him, and fresh crowds gathered to watch him off.
The post-boys knew...and *they* told the post-boys at the next
stage, and the next—Bodmin and Plymouth—not to mention the
boatmen at Torpoint Ferry. But the country-side did not know:
nor the labourers gathering in cider apples heaped under Devon
apple-trees, nor, next day, the sportsmen banging off guns at the
partridges around Salisbury. The slow, jolly life of England on
either side of the high road turned leisurely as a wagon-wheel on
its axle, while between hedgerows, past farm hamlets, church-
towers and through the cobbled streets of market towns, he had
sped and rattled with Collingwood's dispatch in his sealed case.
The news had reached London with him. His last post-boys had
carried it to their stables, and from stable to tavern. To-morrow—
to-day, rather—in an hour or two—all the bells of London would
be ringing—or tolling!...

'He's as tired as a dog,' said the voice of the Secretary. 'Seems
almost a shame to waken him.'

The Lieutenant opened his eyes and jumped to his feet with an
apology. Lord Barham had gone, and the Secretary hard by was
speaking to the night-porter, who bent over the fire, raking it

with a poker. The hands of the Queen Anne clock indicated a quarter to six.

News from the Duchy.

QUESTIONS

(1) Describe the state of the dinner-table in the Board Room, after the dinner-party was over.

(2) In what building was the Board Room situated?

(3) What kind of a clock had it?

(4) When one thing is compared with another which is quite different and the word 'like' is introduced, the resulting figure of speech is called a *simile* [from the Latin *simile*, meaning *like*]. Why does the author of this passage compare the dinner-table with a battlefield? Draw out the comparison still further from the picture of the table that you have in your mind's eye.

(5) You would not use a 'simile' if you were writing a business letter. Why not?

(6) Find two more similes in the foregoing passage and explain them.

(7) Describe Lord Barham, both his appearance and his character. What official position did he hold? Who holds that position to-day?

(8) What two other men were in the room and what were they doing there?

(9) What was the good news contained in the Dispatch handed to Lord Barham and what was the bad news?

(10) How was the Dispatch treated by Lord Barham when he first received it?

(11) Who wrote the Dispatch and what entitled him to do so? What was the name of his flagship?

(12) What was the state of things when the Dispatch-bearer arrived on board? What did he especially notice?

(13) Why was Lieutenant Lapenotière chosen to carry home the Dispatch?

(14) How did the first news of the great naval victory first reach England? How would the news of a great naval victory reach England to-day? How do you think that you would hear it?

(15) To what British port did Lieutenant Lapenotière bring his ship; and how was the news of Trafalgar received there?

(16) Mention any places through which Lieutenant Lapenotière passed on his way from the coast to the Admiralty.

(17) 'All the bells of London would be ringing—or tolling.' Why would the bells be tolled?

(18) What was the name of the Admiral commanding the Combined (Franco–Spanish) Fleet? Name any of the French ships you can.

(19) Who was the Admiral commanding the van of the Combined Fleet?

(20) Say what you have learned about the character of Lord Nelson from reading the passage; and what you have learned about his death.

(21) 'He let some of the wine fall from his glass and trickle along the mahogany (table).' What picture did this present to the Lieutenant?

(22) Explain the following words: 'superscription', 'firmament', 'ineffable aura', 'vacuum'.

(23) What was the name of Lieutenant Lapenotière's ship? and what was her rig?

(24) Substitute other words for the following without alteration of sense: 'decanter', 'askew', 'capacity', 'reconcile', 'tokens', 'trickle', 'momentous', 'wallowing', 'bawling', 'sensations'.

(25) What was the first thing that the Mount's Bay lugger noticed about Lapenotière's ship.

FOR A PRÉCIS

Write a précis of the passage beginning 'Resting there and listening...' and ending '...like pictures on a wall'.

FOR AN ESSAY

(1) Suppose that you have come from the battlefield with Lieutenant Lapenotière and that you are now at home in your father's house.

Describe to your family circle in your own words what the journey was like, how the news was spread by sea and land and how it was received.

(2) Suppose yourself to be the Secretary to the First Lord, and describe the scene in the Board Room up to the time when the Lieutenant faints.

(3) Write home, as if you were Lieutenant Fortescue Kennedy of H.M.S. *Victory*, a vivid account of the battle of Trafalgar and the death of Nelson.

THOMAS CAMPBELL

YE MARINERS OF ENGLAND

Y E Mariners of England,
  That guard our native seas,
Whose flag has braved a thousand years
  The battle and the breeze,
Your glorious standard launch again
  To match another foe;
And sweep through the deep
  While the stormy winds do blow;
While the battle rages loud and long
  And the stormy winds do blow!

The spirits of your fathers
  Shall start from every wave:
For the deck it was their field of fame
  And ocean was their grave.
Where Blake and mighty Nelson fell
  Your manly hearts shall glow,
As ye sweep through the deep,
  While the stormy winds do blow;
While the battle rages loud and long
  And the stormy winds do blow.

Britannia needs no bulwarks,
  No towers along the steep:
Her march is o'er the mountain-waves,
  Her home is on the deep.
With thunders from her native oak
  She quells the floods below,
As they roar on the shore,
  When the stormy winds do blow;
When the battle rages loud and long
  And the stormy winds do blow.

The meteor flag of England
    Shall yet terrific burn,
Till danger's troubled night depart
    And the star of Peace return.
Till then ye ocean-warriors
    Our song and feast shall flow
To the fame of your name
    When the storm has ceased to blow;
When the fiery fight is heard no more
    And the storm has ceased to blow.

QUESTIONS

(1) To whom is the poet referring in the first two lines of the first stanza?

(2) Give an outstanding example of a British naval victory won under cloudless summer skies; and another in which the tempestuous weather was almost more formidable than the enemy.

(3) What pitched battles have there been at sea in the war against Hitler? Where have they been fought and with what result?

(4) What is the proper meaning of the word 'standard' and in what sense is the poet using it here?

(5) How would a 'standard' be launched?

(6) Whom were we fighting upon the seas one thousand years ago?

(7) Whence did they come? and what sort of ships had they?

(8) Who led us to victory against them?

(9) 'Loud and long': what sea-battle, described in this book, may be accepted as the longest on record?

(10) 'Ocean was their grave.' What famous sea-commanders, in addition to Drake, have had a watery grave?

(11) Mention the names of any outstanding sea-commanders who have died fighting at sea in the war against Hitler.

(12) When did oak cease to be used for the building of British battle-ships?

(13) Why should Peace be associated in the poet's mind with a star?

(14) Write afresh in your own way, using the simplest words available:
  (a) 'danger's troubled night.'
  (b) 'thunders from her native oak.'
  (c) 'native seas.'
  (d) 'quells the floods.'
  (e) 'Britannia needs no bulwarks.'
  (f) 'ocean-warriors.'
  (g) 'spirits of your fathers shall start from every wave.'
  (h) 'field of fame.'

(15) What words does the poet use as alternatives for 'sea'? Mention three.

(16) Substitute other words for the following without alteration of sense: 'glow', 'march', 'steep', 'rages', 'match', 'start'.

(17) What do you notice about all the words in the previous question?

FOR AN ESSAY

(1) A meteor is properly a small celestial body travelling through space and appearing to our eyes as a shooting star; but it is applied also to anything that for a time dazzles or strikes the mind with wonder.

The poet in speaking of the 'meteor flag of England' was doubtless thinking of the victories of St Vincent, the Nile, Copenhagen, Trafalgar, Camperdown and the Glorious First of June. With reference to the events of the war against Hitler, show that the phrase is just as applicable to our own epoch as to that of Napoleon.

(2) Under certain conditions of weather, operations by land and in the air become quite impossible. To an old acquaintance, who has never left home, explain that this limitation does not apply to 'ocean-warriors', whose flag must continue to brave the tempest just as much as the enemy.

Illustrate your answer with reference to some of the worst weather experienced by the Royal and Merchant Navies in the war against Hitler.

H.M.S. BELLEROPHON *CAPTURES THE EMPEROR NAPOLEON*

[INTRODUCTORY NOTE. After his defeat at the battle of Waterloo, Napoleon endeavoured to effect his escape from the Continent in the hopes of starting life afresh, with a new Empire over which to rule, in the Middle West of America. Admiral Sir Henry Hotham, however, with his flag in the *Superb*, kept a vigilant watch on the Atlantic seaboard of France with a squadron which had to be fairly widely dispersed. To Captain Maitland of the *Bellerophon* (74) he entrusted the task of guarding the three outlets to the Atlantic from Rochefort. There Napoleon had two frigates, the *Saale* and *Méduse*, awaiting him, but on 3 July 1815 embarked in the even speedier gun-brig, *L'Épervier* (the *Sparrow-hawk*).]

AT break of day, on the 15th July, 1815, *l'Épervier*, French brig of war, was discovered under sail, standing out towards the ship,★ with a flag of truce up; and at the same time the *Superb*, bearing Sir Henry Hotham's flag, was seen in the offing. By half-past five the ebb-tide failed, the wind was blowing right in, and the brig, which was within a mile of us, made no further progress; while the *Superb* was advancing with the wind and tide in her favour. Thus situated, and being most anxious to terminate the affair I had brought so near a conclusion, previous to the Admiral's arrival, I sent off Mr Mott, the First Lieutenant, in the barge, who returned soon after six o'clock bringing Napoleon with him.

On coming on board the *Bellerophon*, he was received without any of the honours generally paid to persons of high rank; the guard was drawn out on the break of the poop, but did not present arms. His Majesty's Government had merely given directions, in the event of his being captured, for his being removed into any of His Majesty's ships that might fall in with him; but no instructions had been given as to the light in which he was to be viewed. As it is not customary, however, on board a British ship of war, to pay any such honours before the colours

★ H.M.S. *Bellerophon*.

are hoisted at eight o'clock in the morning, or after sunset, I made the early hour an excuse for withholding them upon this occasion.

Buonaparte's dress was an olive-coloured great coat over a green uniform, with scarlet cape and cuffs, green lapels turned back and edged with scarlet, skirts hooked back with bugle horns embroidered in gold, plain sugar-loaf buttons and gold epaulettes; being the uniform of the Chasseur à Cheval of the Imperial Guard. He wore the Star, or Grand Cross of the Legion of Honour, and the small cross of that order; the Iron Crown; and the Union, appended to the button-hole of his left lapel. He had on a small cocked hat, with a tri-coloured cockade; plain gold-hilted sword, military boots and white waistcoat and breeches. The following day he appeared in shoes, with gold buckles, and silk stockings—the dress he always wore afterwards, while with me.

On leaving the *Épervier*, he was cheered by her ship's company as long as the boat was within hearing; and Mr Mott informed me that most of the officers and men had tears in their eyes.

General Bertrand came first up the ship's side and said to me, 'The Emperor is in the boat'. He then ascended and, when he came on the quarter-deck, pulled off his hat, and, addressing me in a firm tone of voice, said, 'I am come to throw myself on the protection of your Prince and laws.' When I showed him into the cabin, he looked round and said, 'Une belle chambre' ('This is a handsome cabin'). I answered, 'Such as it is, Sir, it is at your service while you remain on board the ship I command.' He then looked at a portrait that was hanging up, and said, 'Qui est cette jeune personne?' ('Who is that young lady?'). 'My wife,' I replied. 'Ah! elle est très jeune et très jolie' ('Ah! she is both young and pretty'). He then asked what countrywoman she was, begged to know if I had any children, and put a number of questions respecting my country, and the service I had seen. He next requested I would send for the officers, and introduce them to him: which was done according to their rank. He asked several questions of each, as to the place of his birth, the situation he held in the ship, the length of time he had served, and the actions he had been in. He then expressed a desire to go round the ship; but, as the men had not done cleaning, I told him it was customary to clean the lower decks immediately after their breakfast; that they were then so employed; and, if he would defer visiting the ship until they had finished, he would see her to more advantage.

At this time I proposed to him to allow me to address him in English, as I had heard he understood that language, and I had considerable difficulty in expressing myself in French. He replied in French, 'The thing is impossible; I hardly understand a word of your language': and from the observations I had an opportunity of making afterwards, I am satisfied he made a correct statement, as on looking into books or newspapers, he frequently asked the meaning of the most common word. He spoke his own language with a rapidity that at first made it difficult to follow him; and it was several days before I got so far accustomed to his manner of speaking, as to comprehend his meaning immediately.

In about a quarter of an hour, he again intimated a desire to go round the ship; and although I told him he would find the men rubbing and scouring, he persisted in his wish of seeing her in the state she then was. He accordingly went over all her decks, asking me many questions; more particularly about anything that appeared to him different from what he had been accustomed to see in French ships of war. He seemed most struck with the cleanliness and neatness of the men, saying 'that our seamen were surely a different class of people from the French; and that he thought it was owing to them we were always victorious at sea'. I answered, 'I must beg leave to differ with you: I do not wish to take from the merit of our men; but my own opinion is, that perhaps we owe our advantage to the superior experience of the officers; and I believe the French seamen, if taken as much pains with, would look as well as ours. As British ships of war are constantly at sea, the officers have nothing to divert their attention from them and their men; and in consequence, not only is their appearance more attended to, but they are much better trained to the service they have to perform.'

'I believe you are right,' said he. He then went on to talk of several naval actions; adding, 'Your laws are either more severe, or better administered, than ours; there are many instances of French officers having conducted themselves ill in battle, without my being able to punish them as they deserved'; among others, he mentioned the names of two naval officers: and speaking of one of them, said, 'He ought to have suffered death, and I did all I could to bring it about, but he was tried by a French naval court-martial, which only dismissed him the service.' I observed, 'The laws appear sometimes to be administered with more than sufficient severity. I commanded a frigate in the affair of Basque Roads; and in my opinion, the sentence of death on the Captain of the *Calcutta* was unjust: he could do no more to save his ship, and she was defended better and longer than any one there.' He answered, 'You are not aware of the circumstances that occasioned his condemnation; he was the first man to quit his ship, which was fought some time by her officers and crew after he had left her.' He next said, 'I can see no sufficient reason why your ships should beat the French with so much ease. The finest men-of-war in your service are French; a French ship is heavier in every respect than one of yours, she carries more guns, those guns of a larger calibre, and has a great many more men.' I replied, 'I have already accounted for it to you, in the superior experience of our men and officers.' 'I understand,' said he, 'from some Frenchmen who were on board your ship for several days, that you take great pains in exercising your guns, and training your men to fire at a mark.' I answered, 'I did so, because I considered it of the greatest importance': and I added, 'that if the frigates had attempted to put to sea, he would probably have had an opportunity of seeing the effect of it.' He asked me 'if I thought two frigates, with four-and-twenty pounders on their main decks, were a match for a seventy-four gun ship; and whether it was my opinion, if he had attempted to force a passage in the ships at

Isle d'Aix, it would have been attended with success.' I replied, 'that the fire of a two-deck ship was so much more compact, and carried such an immense weight of iron, in proportion to that of a frigate, and there was so much difficulty in bringing two or three ships to act with effect at the same time upon one, that I scarcely considered three frigates a match for one line-of-battle ship;—that, with respect to forcing a passage past the *Bellerophon*, it must have depended greatly on accident, but the chances were much against it; as the frigate would have had to beat out against the wind for three or four leagues, through a narrow passage, exposed to the fire of a seventy-four gun ship, which, from being to windward, would have had the power of taking the position most advantageous for herself.' He then said, reverting to what had passed before about firing at marks, 'You have a great advantage over France in your finances: I have long wished to introduce the use of powder and shot in exercise; but the expense was too great for the country to bear.' He examined the sights on the guns and approved of them highly; asked the weight of metal on the different decks, disapproving of the mixture of different calibres on the quarter-deck and forecastle. I told him the long nines were placed in the way of the rigging, that they might carry the fire from the explosion clear of it, which a carronade would not do: he answered, 'That may be necessary, but it must be attended with inconvenience.' His enquiries were generally much to the purpose, and showed that he had given naval matters a good deal of consideration.

On seeing the additional supply of wads for each deck made up along with the shot boxes in the form of sofas with neat canvas covers, he observed, 'The French ships of war have all the preparations for action that you have, but they have not the way of combining appearance with utility.'

We had breakfast about nine o'clock, in the English style, consisting of tea, coffee, cold meat, etc. He did not each much, or seem to relish it; and when, on enquiry, I found he was accustomed to have a hot meal in the morning, I immediately ordered my steward to allow his Maître d'Hotel to give directions, that he might invariably be served in the manner he had been used to; and after that we always lived in the French fashion, as far as I could effect that object.

During breakfast he asked many questions about English customs, saying, 'I must now learn to conform myself to them, as I shall probably pass the remainder of my life in England.'

Narrative of the Surrender of Buonaparte.

QUESTIONS

(1) What conditions of sea and weather facilitated Captain Maitland's task in capturing Napoleon?

(2) In what ship did Napoleon endeavour to escape? Why did he prefer a ship of this class?

(3) Who was the British Commander-in-Chief on this station and in what ship was his flag flying?

(4) Make a map of the west coast of France showing the position of Rochefort and inserting the Isle de Rhé, Isle d'Aix, Isle d'Oléron and River Charente. Mark with arrows the three alternative routes by which Napoleon might attempt escape.

(5) Describe in a few words the manner of Napoleon's reception on board the *Bellerophon*.

(6) At what hour in the morning did the *Bellerophon* hoist her colours? State precisely to what Captain Maitland referred by the 'colours' of the *Bellerophon*.

(7) 'His Majesty's Government.' What was the name of the King then reigning? And to whom did Napoleon refer as the 'Prince'?

(8) Describe as accurately as possible Napoleon's uniform.

(9) What were the colours of the cockade which he wore in his hat?

(10) What is meant by 'sugar-loaf' as applied to a button?

(11) What change did Napoleon make in his dress after one day on board?

(12) Describe the manner of the farewell paid to Napoleon by his officers and men and account for their feelings.

(13) What was the name of the officer who preceded Napoleon on board the *Bellerophon*?

(14) Why did not Napoleon enjoy the breakfast offered to him?

(15) What was the first request made by Napoleon when he came on board?

(16) Find any three adjectives which you think accurately describe Napoleon's bearing on board the *Bellerophon*.

(17) Tell the true story of the Captain of the *Calcutta* as disclosed for the first time by Napoleon himself.

(18) Give a list of the reasons given by Napoleon to explain why the French fleet was unsuccessful at sea.

(19) What were the real reasons?

(20) Why did Captain Maitland at first decline to take Napoleon round the ship?

(21) When at length he escorted him, how were the ship's company employed?

(22) What opinion did Napoleon form of British sailors?

(23) Name as many battles as you can remember between the French and British navies during the lifetime of Napoleon. Give the dates where possible and the name of the British commander.

(24) From his questions, requests and comments, what sort of a man do you think Napoleon must have been?

(25) Where did Napoleon expect to be taken by the *Bellerophon*? Was his expectation fulfilled; and if not, why not?

(26) Rewrite in your own words, quite simply and with careful attention to stops, the passage beginning 'Thus situated...' and ending '...Napoleon with him'.

(27) Which do you think was the more intelligible, Napoleon's English or Captain Maitland's French?

(28) Give another word or phrase for the following: 'terminate the affair', 'I am satisfied he made a correct statement', 'intimated a desire', 'I proposed to him to allow'.

(29) Why do you think that this formal language was used?

(30) Can you find in this passage any similes or metaphors? Quote examples and comment upon them: or, if you can find none, explain the probable cause of their absence.

FOR A PRÉCIS

Write a précis of the passage beginning 'General Bertrand came...' and ending '...meaning immediately'.

FOR AN ESSAY

(1) Suppose yourself to be a Master's Mate of the *Bellerophon* in 1815 and entering particulars of 14 July in the Log.

What would be your entry concerning the momentous events of the day?

(2) A fellow-officer is on shore and in hospital suffering from a gunshot wound. Write a letter to cheer him up and in the most vivid and graphic manner possible describe to him the sensational news of the capture of the Emperor in Rochefort Roads.

(3) Napoleon asked Captain Maitland whether his two frigates, *Saale* and *Méduse*, would have had any chance against the *Bellerophon*.

What do you think would have been Captain Maitland's comments on the battle of the River Plate? Explain what happened in that spectacular engagement.

(4) In the Tate Gallery, London, there is a picture by W. Q. Orchardson, R.A., showing Napoleon on board the *Bellerophon*. Napoleon has mounted the poop to secure a better view; and his suite, General Bertrand and others, with downcast eyes are standing together at a respectful distance.

As to a friend, unfamiliar with the manner of Napoleon's capture, describe carefully what the scene represents, not forgetting to explain why Napoleon mounted the poop and what must have been the thought passing through his mind as he gazed for the last time on the receding shores of France.

HOME THOUGHTS FROM THE SEA

NOBLY, nobly Cape St Vincent to the North-West died away;
Sunset ran, one glorious blood-red, reeking into Cadiz Bay;
Bluish 'mid the burning water, full in face Trafalgar lay;
In the dimmest North-East distance dawn'd Gibraltar grand and
    gray;
'Here and here did England help me: how can I help England?'
    —say,
Whoso turns as I, this evening, turn to God to praise and pray,
While Jove's planet rises yonder, silent over Africa.

W. M. THACKERAY

'THE FIGHTING TEMERAIRE'

[INTRODUCTORY NOTE. Our first *Temeraire* was captured by Admiral Boscawen at his great victory of Lagos Bay, which helped to make 1759 the 'wonderful year'. The *Temeraire* of this passage, christened in honour of Boscawen and Lagos, was built at Chatham and launched there in 1798. She played a most gallant part at the battle of Trafalgar. She came next astern of the *Victory* and gave Nelson's flagship all the support possible: as Sir Henry Newbolt has sung

> Now the sunset breezes shiver,
> *Temeraire! Temeraire!*
> And she's fading down the river
> *Temeraire! Temeraire!*
> Now the sunset breezes shiver,
> And she's fading down the river,
> But in England's song for ever
> She's the Fighting *Temeraire*.]

I MUST request you to turn your attention to a noble river-piece by J. M. W. Turner, Esq., R.A., 'The Fighting *Temeraire*', as grand a painting as ever figured on the walls of any academy, or came from the easel of any painter. The old *Temeraire* is dragged to her last home by a little, spiteful, diabolical steamer. A mighty red sun, amidst a host of flaring clouds, sinks to rest on one side of the picture, and illumines a river that seems interminable, and a countless navy that fades away into such a wonderful distance as never was painted before. The little demon of a steamer is belching out a volume (Why do I say a volume? Not a hundred volumes could express it) of foul, lurid, red-hot, malignant smoke, paddling furiously, and lashing up the water round about it; while behind it (a cold grey moon looking down on it) slow, sad, and majestic, follows the brave old ship, with death, as it were, written on her. I think my dear Bricabrac (although to be sure, your nation would be somewhat offended by such a collection of trophies) that we ought not, in common gratitude, to sacrifice entirely these noble old champions of ours, but that we should have somewhere a museum of their skeletons, which our children might visit, and think of the brave deeds which were done in them. The bones of the *Agamemnon* and the *Captain*, the *Vanguard*, the *Culloden*, and the *Victory*, ought to be sacred relics, for Englishmen to worship almost. Think of them when alive, and braving the battle and the breeze, they carried Nelson and his heroes victorious by the Cape of St Vincent, in the dark waters of Aboukir, and through the fatal conflict of Trafalgar. All these things, my dear Bricabrac, are, you will say, absurd, and not to the purpose. Be it so: but Bowbellites as we are, we Cockneys feel our hearts leap up when we recall them to memory; and every clerk in Threadneedle Street feels the strength of a Nelson, when he thinks of the mighty actions performed by him.

It is absurd, you will say (and with a great deal of reason), for Titmarsh, or any other Briton, to grow so politically enthusiastic about a four-foot canvas, representing a ship, a steamer, a river, and a sunset. But herein surely lies the power of the great artist. He makes you see and think of a great deal more than the objects before you; he knows how to soothe or to intoxicate, to fire or to depress, by a few notes, or forms, or colours, of which we cannot trace the effect to the source, but only acknowledge the power.

I recollect, some years ago, at the theatre at Weimar, hearing Beethoven's 'Battle of Vittoria', in which, amidst a storm of glorious music, the air of 'God Save the King' was introduced. The very instant it began, every Englishman in the house was bolt upright, and so stood reverently until the air was played out. Why so? From some such thrill of excitement as makes us glow and rejoice over Mr Turner and his 'Fighting *Temeraire*'; which I am sure, when the art of translating colours into music or poetry shall be discovered, will be found to be a magnificent national ode or piece of music.

Art Criticisms.

HELPS

In this passage a typical Briton, Michael Angelo Titmarsh (that is, Thackeray himself), is addressing an imaginary French connoisseur, Monsieur Bricabrac (a name coined by Thackeray from *bric-à-brac*, a French word for curiosities, objects of art, etc.).

QUESTIONS

(1) What epithets does Thackeray apply to the tug?

(2) How does he describe the smoke emerging from the tall smoke-stack of the tug?

(3) At what date did steamers become a common sight on the Thames and other big rivers?

(4) How does Thackeray describe the sun and moon in Turner's picture? Are both often seen in the sky at the same time?

(5) In what words does he suggest the dignified motion of H.M.S. *Temeraire*?

(6) What is the 'moral' of Thackeray's little sermon?

(7) What flattering phrases does he apply to the 'wooden walls of old England'?

(8) The *Agamemnon* was Nelson's first and best loved ship of the line, or battleship, which by his prowess Nelson made famous when he was still a Captain. Thackeray also endeavours to name the four ships that carried his flag or broad pendant in his four most famous battles. Three he names correctly and one incorrectly. Make a list of the four battles in question and set opposite to them the four correct ship names.

(9) What does Thackeray call Trafalgar?

(10) By what two names does he refer to Londoners, himself (Mr Titmarsh) among them?

(11) What effect, in Thackeray's opinion, would the recital of Nelson's actions produce in a clerk in Threadneedle Street? Why does he single out Threadneedle Street?

(12) Wherein, according to Thackeray, does the power of a great artist reside?

(13) Substitute other words for the following without alteration of sense: 'enthusiastic', 'reverently', 'diabolical', 'soothe', 'malignant', 'trophies', 'sacrifice', 'gratitude', 'absurd', 'flaring', 'interminable', 'depress', 'intoxicate'.

(14) Why was Bricabrac likely to be offended by such a collection as Mr Titmarsh proposed?

(15) What was Thackeray's enduring memory of a concert of Beethoven's music at Weimar?

(16) To what does Thackeray compare the effect of Turner's picture on his own mental vision?

FOR AN ESSAY

(1) Think of some big picture which you have seen more than once and admired greatly.

Describe it as vividly as you can in the manner that Thackeray describes 'The Fighting *Temeraire*', giving your reader not only details of its subject but the reasons why the painting has earned your admiration.

(2) Can you think of any easier way to achieve what Thackeray asks for in this passage than to bring to one place all the famous ships which have earned the admiration of patriotic Britons? What would be the chief objections to Thackeray's plan?

(3) Describe as fully as possible a visit you have paid to H.M.S. *Victory*. If you have not yet seen over Nelson's flagship, describe a visit to Trafalgar Square on the twenty-first of October.

THE ENGLISH ADMIRALS

MOST men of high destinies have high-sounding names. Pym
and Habakkuk may do pretty well, but they must not think to
cope with the Cromwells and Isaiahs. And you could not find
a better case in print than that of the English Admirals. Drake
and Rooke and Hawke are picked names for men of execution.
Frobisher, Rodney, Boscawen, Foul-Weather Jack Byron, are all
good to catch the eye in a page of a naval history. Clowdisley
Shovel is a mouthful of quaint and sounding syllables. Benbow
has a bulldog quality that suits the man's character, and it takes
us back to those English archers who were his true comrades for
plainness, tenacity, and pluck. Raleigh is spirited and martial,
and signifies an act of bold conduct in the field. It is impossible
to judge of Blake or Nelson, no names current among men being
worthy of such heroes. But still it is odd enough, and very
appropriate in this connection, that the latter was greatly taken
with his Sicilian title. 'The signification perhaps, pleased him',
says Southey; 'Duke of Thunder was what in Dahomey would
have been called a *strong name*; it was to a sailor's taste, and
certainly to no man could it be more applicable.' Admiral in
itself is one of the most satisfactory of distinctions; it has a noble
sound and a very proud history; and Columbus thought so highly
of it, that he enjoined his heirs to sign themselves by that title as
long as the house should last.

But it is the spirit of the men, and not their names, that I wish
to speak about in this paper. That spirit is truly English; they,
and not Tennyson's cotton-spinners or Mr D'Arcy Thompson's
Abstract Bagman, are the true and typical Englishmen. There
may be more *head* of bagmen in the country, but human beings
are reckoned by number only in political constitutions. And the
Admirals are typical in the full force of the word. They are

splendid examples of virtue, indeed, but of a virtue in which most Englishmen can claim a moderate share; and what we admire in their lives is a sort of apotheosis of ourselves. Almost everybody in our land, except humanitarians and a few persons whose youth has been depressed by exceptionally aesthetic surroundings, can understand and sympathise with an Admiral or a prize-fighter. I do not wish to bracket Benbow and Tom Cribb; but, depend upon it, they are practically bracketed for admiration in the minds of many frequenters of ale-houses. If you told them about Germanicus and the eagles, or Regulus going back to Carthage, they would very likely fall asleep; but tell them about Harry Pearce and Jim Belcher, or about Nelson and the Nile, and they put down their pipes to listen. I have by me a copy of *Boxiana*, on the fly-leaves of which a youthful member of the fancy kept a chronicle of remarkable events and an obituary of great men. Here we find piously chronicled the demise of jockeys, watermen, and pugilists—'Johnny Moore, of the Liverpool Prize Ring; Tom Spring, aged fifty-six; Pierce Egan, senior, writer of *Boxiana* and other sporting works'—and among all these the Duke of Wellington! If Benbow had lived in the time of this annalist, do you suppose his name would not have been added to the glorious roll? In short, we do not all feel warmly towards Wesley or Laud, we cannot all take pleasure in *Paradise Lost*, but there are certain common sentiments and touches of nature by which the whole nation is made to feel kinship. A little while ago everybody, from Hazlitt and John Wilson down to the imbecile creature who scribbled his register on the fly-leaves of *Boxiana*, felt a more or less shamefaced satisfaction in the exploits of prize-fighters. And the exploits of the Admirals are popular to the same degree and tell in all ranks of society. Their sayings and doings stir English blood like the sound of a trumpet; and if the Indian Empire, the trade of London, and all the outward and visible ensigns of our greatness should pass away, we should still leave behind us a durable monument of what we were in these sayings and doings of the English Admirals.

Duncan, lying off the Texel with his own flagship, the *Venerable*, and only one other vessel, heard that the whole Dutch fleet was putting to sea. He told Captain Hotham to anchor alongside of him in the narrowest part of the channel, and fight his vessel till she sank. 'I have taken the depth of the water,' added he, 'and when the *Venerable* goes down, my flag will still fly.' And you observe this is no naked Viking in a prehistoric period; but a Scotch member of Parliament, with a smattering of the classics, a telescope, a cocked hat of great size, and flannel underclothing. In the same spirit, Nelson went into Aboukir with six colours flying; so that, even if five were shot away, it should not be imagined he had struck. He too must needs wear his four stars outside his Admiral's frock, to be a butt for sharp-shooters. 'In honour I gained them', he said to objectors, adding with sublime illogicality, 'in honour I will die with them.' Captain Douglas of the *Royal Oak*, when the Dutch fired his vessel in the Thames, sent his men ashore, but was burned along with her himself rather than desert his post without orders. Just then, perhaps the Merry Monarch was chasing a moth round the supper table with the ladies of his court. When Raleigh sailed into Cadiz, and all the forts and ships opened fire on him at once, he scorned to shoot a gun, and made answer with a flourish of insulting trumpets. I like the bravado better than the wisest dispositions to insure victory; it comes from the heart and goes to it. God has made noble heroes, but he never made a finer gentleman than Walter Raleigh. And as our Admirals were full of heroic superstitions, and had a strutting and vainglorious style of fight, so they discovered a startling eagerness for battle, and courted war like a mistress. When the news came to Essex before Cadiz that the attack had been decided, he threw his hat into the sea. It is in this way that a schoolboy hears of a half-holiday; but this was a bearded man of great possessions who had just been allowed to risk his life. Benbow could not lie still in his bunk after he had lost his leg; he must be on deck in a basket to direct and animate the fight.

I said they loved war like a mistress; yet I think there are not many mistresses we should continue to woo under similar circumstances. Troubridge went ashore with the *Culloden*, and was able to take no part in the battle of the Nile. 'The merits of that ship and her gallant captain', wrote Nelson to the Admiralty, 'are too well known to benefit by anything I could say. Her misfortune was great in getting aground, *while her more fortunate companions were in the full tide of happiness.*' This is a notable expression, and depicts the whole great-hearted, big-spoken stock of the English Admirals to a hair. It was to be in the 'full tide of happiness' for Nelson to destroy five thousand five hundred and twenty-five of his fellow-creatures, and have his own scalp torn open by a piece of langridge shot. Hear him again at Copenhagen: A shot through the mainmast knocked the splinters about; and he observed to one of his officers with a smile, 'It is warm work, and this may be the last to any of us at any moment'; and then, stopping short at the gangway, added, with emotion, 'But, mark you—*I would not be elsewhere for thousands.*'

Virginibus Puerisque.

HELPS

Admiral. The word is derived from the Arabic *Emir-al-Bahr*, ruler of the sea.

Apotheosis (Greek). Literally, release from earthly life and ascension to glory; but also used to imply glorification of a principle or person.

William Hazlitt (1778–1820) and **John Wilson** (1785–1854). Two famous essayists. John Wilson wrote chiefly for *Blackwood's*; Hazlitt for the *Edinburgh Review* and other journals and magazines.

QUESTIONS

(1) Pym and Cromwell: Isaiah and Habakkuk. Which of these does Stevenson select as high-sounding names?

(2) Which names of British Admirals does he select as 'picked names for execution'?

(3) What other high-sounding names does he fix upon?

(4) Which Admiral, in Stevenson's opinion, had a name of 'quaint and sounding syllables'?

(5) Which name had a 'fitting bulldog quality'?

(6) What was Admiral Byron's nickname?

(7) What does the word 'Raleigh' signify? If used in its original sense, how would it be spelled to-day?

(8) Which two English Admirals does Stevenson rate higher than all the rest? Do you agree with his choice?

(9) What was Nelson's Sicilian title and why did it please him?

(10) Where is Dahomey?

(11) What distinction did Columbus prefer before all others?

(12) What words does Stevenson select to describe
  (a) commercial travellers;
  (b) industrial workers of Lancashire?

(13) In what periodical were pugilistic encounters once recorded in full?

(14) What prize-fighters does Stevenson mention by name?

(15) To what religious leaders does Stevenson refer?

(16) What epic poem does Stevenson mention as unlikely to appeal to all classes of readers?

(17) What was the name of Duncan's flagship when he was blockading the Dutch fleet in the Texel?

(18) What ship did Troubridge command in the Nile campaign of 1798?

(19) By what other name does Stevenson refer to the battle of the Nile?

(20) Provide other ways of expressing 'frequenters of ale-houses', 'youthful member of the fancy', 'had a strutting and vainglorious style'.

(21) Explain 'obituary', 'humanitarians', 'aesthetic', 'demise', 'illogicality', 'annalist', 'signification'.

(22) To what Admirals is Stevenson referring in the following:
  (a) 'On deck in a basket to direct and animate the fight.'
  (b) 'God has made noble heroes, but he never made a finer gentleman.'
  (c) 'English archers...were his true comrades for plainness, tenacity and pluck.'
  (d) 'A Scotch member of Parliament, with a smattering of the Classics, a telescope, a cocked hat of great size and flannel underclothing.'
  (e) 'The merits of that ship and her gallant captain are too well known to benefit by anything I can say.'
  (f) 'It was in the full tide of happiness to have his own scalp torn open by a piece of langridge shot.'
  (g) 'This was a bearded gentleman of great possessions who had just been allowed to risk his life.'

(23) In the same style as the above write brief descriptions of any three of the following: Hawkins, Drake, Grenville, Blake, Howard of Effingham, Albemarle, Anson and Hawke.

(24) Substitute other words for the following without alteration of sense: 'destinies', 'martial', 'current', 'distinctions', 'applicable', 'sympathize', 'kinship', 'imbecile', 'notable', 'typical', 'depicts', 'exploits', 'sublime', 'startling', 'woo'.

(25) Write sentences of your own invention introducing the words 'cope', 'enjoined', 'durable', 'bravado', 'smattering'.

FOR AN ESSAY

(1) If Stevenson is right in arguing that the average Briton puts, or used to put, Admirals and pugilists in the same class because both exhibit, or have exhibited, pluck in the same exceptional degree, is he also correct in maintaining that this virtue is one in which all Britons can claim some share? Support your argument with examples to illustrate your meaning.

(2) Some maintain that boxing is the noblest of all sports. If you agree, explain how and why this happens to be the case. If you do not agree, say which alternative form of sport you prefer with full reasons for your preference.

(3) Write a continuation of Stevenson's essay on the 'English Admirals' citing other endearing characteristics not mentioned by him, and quoting instances of their humour, gallantry, or singularity, not already made use of in the passage above.

(4) Describe in some detail any exciting boxing match which you have witnessed.

R. E. VERNÈDE

ENGLAND TO THE SEA

[INTRODUCTORY NOTE. When Germany threatened the world with an aggressive despotism more menacing than that of Napoleon, this country found itself faced with enemies who buttressed the reality of their immense military might with a Propaganda-machine which insisted on the legend of German invincibility and racial superiority over all other Nations. Repetition being more convincing than argument, many besides the Germans came to believe that British pre-eminence at sea was a thing as obsolete as the wooden man-of-war, and that the zest and keenness of British seamen had degenerated and their skill, courage and experience fallen into a decline. To offset this erroneous creed, the following poem, by one who soon afterwards died fighting for his country, appeared in the early days of August 1914.]

HEARKEN, O Mother, hearken to thy daughter!
 Fain would I tell thee what men tell to me,
Saying that henceforth no more on any water
 Shall I be first or great or loved or free,

But that these others—so the tale is spoken—
 Who have not known thee all these centuries
By fire and sword shall yet turn England broken
 Back from thy breast and beaten from thy seas,

Me—whom thou barest where thy waves should guard me,
 Me—whom thou suckled'st on thy milk of foam,
Me—whom thy kisses shaped what while they marred me,
 To whom thy storms are sweet and ring of home.

'Behold,' they cry, 'she is grown soft and strengthless,
 All her proud memories changed to fear and fret.'
Say, thou, who hast watched through ages that are lengthless,
 Whom have I feared, and when did I forget?

What sons of mine have shunned thy whorls and races?
 Have I not reared for thee time and again
And bid go forth to share thy fierce embraces
 Sea-ducks, sea-wolves, sea-rovers, and sea-men?

Names that thou knowest—great hearts that thou holdest,
   Rocking them, rocking them in an endless wake—
Captains the world can match not with its boldest,
   Hawke, Howard, Grenville, Frobisher, Drake?

Nelson—the bravest of them all—the master
   Who swept across thee like a shooting star,
And, while the Earth stood veiled before disaster,
   Caught Death and slew him—there—at Trafalgar?

Mother, they knew me then as thou didst know me;
   Then I cried, Peace, and every flag was furled:
But I am old, it seems, and they would show me
   That never more my peace shall bind the world.

Wherefore, O Sea; I, standing thus before thee,
   Stretch forth my hands unto thy surge and say:
'When they come forth who seek this empire o'er thee,
   And I go forth to meet them—on that day

God grant to us the old Armada weather,
   The winds that nip, the heavens that stoop and lour—
Not till the Sea and England sink together,
   Shall they be masters! Let them boast that hour!'

ADMIRAL OF THE FLEET LORD CHATFIELD,
G.C.B., O.M., K.C.M.G., C.V.O., D.C.L.

THE BATTLE OF HELIGOLAND
28 AUGUST 1914

ON August 27th we* left Scapa for a cruise or sweep in the North Sea. The second Cruiser Squadron, under Commodore William Goodenough,† was with us, but we had no destroyers. Beatty had orders to proceed towards the Heligoland Bight; Rear Admiral Tyrwhitt,‡ in command of the Harwich destroyer force, was carrying out a raid on German light forces off Heligoland. During the early morning of the 28th Goodenough was sent in to support him, as he seemed to be in trouble.

About noon on the 28th we intercepted a message from Tyrwhitt in the *Arethusa*, which implied that he was in some difficulty and hotly engaged by German light cruisers. Beatty's force was then some forty miles north of Heligoland. The Bight was not a pleasant spot into which to take great ships; it was unknown whether mines had been laid there, submarines were sure to be on patrol, and to move into this area so near to the great German base at Wilhelmshaven was risky. Visibility was low, and to be surprised by a superior force of capital ships was not unlikely. They would have had plenty of time to leave harbour since Tyrwhitt's presence had been first known.

Beatty was not long making up his mind. He said to me, 'What do you think we should do? I ought to go and support Tyrwhitt, but if I lose one of these valuable ships, the country will not forgive me.'

Unburdened with responsibility, and eager for excitement,

---

* The Battle-Cruiser squadron.
† Now Admiral Sir William Goodenough, G.C.B., M.V.O.
‡ Now Admiral of the Fleet Sir Reginald Tyrwhitt, Bart., G.C.B., D.S.O.

I said, 'Surely we must go'. It was all he needed, but whatever I had said would have made little difference. We steamed towards Tyrwhitt at twenty-five knots, the Second Cruiser Squadron five miles ahead.

Here, we thought, is the real thing at last. The four battle-cruisers *Lion, Princess Royal, New Zealand* and *Indefatigable*, steaming at high speed, black smoke streaming from their great funnels, was always an impressive sight and gave one a feeling of strength and invincibility. As we approached, everyone was at action stations, the guns loaded, the range-finders manned, the control alert, the signalmen's binoculars and telescopes scouring the misty horizon. It became still more misty until one could hardly see two miles. Suddenly the report of guns was heard. Wireless in those days was still in its infancy, and reports in code took a long time to come through; we had nothing from Commodore Goodenough, yet felt he was in action. The sound of the guns got closer, a regular cannonade.

Suddenly on our port bow we saw that memorable sight, the flash of guns through the mist. Beatty stood on the bridge by the compass, his glasses scanning the scene. At length we made out the hulk of a cruiser;* indeed she was little more than a hulk; her funnel had fallen and her foremast had been shot away, a fire raged on her upper deck. She was evidently German and had been engaged by all four ships of Goodenough's squadron. We swung round ninety degrees to port. 'Leave her to them,' said Beatty. 'Don't fire.'

Soon we sighted another German cruiser fine on the port bow. I pointed it out to Longhurst† in the control position. 'Enemy cruiser almost right ahead crossing to port. Open fire.' The turrets swung round and the German cruiser altered course away and towards Heligoland. Instantly our turret guns opened fire, followed by those of the squadron. In a few moments the German (it was the cruiser *Köln*) was hit many times by heavy

---

* The *Mainz*.
† Lieutenant-Commander Longhurst, gunnery officer of H.M.S. *Lion*.

shell; she bravely returned our fire with her little four-inch guns aiming at our conning tower. One felt the tiny four-inch shell spatter against the conning-tower armour, and the pieces 'sizz' over it. In a few minutes the *Köln* was also a hulk.

At that moment we descried a small German ship a mile on the starboard bow. Sighting us, she made off at right-angles zigzagging. Pointing her out to Longhurst, I told him to cease firing at the *Köln* and to engage her before she could torpedo us. He rapidly swung the 13·5-inch turrets round from the port to the starboard beam and re-opened fire. Three salvoes were enough and the German (the *Ariadne*) disappeared from sight; an explosion was seen and a mass of flame. It is known she sank almost immediately.

By now we were getting near the fortress. Beatty told me to lead round to the northward, the other ships following. We had sighted Tyrwhitt for a moment. He had had no information that we were at sea but he was, no doubt, glad to see us; we had relieved the pressure his force was undergoing. We retraced our tracks and soon re-sighted the *Köln* ahead. She lay like a hulk and the Admiral told me to sink her. We put two salvoes from the two foremost turrets into her; she sank beneath the waves stern first. A submarine was reported by one of the battle-cruisers. We had done enough, and ordering Goodenough to rejoin after he had saved such German sailors as he safely could, we steered north for safer waters.

It had been a thrilling and busy twenty minutes or so; we felt satisfied. The men came rushing up on deck and cheered the Admiral. It was no great naval feat, but carried out under the nose of the German Commander-in-chief, it actually meant a good deal both to Germany and to England. We had shown our sea ascendancy, our will to seek every opportunity of engaging the enemy even at his very front door. We had not met either mine or torpedo.

Success rightly forgives all risks taken. David Beatty had shown himself the leader needed, ready to dare risks, not light-heartedly but with a full sense of responsibility. He had mentally measured them and proved by his success that his judgment was correct.

The Navy and Defence.

QUESTIONS

(1) Where is Scapa Flow? What was its significance in August 1914?

(2) Who was Commander-in-Chief of the Grand Fleet in August 1914?

(3) What kind of a ship is a Battle-Cruiser?

(4) Who commanded the Battle-Cruiser squadron?

(5) What was the name of his flagship?

(6) Who was his Flag Captain?

(7) Who commanded the Destroyer force at Harwich?

(8) In what ship did he wear his broad pendant?

(9) What nickname would you consider appropriate for this ship and why?

(10) What orders did the Battle-Cruiser squadron receive on 27 August 1914?

(11) Give the name of the ships comprising the Battle-Cruiser squadron on that date.

(12) What were the conditions then prevailing which led to the issue of these orders?

(13) What was the objective (or target) of the Commodore (D) Harwich?

(14) What orders had already been issued to the Second Cruiser squadron?

(15) Who was in command of this squadron?

(16) Where is Heligoland?

(17) What information did the Battle-Cruiser squadron receive when forty miles north of Heligoland?

(18) What is the name of the great German naval base situated in Heligoland Bight?

(19) What particular risks attended an incursion into the Bight in August 1914?

(20) What question did the Admiral commanding the Battle-Cruiser squadron put to his Flag Captain on receipt of the information mentioned in Question 17 above?

(21) What was the Flag Captain's reply?

(22) What was the speed of the Battle-Cruiser squadron?

(23) How was it situated with reference to Heligoland and to the Second Cruiser squadron?

(24) Describe the preparations for battle.

(25) How good was the visibility?

(26) To what extent had wireless developed in August 1914?

(27) What replaced at Heligoland the telescope used by senior officers in Nelson's day?

(28) In what direction was gun-fire first spotted?

(29) What was the first German ship discovered and what was her condition?

(30) What was the next German ship encountered and how did she fare at the hands of the Battle-Cruiser squadron?

(31) Where was the *Ariadne* first sighted and what was her fate?

(32) How did the ship's company of the *Lion* show their feelings at the close of the engagement?

(33) What order did the Admiral commanding the Battle-Cruiser squadron give to the Second Cruiser squadron when victory had declared itself?

(34) What was the final measure of the British success, both moral and material?

(35) Explain 'zigzagging', 'conning tower', 'salvoes', 'range-finders', 'turrets'.

(36) Substitute other words for the following without alteration of sense: 'invincibility', 'retraced', 'scanning', 'pressure', 'unburdened', 'memorable', 'ascendancy', 'light-heartedly', 'spatter', 'mentally'.

FOR A PRÉCIS

Write a précis of the passage beginning 'About noon on the 28th...' and ending '..."Don't fire"'.

FOR AN ESSAY

(1) Draw out points of resemblance and points of difference as between the battle of Heligoland and a battle of Hawke's day or Nelson's, more especially in regard to speed, weapons, range, risks, and mechanical appliances.

(2) From what you know of, or can ascertain concerning, the war of 1914–18, in which class of ships would you prefer to have served, battle-ships, battle-cruisers, light-cruisers, destroyers or submarines?

(3) When the war of 1914–18 began, two mighty forces stood out pre-eminent—the German Army and the British Navy. How far is it true to say that, when it ended, the German Army had failed in the most decisive manner, while the British Navy continued to maintain the highest and noblest traditions of the past?

THE RT HON. WINSTON S. CHURCHILL, C.H.

'THE NAVY IS HERE!'*

[INTRODUCTORY NOTE. The second war of German aggression began on Sunday, 3 September 1939, and the Germans instantly opened a violent attack on the merchant navy of Great Britain. One of their most formidable surface-raiders was the 'pocket battleship', *Graf von Spee*, which, after sinking nine valuable merchantmen in the South Atlantic and Indian Ocean, was brought to battle by Commodore Harwood on Wednesday, 13 December 1939, off the River Plate.

The officers and men, taken prisoner from the merchantmen sunk by the German pocket battleship, were confined in the auxiliary vessel *Altmark*, which accompanied the *Graf von Spee* on her marauding career. The *Altmark* subsequently endeavoured to slink home to Germany with her captives by making illegitimate use of the neutral waters off Norway's western coast. On Friday, 16 February 1940, H.M. destroyer *Cossack* intercepted the *Altmark* in Joessing Fiord and rescued 299 British seamen. A week later the Lord Mayor of London gave a luncheon party at the Guildhall to officers and ratings of H.M.S. *Exeter* and *Ajax*, two of the participants in the River Plate battle, and Mr Churchill delivered the following memorable speech.]

MY colleagues of the Board of Admiralty and of the War Cabinet are grateful to you for inviting us here to-day to share the hospitality which the City of London has extended to the victors of the River Plate. It is an occasion at once joyous, memorable and unique. It is the highest compliment your ancient Corporation could give to the officers and men of the *Exeter* and *Ajax* and through them to the whole of our Navy, upon whom under Providence our lives and State depend from hour to hour.

I do not suppose that the bonds which unite the British Navy to the British nation—and they have taken a long time to form— or those which join the Navy and the Mercantile Marine were ever so strong as they are to-day. The brunt of the war so far has fallen upon the sailormen, and their comrades in the Coastal Air Force, and we have already lost nearly 3000 lives in a hard, unrelenting struggle which goes on night and day and is going

---

* Speech delivered at the Guildhall, 23 February 1940.

on now without a moment's respite. The brilliant sea fight which Admiral Harwood conceived, and which those who are here executed, takes its place in our naval annals, and I might add that in a dark, cold winter it warmed the cockles of the British heart. But it is not only in those few glittering, deadly hours of action, which rivet all eyes, that the strain falls upon the Navy. Far more does it fall in the weeks and months of ceaseless trial and vigilance on cold, dark, stormy seas from whose waves at any moment death and destruction may leap, with sullen roar. There is the task which these men were discharging and which their comrades are discharging. There was the task from which, in a sense, the fierce action was almost a relief.

Here let me say a word for the naval members of the Board of Admiralty and especially for the First Sea Lord, Sir Dudley Pound, and his Deputy-Chief of Naval Staff (the newly promoted Vice-Admiral Phillips) for the skilful combination for which they have been responsible. You must remember that for one stroke that goes home, for one clutch that grips the raider, there are many that miss their mark on the broad oceans; for every success there are many disappointments. You must never forget that the dangers that are seen are only a small part of those that are warded off by care and foresight, and therefore pass unnoticed. The Admiralty and the Fleet are learning together the special conditions of this hard and novel war, and although mistakes and accidents will certainly occur, and sorrow will fall from time to time upon us, we hope that from Whitehall the sense of resolution and design at the centre will impart itself to all afloat, and will lighten the burden of their task and concert the vigour of their action. It is not, for instance, a mere coincidence that has brought the *Achilles* out of the vast Pacific Ocean to the shores of far-off New Zealand, in order to receive in the Antipodes the same warm-hearted welcome as her sisters the *Ajax* and the *Exeter* are receiving now in dear old London.

The spirit of all our forces serving on salt water has never been more strong and high than now. The warrior heroes of the past may look down, as Nelson's monument looks down upon us now, without any feeling that the island race has lost its daring or that the examples they set in bygone centuries have faded as the generations have succeeded one another. It was not for nothing that Admiral Harwood, as he instantly at full speed attacked an enemy which might have sunk any one of his ships by a single successful salvo from its far heavier guns, flew Nelson's immortal signal of which neither the new occasion, nor the conduct of all ranks and ratings, nor the final result were found unworthy.

To the glorious tale of the action off the Plate, there has recently been added an epilogue—the rescue last week by the *Cossack* and her flotilla, under the nose of the enemy and amid the tangles of one-sided neutrality, of the British captives taken from the sunken German raider. Their rescue at the very moment when these unhappy men were about to be delivered over to German bondage, proves that the long arm of British sea power can be stretched out, not only for foes but also for faithful friends. And to Nelson's signal of 135 years ago, 'England expects that every man will do his duty', there may now be added last week's not less proud reply: 'The Navy is here!'

Into Battle.

QUESTIONS

(1) What was the date on which this speech was delivered?
(2) What post in the Cabinet did Mr Churchill then fill?
(3) When did he become Prime Minister?
(4) Whom did he succeed?
(5) Who followed him in the post which he vacated to become Prime Minister?
(6) What is meant by 'War Cabinet'?
(7) What casualties were suffered by the sea forces of the Crown during the first six months of the war?
(8) What was the date of the battle of the River Plate?
(9) Trace the circumstances leading to that memorable encounter.
(10) What British ships were engaged, and with whom?
(11) What kind of vessel was the German ship?
(12) Who was the British Commander-in-Chief?
(13) What kind of ships did he command?
(14) With what other forces of the Crown does Mr Churchill in this speech associate the Royal Navy?

(15) Which members of the Board of Admiralty did Mr Churchill mention in his speech and for what qualities did he say that the Navy was indebted to them?

(16) Which of them afterwards died in battle at sea and what was the occasion of his death?

(17) Where did the *Achilles* repair after the battle of the River Plate?

(18) In which ship did the British Commander-in-Chief fly his Broad Pendant?

(19) What signal did he hoist before engaging the enemy?

(20) What was Mr Churchill's comment upon the use of this signal?

(21) What was the name of the German ship at the battle of the River Plate and what eventually became of her?

(22) What became of the prisoners taken by the German ship?

(23) How, where, and by whom were they rescued?

(24) By means of what epithets or adjectives does Mr Churchill describe
    (a) 'the hours of action' (battle at sea)?
    (b) 'the occasion of the Guildhall banquet'?
    (c) 'the strain and struggle of watching at sea'?
    (d) 'the war against the Nazis'?
    (e) 'the spirit of those serving on salt water'?

(25) Explain what is meant by 'epilogue', 'ancient Corporation', 'Antipodes', 'cockles of the heart', 'The Island Race', 'tangle of one-sided neutrality', 'Nelson's immortal signal'.

(26) Substitute other words for the following without change of sense: 'victors', 'vigour', 'hospitality', 'unique', 'vigilance', 'resolution', 'colleagues', 'joyous', 'brunt', 'bonds', 'respite', 'unrelenting', 'bondage', 'rivet', 'foresight', 'concert', 'coincidence'.

(27) Who first employed the expression, 'The Navy is here'?

(28) Mention two or more naval victories since Mr Churchill became Prime Minister?

(29) Mention any two books written by Mr Churchill.

(30) What do you know of 'Mr Bullfinch'?

FOR A PRÉCIS

Write a précis of the passage beginning 'Here let me say a word...' and ending '...dear old London'.

FOR AN ESSAY

(1) Prove with full particulars of names, dates and episodes the truth of Mr Churchill's statement that the burden of the War during the first six months fell upon the 'sailormen'.

(2) Write a biography of Mr Churchill bringing out the wide and varied experience he has had as soldier, author and statesman.

(3) Describe as vividly as possible the events leading up to the battle of the River Plate, the course of the action itself, and the events that followed it.

(4) Imagine yourself to be one of the prisoners of the *Altmark*, and describe in a letter to a cousin in Canada your experiences in German hands and the joyous occasion of your rescue.

J. G. WHITTIER

THE THREE BELLS

[INTRODUCTORY NOTE. For years before the second German war of aggression broke out, Hitler boasted of a 'secret weapon'; and this, when war came, proved to be the dire and deadly 'magnetic mine'. On 18 November 1939, six merchantmen were sunk by this diabolical device within 24 hours; and of the six victims five were neutrals. Thus, months before the Continent was introduced to the benefits of the New Order, the seaways were reminded of the ruthless savagery and barbarous brutality which had terrorized seafaring men before the acceptance of Christianity.

Meditating on these events, the reader needs to remind himself that from 1815 until the rise of German despotism, Great Britain did actually exercise a veritable sea-supremacy, which some opposed, but none denied; a supremacy which enabled those who exercised it to impose upon the ocean-world whatever code of laws they cared to ordain. On what basis did this supremacy rest?

In Blake's day a permanent force of British fighting ships was established; and this force, under Charles II, was permitted by the Crown to adopt the time-honoured title of the 'Royal Navy'. From that day to this Divine Service has been said on board all the King's ships: and this is the Navy's own prayer:

'O Eternal Lord God, who alone spreadest out the Heavens and rulest the raging of the seas; who hast compassed the waters with bounds until day and night come to an end; be pleased to receive into thy Almighty and most gracious protection the persons of us thy servants and the fleet in which we serve. Preserve us from the dangers of the sea and from the violence of the enemy; that we may be a safeguard unto our most gracious Sovereign Lord the King and his dominions, and a security for such as pass on the seas upon their lawful occasions; that the inhabitants of our island may in peace and quietness serve Thee, our God: and that we may return in safety to enjoy the blessings of the land with the fruits of our labours, and with a thankful remembrance of Thy mercies to praise and glorify Thy holy Name.'

This, then, in contrast to the German 'New Order', is the ideal, to which British sea-governance has in the past attempted to guide the world— 'security for such as pass on the seas upon their *lawful* occasions'; a brotherhood of all ocean-toilers irrespective of race, creed, colour or nationality; a confraternity of all who go down to the sea in ships and do their business in great waters.

The spirit thus inculcated is well brought out in the following poem which dates from Victorian times and which, it should be carefully noted, is *not* (like all the other passages in this book) by a British-born writer, but by an American.]

BENEATH the low-hung night cloud
  That raked her splintering mast
The good ship settled slowly,
  The cruel leak gained fast.

Over the awful ocean
  Her signal guns pealed out.
Dear God! was that an answer
  From the horror round about?

A voice came down the wild wind,
  'Ho! ship ahoy!' its cry:
'Our stout *Three Bells* of Glasgow
  Shall lay till daylight by!'

Hour after hour crept slowly,
  Yet on the heaving swells
Tossed up and down the ship-lights,
  The lights of the *Three Bells*.

And ship to ship made signals,
  Man answered back to man,
While oft to cheer and hearten
  The *Three Bells* nearer ran;

And the Captain from her taffrail
  Sent down his hopeful cry.
'Take heart! Hold on!' he shouted,
  'The *Three Bells* shall lay by!'

All night across the waters
  The tossing lights shone clear;
All night from reeling taffrail
  The *Three Bells* sent her cheer,

And when the dreary watches
  Of storm and darkness passed,
Just as the wreck lurched under,
  All souls were saved at last.

Sail on, *Three Bells*, for ever,
  In grateful memory sail!
Ring on, *Three Bells* of rescue
  Above the wave and gale.

Type of the Love eternal,
  Repeat the Master's cry,
As tossing through our darkness
  The lights of God draw nigh.

FOR AN ESSAY

A friend, employed on civil defence duties, has written to you, commenting upon the inhuman cruelty of the Germans to merchant seamen and insisting that, when enemy ships scuttle themselves, their crews should properly be left in their boats to look after themselves. Write a closely reasoned reply showing that such reprisals would be entirely contrary to the British ideal, which all serving at sea desire to maintain unsullied until the days of Peace return.

FOR FURTHER READING

GENERAL

R. C. AND ROMOLA ANDERSON	The Sailing Ship
FRANK C. BOWEN	Sea Slang
TRYSTAN EDWARDS	British Bluejacket
ERNEST GRAY	Surgeon's Mate
L. G. C. LAUGHTON AND V. HEDDON	Great Storms
R. C. LESLIE AND C. R. L. FLETCHER	Old Sea Wings, Ways and Words in the days of Oak and Hemp
ADMIRAL SIR WILLIAM JAMES	Blue Water and Green Fields
PROFESSOR MICHAEL LEWIS	England's Sea Officers
G. E. MANWARING AND B. DOBREE	The Floating Republic
COMMANDER HILARY MEAD, R.N.	Trafalgar Signals

HISTORY

SIR GEOFFREY CALLENDER	The Naval Side of British History
SIR GEOFFREY CALLENDER	The Story of H.M.S. *Victory*
ADMIRAL OF THE FLEET LORD CHATFIELD	The Navy and the Nation
W. H. FITCHETT	Fights for the Flag
EDWARD FRASER	Famous Fighters of the Fleet
EDWARD FRASER	*Londons* of the British Fleet
EDWARD FRASER	*Bellerophon* the Bravest of the Brave
EDWARD FRASER	The Sailors whom Nelson led
J. A. FROUDE	England's Forgotten Worthies [Short Studies]
J. A. FROUDE	English Seamen in the Sixteenth Century
J. R. HALE	The Great Armada
BASIL LUBBOCK	The Log of the *Cutty Sark*
ADMIRAL SIR F. MAITLAND	The Surrender of Napoleon
JOHN MASEFIELD, O.M.	On the Spanish Main
JOHN MASEFIELD, O.M.	The *Conway*
JOHN MASEFIELD, O.M.	Sea Life in Nelson's day
C. FOX SMITH	Ocean Racers
C. FOX SMITH	A Book of Famous Ships
C. FOX SMITH	The Return of the *Cutty Sark*

BIOGRAPHY

SIR GEOFFREY CALLENDER	Sea Kings of Britain
SIR JULIAN CORBETT	Drake [English Men of Action]
W. H. FITCHETT	Nelson and his Captains

HON. JOHN FORTESCUE	Dundonald [English Men of Action]
LT.-CMDR. RUPERT GOULD, R.N.	Captain Cook
LORD PONSONBY	Samuel Pepys
LORD RENNELL OF RODD	Sir Walter Raleigh [English Men of Action]

SEAFARING

HILAIRE BELLOC	The Cruise of the *Nona*
JOSEPH CONRAD	The Mirror of the Sea
R. H. DANA	Two Years before the Mast
CAPTAIN TAPPRELL DORLING, R.N. (Taffrail)	Pincher Martin, O.D.
BASIL LUBBOCK	Round the Horn before the Mast
BASIL LUBBOCK	Barlow's Journal
HERMAN MELVILLE	White Jacket
HERMAN MELVILLE	Moby Dick
SIR ARTHUR QUILLER-COUCH	Dead Man's Rock
SIR ARTHUR QUILLER-COUCH	I saw Three Ships
SIR ARTHUR QUILLER-COUCH	The Ship of Stars
PAY-CAPTAIN RITCHIE, C.V.O., R.N. (Bartimeus)	Naval Occasions
PAY-CAPTAIN RITCHIE, C.V.O., R.N. (Bartimeus)	A Tall Ship
PAY-CAPTAIN RITCHIE, C.V.O., R.N. (Bartimeus)	The Navy Eternal
MICHAEL SCOTT	Tom Cringle's Log
MICHAEL SCOTT	The Cruise of the *Midge*
R. L. STEVENSON	Treasure Island
R. L. STEVENSON (with Lloyd Osbourne)	The Ebb-Tide
H. M. TOMLINSON	Gallion's Reach
JULES VERNE	Twenty Thousand Leagues under the Sea
RICHARD WALTER	A Voyage round the World by Lord Anson

POETRY

SIR GEOFFREY CALLENDER	Realms of Melody
S. T. COLERIDGE	The Ancient Mariner
RUDYARD KIPLING	Collected Poems, especially The Flag of England, Big Steamers, Minesweepers
JOHN MASEFIELD, O.M.	Salt Water Ballads
JOHN MASEFIELD, O.M.	A Mainsail Haul
JOHN MASEFIELD, O.M.	Dauber
JOHN MASEFIELD, O.M.	A Sailor's Garland

SIR HENRY NEWBOLT	Poems New and Old
ALFRED NOYES	Drake, an English Epic
ALFRED NOYES	A Salute from the Fleet
C. FOX SMITH	Sea Songs and Ballads
C. FOX SMITH	A Book of Shanties
LORD TENNYSON	Enoch Arden
LORD TENNYSON	The Voyage of Maeldune

FICTION

R. M. BALLANTYNE	Coral Island
R. M. BALLANTYNE	Martin Rattler
MRS BARRINGTON	Divine Lady
R. D. BLACKMORE	Springhaven
WINSTON CHURCHILL	Richard Carvel
JOSEPH CONRAD	Youth
JOSEPH CONRAD	The Nigger of the *Narcissus*
DANIEL DEFOE	Robinson Crusoe
DANIEL DEFOE	Captain Singleton
LT.-COL. DRURY, C.B.E., R.N.	The Passing of the Flagship
LT.-COL. DRURY, C.B.E., R.N.	The Shadow on the Quarter-Deck
LT.-COL. DRURY, C.B.E., R.N.	The Tadpole of an Archangel
C. S. FORESTER	Captain Hornblower
C. S. FORESTER	Brown on Resolution
C. S. FORESTER	The Ship
THOMAS HARDY, O.M.	The Trumpet-Major
IAN HAY AND STEPHEN KING-HALL	The Middle Watch
EDWARD HOWARD	Rattlin the Reefer
CHARLES KINGSLEY	Westward Ho !
W. H. G. KINGSTON	Peter the Whaler
W. H. G. KINGSTON	The Three Midshipmen
CAPTAIN MARRYAT, R.N.	Peter Simple
CAPTAIN MARRYAT, R.N.	Mr Midshipman Easy
CAPTAIN MARRYAT, R.N.	The King's Own
JOHN MASEFIELD, O.M.	Captain Margaret
JOHN MASEFIELD, O.M.	Lost Endeavour

GLOSSARY

OF NAUTICAL TERMS OCCURRING IN THE PASSAGES QUOTED

ABAFT. The hinder part of a ship, or all those parts which lie towards the stern. Used relatively, it signifies farther aft, or nearer the stern.

ABEAM. In a line at right angles to the ship's length: opposite the centre of a ship's side.

ABLE SEAMAN. The highest grade of seaman other than LEADING SEAMAN.

ACTION STATIONS. Assigned positions for battle at sea.

ADMIRAL. Naval officer in charge of a fleet, or part of a fleet. The word is derived from the Arabic *Emir-al-Bahr*, ruler of the sea.

ADRIFT. The state of a vessel broken loose from her moorings. (Slang) Late or behind time.

AFTER HOLD. The after part of the hold.

AHEAD. Farther onward, or immediately in front of a ship; opposed to ASTERN (q.v.).

ALTER COURSE. To change the direction of the ship's head.

ALTITUDE. See TAKE AN ALTITUDE.

ASTERN. Any position behind a vessel; opposed to AHEAD, which is before her.

AVAST! An order to pause in any operation.

BACKSTAYS. Ropes extending from the topmast heads to the sides of the ship, and slanting a little backwards to second the shrouds in supporting the mast.

BALLAST. Stone, iron, gravel or any such material, deposited in a ship's hold, when she has no cargo on board, or not sufficient to bring her low enough in the water to prevent her from capsizing.

BARE POLES, UNDER. No sails set.

BATTERY. A number of cannon with their equipment.

BATTLE CRUISERS. First adopted in 1911 and introducing into the large type of ARMOURED CRUISER the DREADNOUGHT principle of all-heavy guns.

BEAM. The measurement of a ship at her greatest breadth. *Abaft the beam* implies any direction aft of a transverse line amid-ships, whether in or out of the ship. *Before the beam* implies any direction forward of the same.

BEAR DOWN, TO. See BEAR UP, TO.

BEAR UP, TO. To keep farther away from the wind by putting the helm up. When a ship or fleet performed this manœuvre, with a view to engage, she was said to 'BEAR DOWN' on the foe, so that *bear up* and *bear down* are not opposite in meaning but akin.

BEAT, TO. Said of a ship when she strives to make headway against the wind by changing alternately from one tack to another.

BELAY, TO.   To secure or fasten; to cancel.

BINOCULARS.   Field-glass with twin eye-pieces.

BLOCK.   A pulley together with its framework.

BOATSWAIN.   The warrant officer who in the old Navy was responsible for all the gear that set the ship in motion and all tackle that kept her at rest.

BOMB-KETCH, BOMB-SHIP, BOMB-VESSEL, MORTAR-BOAT, MORTAR-VESSEL.   A two-masted vessel, mounting mortars (q.v.) in her bows; stoutly built and often stuffed with junk and shavings to counteract the downward recoil of the guns. First used 1682.

BOS'N.   See BOATSWAIN.

BOW, BOWS.   Foremost end of a vessel.

BOWSPRIT.   A large spar projecting over the stem and ranking on an equality with the lower masts; setting one or more sails of its own and taking much of the forward rigging. Corruption of BOLT-sprit, a sprit or tilted boom secured by a bolt.

BOXING THE COMPASS.   Reciting the points of the compass from North, clockwise or anti-clockwise.

BOY.   The lowest rating in a man-of-war.

BRACES.   Ropes rove through blocks at the end of a yard to fix or change its position.

BREAK OF POOP.   The foremost part where its planking is cut short; fenced in by the poop-rails.

BRIDGE.   The narrow raised platform athwart the ship whence the Captain issues his orders.

BRIG.   A two-masted square-rigged vessel.

BROAD PENDANT.   A swallow-tailed banner, the distinctive mark of a Commodore (q.v.).

BROADSIDE.   The simultaneous discharge of all the artillery on one side of a ship.

BULWARK.   The planking or woodwork round a vessel above the level of her uppermost deck; figuratively, a fortification or rampart; any means of defence or security.

BUNK.   A sleeping berth anywhere, more properly in a ship's cabin.

BUOY THE CABLE, TO.   When the cable has been slipped (q.v.), to mark the position by a buoy attached to it, so that the cable may be subsequently recovered.

CABIN.   A room or apartment in a ship, set aside for the use of officers.

CABLE.   A strong rope, or chain, of considerable length, to hold the ship when at anchor.

CABLE.   (Measure of distance.) One hundred fathoms or 600 ft.

CALIBRE.   The size of the bore of a gun.

CANNONADE.   An attack with artillery; the simultaneous discharge of heavy guns.

CANVAS.   Used as the equivalent of SAILS: 'to set their canvas' means 'to make sail'.

CAPITAL SHIP.   A ship of modern times, powerful enough to be in the line of battle. The term has fallen into disuse since 1918.

CAPTAIN.   The principal officer in command of a ship.

CARPENTER. One of the warrant officers of an old man-of-war: responsible for the upkeep of the ship and the repair of her fabric and appurtenances: replaced in modern times by the SHIPWRIGHT.

CARRONADE. A gun for use at close quarters and mounted on the upper deck. Range being no object, it was short and stumpy, but could discharge a 68 pound shot when the biggest long-range gun was a 32 pounder.

CHANNEL. The deeper part of a strait, bay, or harbour.

CHART. A marine map, by means of which the Navigator of a ship may shape her course.

CHASE-GUNS. Guns mounted either in the bow or stern of an old time man-of-war to be employed in pursuit of an enemy's ship or in defence of one's own.

CHOCK-A-BLOCK. Full to capacity.

CLOSE ACTION. In Nelson's day this meant battle at half pistol shot, that is, about thirty yards.

CLUB-HAUL, TO. To tack by dropping a lee anchor and slipping the cable.

CLUE. The lower corner of a square sail and the aftmost corner of a staysail.

COASTER. A vessel that on account of her size keeps near the coast and hesitates to lose sight of land.

COCKED HAT. The old-fashioned three-cornered hat; or the triangular pointed hat which took the place of the three-cornered variety.

COCKPIT. The after part of the ORLOP (q.v.); in time of battle the place where the wounded received attention; the residence of the Surgeon and his mates: at other times the berthing place of the elder Midshipmen and some of the warrant officers.

COEHORN. A very small and handy mortar, made of brass and named after the Dutch engineer who invented it.

COME TO AN ANCHOR, TO. Equivalent to anchoring.

COMMANDER-IN-CHIEF. The senior officer in any port or on any station, appointed to hold command over his own and all other vessels within the limits assigned to him.

COMMISSION, TO. To take charge of a fighting ship, at the instance of the Admiralty or Lord High Admiral, and get her ready for sea; said of a CAPTAIN appointed to a new command, his COMMISSION lasting till his ship is PAID OFF.

COMMODORE. A courtesy title given to the senior officer in command of a detached squadron, that officer being beneath the rank of a Rear-Admiral. See also BROAD PENDANT.

COMPASS POINTS. The compass card is divided into thirty-two equal parts by lines drawn from the centre to the circumference called RHUMB LINES, the extremities of which are called POINTS. The intervals between may be divided into halves and quarters, called HALF POINTS and QUARTER POINTS: e.g., E. by N. $\frac{1}{4}$ N., W. $\frac{1}{2}$ S., etc. The circumference is also divided into 360 degrees, so that the angle subtended by two Rhumb lines is equal to 11 degrees 15 minutes.

CON, TO. To direct the steerage of a ship.

CONNING TOWER. A heavily armoured citadel in a man-of-war whence orders can be issued in time of battle.

CONSORT. Any vessel keeping company with another.

CONTROL POSITION. The ship's bridge, or other position, where voice-pipes, bells, and mechanical contrivances enable the Captain of a ship to convey orders to those waiting for them.

COURSES. The sails that hang from the lower yards. A ship is said to be 'under her courses' when she has no sail set but the foresail, mainsail and mizzen. (COURSE is a corruption of 'corps', the body of the sail, when canvas was increased, not by topsails etc., but by bonnets.)

CRAFT. A word of general description applied to ships, more especially to small ships.

CRANK. Used by a ship incapable of bearing her sails without danger of overturning.

CRUISE, TO. To sail to and fro on a wandering voyage in search of the enemy's vessels or for the protection of one's own.

CRUISER. Like the frigate of olden days the cruiser relies primarily on her speed; and is employed to protect the trade routes, to glean intelligence, and to act as the 'eyes of the fleet'.

CURRENT. A volume of water moving in a certain direction.

CUTTER. The favourite greyhound of the fleet in Nelson's day; setting one fore-and-aft sail, square topsail and triangular headsails.

DEAD-RECKONING. To ascertain the position of a ship by measurement of the distance run. See LOG.

DECKS. The planked floors of a ship, which connect the sides together and serve as platforms to lodge the men and support the artillery.

DEEP. Deep water; used generally also of the sea or ocean.

DEPARTURE. The navigator's last professional sight of land.

DESTROYERS. Towards the close of last century a very fast small ship armed with torpedoes made a menacing appearance and the TORPEDO-BOAT-DESTROYER was evolved to hunt her off the seas. When the submarine rendered other forms of torpedo-craft obsolete, the DESTROYER grew and developed as the ideal ship to hunt the submarine.

DISEMBARK, TO. To quit a ship; to go ashore.

DISMASTED. Deprived of a mast, or masts.

DIVISION. A portion, or section, of a squadron.

DOCK. An enclosure or artificial basin near a harbour or river for the reception of ships for repair, etc.

DREADNOUGHT. Until the advent of this ship in 1907, battleship design had proceeded on very similar lines for many years: viz. four large guns in two TURRETS (q.v.), one forward and one aft, and a battery of smaller guns disposed along the broadside. The DREADNOUGHT mounted ten large guns in five turrets and established the 'all big-gun' principle.

DROP ANCHOR, TO. The correct sea term for to anchor.

EBB, EBB-TIDE. The retiring or outflowing tide.

EMBARK. To go on board (French: em, 'in', and barque, 'a ship').

END ON. The opposite of broadside on.

ENSIGN (pronounced ENS'N). A large banner hoisted on a high pole extended over the stern and called the ENSIGN-STAFF; used to distinguish the ships of different nations and in old days to characterize the different squadrons of a fleet.

ENSIGN-STAFF.   See ENSIGN.
EXPRESS.   With haste.

FAG END.   When only the extreme end of a rope remains.
FAIR (of weather or wind).   Favourable.
FATHOM.   Six feet.   One hundred fathoms make approximately one
  CABLE, and ten CABLES one NAUTICAL MILE or KNOT, i.e., 6080 feet.
  All soundings are made in fathoms unless otherwise stated.
FIGUREHEAD.   The carved emblem beneath a ship's bowsprit.
FIRESHIP.   An old ship filled with combustible materials such as sulphur,
  resin, tallow and pitch and designed for the destruction of the
  enemy.
FLAG.   (1) Used loosely to signify the National Colours or other fluttering
  device.
      (2) Properly the banner by which at sea an Admiral is distinguished
  from the inferior ships of his squadron.
FLAG-OFFICERS.   Naval officers of flag rank, i.e., Admirals of the Fleet,
  Admirals, Vice-Admirals and Rear-Admirals.   In the old days when
  a fleet was divided into three squadrons, flying Red, White and Blue
  Ensigns (q.v.), Flag-officers were graded according to colour, Admirals
  of the Red, White and Blue; Vice-Admirals of the Red, White and
  Blue; and Rear-Admirals of the Red, White and Blue.   It was unlikely,
  however successful an officer might be, that he would climb from
  Rear-Admiral of the Blue to Admiral of the Red.
FLAGSHIP.   A man-of-war wearing the banner of an Admiral, Vice-
  Admiral or Rear-Admiral.
FLAT BOTTOMS.   Abbreviation for flat-bottomed boats.
FLOOD, FLOOD TIDE.   The top of the rising or inflowing tide.
FLOTILLA.   A fleet or squadron of small ships: e.g., a British destroyer
  flotilla consists of eight destroyers and one leader, or of eight all told.
FLY BOAT.   A big merchantman, originally Dutch; the type is now
  obsolete.
FO'C'SLE.   Abbreviation of FORECASTLE.
FORE-AND-AFT.   Throughout the whole ship's length; lengthways of the
  ship.
FORECASTLE.   A short deck situated in the fore part of the ship, above the
  upper deck; the forepart of the ship under the maindeck; the quarters
  of the crew.
FORESAIL.   The COURSE or lowest sail set on the foremost of a ship's masts.
FOUL.   A term generally used in contrast to clear, and implies entangled,
  embarrassed or contrary to: e.g., *to foul the helm*, to find steerage
  impracticable owing to the rudder becoming entangled with rope or
  other gear.
FOUR-INCH SHELL.   Shell of four-inch calibre.
FRIGATE.   The counterpart in a sailing navy of the cruiser of to-day;
  a light nimble vessel built for speed; employed in particular for the
  gleaning of intelligence and the protection and assault of trade-routes.
  In battle the frigates took station on the disengaged side of the fleet,
  where they repeated signals, sped on messages, and succoured the
  distressed.

FUTTOCKS, FUTTOCK SHROUDS. Short shrouds connecting the lower rigging with the rims of the tops by which seamen climbed to the topmast shrouds without passing through the lubber's hole.

GALLEASS (or GALLEASSE). An oared battleship like the GALLEY, but with broadside guns on the deck above.

GALLEON. The accepted term for the type of ship which the Spaniards used in 1588; that is, an armed merchantman of exceptional quality, combining the strength of the mediaeval trader with some of the finer lines and fighting features of the GALLEY.

GALLERY. A balcony built outside the body of a ship; either at the stern, STERN-GALLERY, or on the quarter, QUARTER-GALLERY; used for the convenience of officers.

GALLEY. (1) A fighting ship propelled by oars; (2) the ship's kitchen.

GANGWAYS. In the old Navy narrow platforms on either side of the ship, leading from the quarter-deck to the forecastle and bridging the waist.

GLASS. (Abbreviation for watch-glass.) A division of a WATCH (q.v.) as measured by a half-hour sand-glass. 'We fought for 5 glasses' would mean 'We fought for 2½ hours'.

GRAPE-SHOT. Three tiers of cast-iron balls, generally three in a tier and weighing two pounds apiece, between four parallel iron discs connected by a central pin.

GRAPPLE. To lay fast hold of; or to contend in close fight.

GROG. Rum and water mixed in the ratio 2 of water to 1 of rum. So called after 'Old Grog', otherwise the nickname of Admiral Vernon, who first watered the seamen's rum and wore a grogram foul-weather coat.

GUN BRIG. A BRIG armed with small cannon: see BRIG.

GUNNER. One of the principal warrant officers; responsible for all the ordnance on board, all the ammunition, and all the small arms: responsible also for the instruction of the seamen in the art and practice of gunnery.

GUNWALE (pronounced 'gunnel'). The thick strake which bounds the uppermost plank of a ship or a boat.

HALF MUSKET-SHOT. About forty to fifty yards.

HALF PISTOL-SHOT. About twenty-five to thirty yards.

HALF-PIKE. A weapon of the same species as a PIKE (q.v.) but with a short staff for fighting at close quarters.

HALF-PORT. Half a PORT-LID (q.v.) made as such, like the folding doors of domestic architecture.

HALLIARD (or HALYARD). A rope or purchase used for hoisting or lowering a sail, yard or flag.

HANDING. The same as furling.

HANDS. Apart from the wheel and the capstan, there was from 1588 to 1805 no machinery in use on board ship. All the work, including the movement of guns, was done by *manual labour*. The members of the ship's company were therefore known as 'hands'.

HANDSOMELY. Carefully and slowly.

HANGER. A short sword, curved near the point.

HATCH. The covering of a hatchway.

HATCHWAY. An opening in a ship's deck. There were as a rule in the wooden men-of-war three stairways on every deck, fore hatchway, main hatchway and after hatchway.

HAUL, TO. To tug, to try to draw something; HAUL-OFF, to alter a ship's course.

HEAVE-TO, TO. To bring a vessel to a standstill; to make her lie to.

HEAVING THE LEAD. See LEAD.

HELM. The instrument by which a ship is steered: it includes the rudder, the tiller, and the wheel.

HOIST, TO. To raise by means of halliards or tackles.

HOLD. All that part of the inner cavity of a ship comprehended between the bottom timbers and the lowest deck; supplying space for ballast, provisions and stores.

HOOKER. A contemptuous reference to a ship.

HORIZON. The circular line formed by the apparent meeting of the sea and sky.

HULK. In the sixteenth century the large merchantman of the northern nations. As she grew obsolete, her name was applied in derision to all crank vessels, until it came to be degraded to its present use, i.e., any old vessel unfit for further employment.

HULL. The frame or body of a ship, exclusive of masts, yards, sails and rigging.

HULL DOWN. The earth being spherical in shape, the hull of a ship drops behind the horizon while her masts still remain visible.

IN STAYS. The position of a sailing ship when about to change from one tack to another.

JACK. The Union Flag. Displayed right forward in one of H.M. ships: formerly at the jack-staff on the bowsprit. MERCHANT JACK, a small Union Flag with a white border and worn at the jack-staff of merchantmen.

JACOB'S LADDER. A rope or wire ladder with wooden bars for steps.

JUNK. Condemned rope.

JURY MAST. A temporary or occasional mast, erected in a ship in the place of one which has been carried away by accident.

KETCH. A vessel equipped with two masts, viz. main and mizzen; adopted by the Royal Navy about 1650 on account of its speed and consequent usefulness as a dispatch boat.

KILLICK. The stone-weighted wooden hook, the anchor of primitive folk. (Slang) Leading Seaman, so called from his badge, an anchor.

KNOTS. The speed of a ship; e.g., a ship of 10 knots is a vessel which covers ten nautical miles in an hour. The word is derived from the knots that marked the log-line which in conjunction with the sand-glass was employed for determining the velocity of a ship. In the olden days the word 'knot' was used as the equivalent of a nautical mile, i.e., 6080 feet. Roughly one knot equals 1¼ land miles per hour. Ten knots equal 11·515 miles per hour; 25 knots, 28·787 miles per hour.

LANDFALL. The first land to be sighted after a long voyage—a mountain perhaps, a rocky headland, or a stretch of sand dunes.

LANGRIDGE. Scrap iron used instead of shot for employment against sails.

LARBOARD. The left side of a ship when the spectator's face is turned towards the bow. To avoid confusion with 'starboard', the word PORT was substituted in 1849.

LAUNCH. After 1800, equivalent to LONG BOAT (q.v.), the principal or largest boat of a man-of-war; loosely used of a vessel of any kind.

LEAD, LEADLINE. The plummet used for ascertaining the depth of water when near or nearing the land. At 2 fathoms (12 feet) from the bottom end the line is marked with a piece of leather with two prongs; at 3 fathoms, with a piece of leather with three prongs; at 5 with a piece of white bunting; at 7 with a piece of red bunting; at 10, with a piece of leather with a hole in it; at 13 with a piece of blue bunting; at 17 with a piece of red bunting; and at 20 with a piece of cod line with two knots. These are known as 'Marks', the intermediate numbers being 'Deeps'. Thus the Quarter-Master may call out 'By the mark, seven', 'By the deep, nine'.

LEADING SEAMAN. A higher grade of ABLE SEAMAN; intermediate between ABLE SEAMAN and PETTY OFFICER.

LEE. That part of the hemisphere to which the wind is directed, to distinguish it from the other part, which is called TO WINDWARD.

LEE-SHORE. The shore on, or facing, the leeside of a ship.

LEEWARD, TO LEEWARD. The opposite of WINDWARD, TO WINDWARD (q.v.); on the sheltered side of the ship, or the side opposite to that from which the wind is blowing.

LIE-TO, TO. See LYING TO.

LIEUTENANT. Originally a highly placed officer, deputising for the Captain. (French: *tenant*, 'holding'; *lieu*, 'place of'): latterly every officer borne on the books of a man-of-war below the rank of Commander or Lieutenant-Commander and above the rank of Sub-Lieutenant, Mate or Midshipman.

LIGHT CRUISER. A fighting ship less closely related to the eight-inch-gun ships than to the large DESTROYERS which they closely resemble.

LIGHT FORCES. Equivalent to FLOTILLAS (q.v.).

LINE ABREAST. See LINE OF BATTLE.

LINE AHEAD. See LINE OF BATTLE.

LINE OF BATTLE. The disposition of a fleet in battle array.

    (a) LINE ABREAST. The disposition of a fleet when all the ships composing it have their keels parallel one to another, and when a straight line passing through the mainmast of each ship makes, with the line of the ships' advance, a right angle.

    (b) LINE AHEAD. The disposition of a fleet when all the ships composing it have their keels in one and the same straight line.

LINE OF BATTLE SHIP. Equivalent to SHIP or SAIL OF THE LINE (q.v.).

LOG. The machine or instrument by which the ship's rate of motion is ascertained.

LONG BOAT. The principal and largest boat towed or carried by a man-of-war (1340–1800).

LORD HIGH ADMIRAL. A highly placed Government official responsible from early times for the duties now performed by the Board of Admiralty.

LOWER DECK. Equivalent to GUN DECK when the latter term is properly used; in Nelson's day the position of the heaviest batteries and the berthing-place of the crew. To-day equivalent to MESS-DECKS.

LUBBER. Deficient in the qualities of a seaman.

LUG. A square sail bent to a yard that hangs obliquely to the mast. To LUG, to pull or haul with difficulty.

LUGGER. A small vessel with square or quadrilateral sails set fore and aft: very speedy and used in the old days as intelligence vessels and smugglers.

LYING TO. The retardation of a ship's course by arranging the sails so that they counteract each other and render the vessel herself almost immovable.

MAGAZINE. Storeroom for explosives; embedded deep in the hold where the enemy's fire should not be able to penetrate.

MAIN. Properly the mainland of South America as contrasted with the islands of the West Indies: loosely used of the sea or ocean.

MAIN MAST. The central mast of a ship. The term is reminiscent of a time when the biggest ship had but one big mast and a couple of overgrown flag-staffs.

MAKE APPLICATION FOR A WARRANT. See WARRANT OFFICER.

MAN-OF-WAR. A fighting ship; to-day commonly referred to as a 'warship'.

MARINES. A body of officers and soldiers raised to serve on board ship and trained to fight either at sea or on shore: till Anson's day part of the Regular Army.

MASTER. The warrant officer responsible for the navigation of the ship, for the care of all charts and instruments and for the stowage of the hold.

MASTS. In a SHIP proper, that is to say, a three-masted, square-rigged vessel, the masts, reckoning from the stem, are styled FORE, MAIN, MIZZEN. Above the LOWER MASTS come the TOPMASTS; above the TOPMASTS, the TOP-GALLANTS; and above the TOP-GALLANTS, the ROYALS.

MAT'LOT. Sailor; from the French *matelot*.

MERCHANTS. Often used as the equivalent of MERCHANTMEN.

MESS-DECKS. The living quarters of the crew.

MIDDLE WATCH. See WATCHES.

MIDSHIPMAN. Originally a petty officer serving amidships, gradually the title came to be applied to young officers qualifying for commissions, who (it was presumed) had already qualified as ABLE SEAMEN.

MINE. A floating or submerged charge of high explosives designed to blow a ship to pieces on contact.

MIZZEN. The aftermost mast of a three-masted ship.

MOOR. To secure a ship with two anchors and cables.

MORTAR. A short piece of ordnance designed to secure a vertical fall of the projectile. Fired at a fixed angle of elevation, generally 45°.

MORTAR BOAT. See BOMB-KETCH.

MUSKET or MUSQUET. The predecessor of the rifle; a smooth bore weapon. Its range was from eighty to one hundred yards, though hits were occasionally made at one hundred and fifty yards. No hit was ever, by steady aim, secured at two hundred yards.

NAVIGATION. The art of conducting a ship from her starting-place to her destination.

NETTING. The iron stanchions and network on top of the gunwale for the stowage of the hammocks.

OFFING. Out at sea, or at an adequate distance from the land; between the shore and the horizon.

ON BOARD THE ADMIRAL. Equivalent to on board the Flagship.

ORDINARY SEAMAN. The first step in a sailor's upward career: see BOY.

ORLOP. The uppermost portion of a ship's hold; floored and appointed like an ordinary deck, but accommodating storerooms instead of guns.

PASSAGE. A ship's journey from starting-point to destination. See VOYAGE.

PATROL, TO. To keep watch and afford protection to a specified route or area by constant movement over the location.

PEDEREROES. Equivalent to STONE GUNS, that is artillery, discharging stone or granite cannon-balls.

PENDANT (pronounced PENNANT). A long, narrow banner worn at the main-mast head, the badge of a man-of-war; hoisted by the officer who commissions the ship.

PETTY OFFICER. A naval officer with rank corresponding to that of a non-commissioned officer in the army.

PIKE. The ancestor of the bayonet; a blade at the end of a staff, measuring 16 to 18 feet.

PINNACE. In Elizabeth's reign a fast little ship like the gun brig or schooner of Nelson's day: not to be confused with the boat of to-day.

PIPE DOWN. The last pipe of the day; the end of all activities.

PIPE THE SIDE. A Naval salute with the Boatswain's Pipe.

PITCH. The solid black shining substance obtained by boiling down ordinary tar.

PLY, TO. To work at steadily; to make regular passages between two ports; to make way against the wind by tacking.

P.O. Petty officer (q.v.).

POINT. A subdivision of the compass face; $11° 15'$ or $\frac{1}{32}$ of a complete turn or revolution.

POINT, TO. (Gunnery phrase.) To take careful aim.

POOP. The highest and aftermost deck of a ship, connected by stairways with the quarter-deck.

PORT-LID. The shuttering or cover of a gun-port.

PORTS. The embrasures or openings in the sides of a man-of-war, wherein the artillery is ranged upon the decks above and below.

POST-SHIP. A ship of the Royal Navy of sufficient importance to confer the rank of POST CAPTAIN on her commanding officer. Some ships are commanded by Lieutenants, who might be referred to as 'Captain' but do not thereby attain POST RANK.

POWDER ROOM. In the old Navy a carefully insulated compartment near the MAGAZINE where the gunpowder could be made up into cartridges.

PULL, TO. To propel a boat by rowing or tugging at an oar.

PURSER. One of the warrant officers of the old Navy; responsible for the whole internal economy of the ship, the issue of provisions and other stores, and the record of work done by each member of the ship's company.

QUARTER. In an old wooden wall that part of a vessel's side from abaft the mainmast to the stern; its equivalent in a modern man-of-war.

QUARTER-DECK. In an old wooden wall that part of the upper deck between the break of the poop and the mainmast; the habitat or headquarters of the officers.

QUARTERS. The name given at sea to the several stations where the officers and men are posted when on duty.

RAKE. Any deviation of masts from the vertical.

RAKE, TO. To sweep a vessel from stern to stem or stem to stern with broadside fire.

RANGE-FINDER. An instrument for determining the range or distance of an object by taking sights.

RANGE, TO. To sail in a direction parallel to.

RATLINES. Small lines which traverse the shrouds horizontally at regular intervals and so provide a ladder up aloft.

REACH. The distance traversed between tacks.

'RED DUSTER' (Slang). The Red Ensign of the British Merchant Navy.

REEF. A certain portion of a sail comprehended between the top or bottom and a row of eyelet holes parallel thereto. The intention of the reef is to reduce the surface of the sail in proportion to the increase of the wind. Thus there are several reefs parallel to each other in the superior sails: e.g., the topsails of a ship are generally furnished with three or four.

REEFER. Equivalent in the sailing navy to Midshipman.

RENDEZ-VOUS. An appointed place of meeting. (French, *Rendez*, 'render'; *vous*, 'yourselves'.)

RIDE, TO. To be held in a particular position by one or more anchors and cables.

RIGGING. Ropes and tackles.

ROAD. See ROADSTEAD.

ROADSTEAD. A bay or place of anchorage at some distance from the shore, and therefore 'open', or exposed, to wind and gales.

ROBANDS. Small plaited lines to be rove through eyelet holes, whereby the sails (after the earings are secured) are bent to the yard.

ROUND SHOT. The solid iron cannon-ball of various weights used by the Navy from Elizabethan times till the time of the Crimean War.

SAIL. Often used as the equivalent of SHIP, e.g., 'thirty sail of men-of-war'.

SAIL OF THE LINE, SHIP OF THE LINE. A fighting ship of sufficient strength to take her place in the battle line: i.e., the equivalent of a battleship to-day.

SALVO. A simultaneous discharge of a ship's guns.

SCALDINGS. The old popular call for a passage along the deck, from the popular name for pea-soup.

SCUPPER. A hole in a ship's side to drain off water from the deck or decks.

SEAMANSHIP. The art of handling a vessel under sail or under any other form of propulsion.

SELVAGEE. An untwisted skein of rope yarn marled together.

SERVICE, THE. Alternative expression for the Royal Navy or the Merchant Navy.

SEVENTY-FOUR. One of the two varieties of third-rate ships of the line, from Anson's day onward: mounting 28 thirty-two pounders on the lower deck, 28 eighteen-pounders on the upper deck, 14 nine-pounders on the quarter-deck and 4 nine-pounders on the forecastle. In a manner of speaking, the *typical battleship* of Nelson's day.

SHARP-SHOOTERS. The equivalent of modern SNIPERS.

SHEET. Tackle attached to one or both clues, or lower corners, of a square sail to spread and to curb the canvas. When a ship sails with a side wind, the lower corners of the main and foresails are fastened by a TACK and a SHEET, the former being to windward and the latter to leeward.

SHIP'S COMPANY. The whole crew of any ship including both officers and men.

SHOAL. A place where sea water is not deep; an unseen sandbank.

SHROUDS. A range of large ropes extended from the mast-head to the right and left sides of a ship to support the masts and enable them to carry sail. They receive their proper designation from the masts to which they belong: e.g., mizzen shrouds, fore topmast shrouds, etc.

SIGNAL LIEUTENANT, THE. Officer in charge of communications.

SIGNALMAN. One who makes signals or interprets those made.

SHALLOW. See SHOAL.

SIXTY-FOUR. One of the two varieties of third-rate ships of the line, from Anson's day onwards. Mounting 26 twenty-four pounders on the lower deck, 26 twelve-pounders on the upper deck, 10 six-pounders on the quarter-deck and 2 six-pounders on the forecastle. See SEVENTY-FOUR.

SLIP THE CABLE. To allow the cable to run quite out when there is not time to weigh the anchor. (Slang) To die.

SLOOP. The smallest vessel employed for fighting purposes during the eighteenth century.

SMALL ARMS. The muskets, pistols, cutlasses, tomahawks and boarding-pikes, kept under charge of the GUNNER, in the gun-room.

SNOTTY. A Midshipman.

SPAR. General term for all masts, yards, booms, gaffs, etc.

SPLICE THE MAIN BRACE (Slang). To serve out an allowance of drink to all hands to celebrate a special occasion.

SPRING ON THE CABLE. If a ship rode at anchor with her head northerly and it was required to bring her batteries to bear on an object directly south, a hawser was run out of her stern and attached to the cable at a distance from the ship. The hawser was then tautened; and the cable being slackened, the ship turned her side towards the object to be battered.

SPRITSAIL. A sail attached to the yard which hung under the bowsprit.

SQUADRON. Properly a subdivision of a fleet; used loosely for a small fleet or any detachment of ships from the main body.

STANDARD. Abbreviated for ROYAL STANDARD, the personal banner of the reigning Sovereign, worn whenever His Majesty may be on board. In old days hoisted also on His Majesty's birthday; and one of the three colours worn at the launch of one of H.M. ships.

STAND BY. The warning to be ready for instant action when the command is given.

STARBOARD. The right side of a ship when the spectator's face is turned towards the bow.

STATION. Appointed place or position of a ship.

STAY. A large strong rope employed to support a mast on its forward side.

STEM. The forward end of a ship, opposite to stern.

STEM, TO. To cut as with the stem of a vessel.

STERN. The after part of a vessel, or that part which is presented to the view of a spectator immediately in her wake (q.v.).

STERN CHASE. The tedious process of pursuing an enemy whose only idea is to escape.

STRAND. The sea beach.

STRIKE, TO. To lower or let down anything; used emphatically to denote the lowering of colours in token of surrender.

SUBMARINES. The first submarines were commissioned by the Royal Navy in 1902 and were small boats capable of remaining under water for three hours, with no living quarters for the crew, which numbered six.

SWINGING THE LEAD. See LEAD.

TACK. A rope attached to the lower corner of a sail on its weather side to confine the canvas in board when sailing on a wind. See also SHEET.

TACK, TO. To turn a ship's head round, against, and in opposition to the direction of the wind. See WEAR.

TACK ABOUT, TO. To put about on the opposite tack.

TACKLE, TACKLING. A mechanical contrivance consisting of a rope with an assemblage of blocks and known in mechanics by the name of pulley.

TAKE AN ALTITUDE, TO. To determine the position of a ship by observing with the help of navigational instruments (cross-staff, back-staff, quadrant, sextant, nocturnal, etc.) the height of the sun at noon, or of the pole star or other celestial body at night.

TAR (Slang). A sailor; abbreviated from TARPAULIN in reference to his foul-weather attire.

THIRTEEN-POINT-FIVE-INCH TURRETS. Turrets mounting guns of 13·5 in. calibre.

THREE SHEETS IN THE WIND (Slang).   Slightly intoxicated.

TIDDLY (Slang).   Smart or ship-shape.

TIDE.   The regular flux and reflux or rhythmic ebb (q.v.) and flow of the sea.

TIER.   The name given to the row or battery of cannon mounted on one side of a ship's deck.

TOMPION.   A circular plug of wood used to stop the muzzle of a gun and thereby keep out the wet.

TOP.   A platform surrounding the lower masthead, from which it projected on all sides like a scaffold. It was fenced in with a rail; and used (1) to extend the topmast shrouds; (2) as a vantage-post for observation; and (3) as a battle station for small-arm parties.

TOP-GALLANT SAILS, TOP-GALLANTS.   The third sails above the deck; set above the topsail yards in the same manner as the topsails were set above the lower yards. Not introduced into the Royal Navy until the seventeenth century and not much used during the First Dutch War.

TOPMASTS.   See MASTS and TOPSAILS.

TOP-MEN.   Small-arms party serving in the TOPS.

TOPSAILS.   The second sails above the deck; extended across the topmasts by the topsail yards above and by the lower yards below; fastened to the former by earings and robands and to the latter by topsail sheets, which, passing through blocks fixed on the extremities of the sail and similar blocks fixed on the inner part of the yard, lead downwards to the deck.

TORPEDO.   A self-propelled weapon of offence, usually cigar-shaped, carrying a charge of gun-cotton, and detonating upon impact with a ship or other target.

TRICK.   A spell at the wheel or on look-out.

TROOPS (Slang).   A term applied to the crew.

TRUCK.   (1) A circular cap on the upper masthead, holding a pulley through which signal halliards are rove; (2) the wheel of a gun-carriage.

TURRET.   A revolving citadel wherein a battleship's heaviest guns are mounted. Prior to the DREADNOUGHT of 1907 the heaviest guns were 9·2 in. The *Dreadnought* mounted ten 12 in. guns: and in subsequent classes the big guns increased from 12 in. to 13·5 in., from 13·5 in. to 15 in., and in the *Nelson* and *Rodney* from 15 in. to 16 in., with the turrets mounting three guns instead of two.

UNDER SAIL.   With sails or canvas set.

UNDER WAY.   A ship is 'under way' when she is not anchored or moored, but moving through the water.

UPPER DECK.   Such parts of the uppermost deck of a ship as are not otherwise designated.

VAN.   The leading division of a fleet.

VEER, TO.   To pay out cable. *The wind veers* when it goes round with the sun; when it shifts in opposition to the sun it is said *to back*.

VOYAGE.   A ship's journey from starting-place to destination and back again.

WAD. A mass of paper, tow or the like, to keep the charge in a gun.

WAIST. That part of a ship which is contained between the quarter-deck and the forecastle.

WAKE. The smooth print or track impressed by the course of a ship on the surface of the water. The ship is said to be *in the wake* of another when she follows in the same track.

WARD-ROOM. The commissioned officers' mess-room; in the old wooden walls situated aft of the main deck.

WARRANT OFFICER. An officer appointed to preside over and superintend some particular department of a ship. The principal warrant officers of the old navy were the Master, Surgeon, Purser, Boatswain, Gunner and Carpenter (q.v.).

WATCH. The division of a ship's company into two parties so that work may be continuous. The two divisions are known as the Starboard Watch and the Port. The word is also applied to the time during which the watch remains on deck. See WATCHES.

WATCHES. Divisions of the working day. The period from midnight to 4 a.m. is the 'Middle' watch; from 4 a.m. to 8 a.m. the 'Morning'; from 8 a.m. to noon the 'Forenoon'; from noon till 4 p.m. the 'Afternoon'. The next four hours are split up into two watches known as 'Dog' watches. They are from 4 p.m. to 6 p.m. the 'First Dog', and from 6 p.m. till 8 p.m. the 'Last Dog'. The final watch of the day from 8 p.m. till midnight is, paradoxically enough, the 'First Watch' (i.e. of the Night). 'Dog' is not improbably a corruption of 'Docked', i.e., if a pun be allowed, CUR-TAILED.

WATERLINE. The line made by the water's edge when a ship has received her full complement of stores.

WEAR, TO. Reverse of to tack; to turn a ship round by going *from* the wind and hauling to it again gradually; or, as it is termed, coming to the wind on the new tack.

WEATHER GAUGE. In battle the position of that fleet, squadron, or ship, which lay nearer the wind than its adversary.

WEATHER SHROUDS. The shrouds on the windward side of a ship.

WEATHER, TO. To sail to windward of some headland, ship, or other obstacle.

WEIGH, TO. To set a ship in motion by raising the anchor.

WINDWARD, TO WINDWARD. On the side of the ship from which the wind is blowing.

YARD. A long timber suspended upon a mast to spread the sail. Yards are termed (1) square, or (2) lateen; the first being suspended across the mast at right angles, the second obliquely. Square yards taper from the middle (called the SLINGS) to the extremities which are termed the YARD-ARMS.

ZIG-ZAGGING. Altering course as a defensive move against torpedo attacks by submarine.

INDEX

www.ingramcontent.com/pod-product-compliance
Ingram Content Group UK Ltd.
Pitfield, Milton Keynes, MK11 3LW, UK
UKHW042143280225
455719UK00001B/55